Hui

Hui

A Study of Maori
Ceremonial Gatherings

Anne Salmond

A RAUPO BOOK
Published by the Penguin Random House Group

UK | USA | Canada | Ireland | Australia
India | New Zealand | South Africa | China

First published by Reed Publishing (NZ) Ltd, 1975

Penguin
Random House
New Zealand

Second edition 1976
Reprinted 1983, 1985, 1987, 1990, 1994, 1996

First published by Penguin Group (NZ) Ltd, 2009

This edition published by the Penguin Random House Group, 2015

Copyright © Anne Salmond

The author asserts her moral rights to this work.

Cover design by Cheryl Rowe
Printed and bound in Australia by Griffin Press,
an Accredited ISO AS/NZS 14001 Environmental Management Systems Printer

All rights reserved. Without limiting the rights under copyright reserved above,
no part of this publication may be reproduced, stored in or introduced into a retrieval
system, or transmitted, in any form or by any means (electronic, mechanical,
photocopying, recording or otherwise), without the prior written permission of
both the copyright owner and the above publisher of this book.

A catalogue record for this book is available
from the National Library of New Zealand.

ISBN 978-0-143-20302-5

penguinrandomhouse.co.nz

This book is dedicated to
Eruera and Amiria Stirling,
who made it possible.

"*E paru i te tinana, e mā, i te wai,*
E paru i te aroha, ka mau tonu e."

CONTENTS

LIST OF MAPS AND FIGURES	vii
PREFACE TO THE 2004 EDITION	viii
ACKNOWLEDGEMENTS	x
1. INTRODUCTION	1
Fieldwork	4
Outline of Contents	6
2. HISTORY	10
Pre-contact	10
Post-contact	18
3. THE SETTING: "A place to stand"	31
The *Marae*	31
Establishing a *Marae*	56
Opening the *Marae*	70
Historical Development of the *Marae*	77
Urban *Marae* in Auckland	82
Orākei *Marae*	84
Māngere *Marae*	85
The Maori Community Centre	86
Te Unga Waka	87
Te Tira Hou	88
Ngā Hau e Whā	88
Te Māhurehure Community Centre	89
4. STAGING	91
Organisers	91
Before the *Hui*	94
During the *Hui*	103
After the *Hui*	113

5.	**THE RITUALS OF ENCOUNTER**	115
	Introduction	115
	Actors	120
	Language	128
	Ritual Units	131
	Waerea (protective incantation)	131
	Wero or *Taki* (ritual challenge)	132
	Karanga (call)	137
	Poroporoaki (farewell)	141
	Pōwhiri (action chant of welcome)	142
	Tangi (weeping)	145
	Whaikōrero (oratory)	147
	Hongi (pressing noses)	176
6.	**CENTRAL ACTIVITIES AND HUI TYPES**	179
	Tangihanga (Tangi)	180
	Kawe Mate ("carry the death")	188
	Hurahanga / *Whakaara* } *Kōhatu* (unveiling)	192
	Mārenatanga (wedding)	193
	Tomo (formal request for permission to marry)	193
	Mārenatanga (wedding ceremony)	194
	Hākari (feast, wedding breakfast)	195
	Birthdays and Wedding Anniversaries	196
	Church Gatherings	197
	Hui Tōpu (Church of England)	198
	Ringatū Gatherings	200
	Te Whiti Gatherings	202
	King Movement Gatherings	203
	Poukai	203
	Koroneihana (Coronation)	206
	Ceremonial Welcome	207
	Meetings and Conferences	208
7.	**EPILOGUE**	210
	BIBLIOGRAPHY	214
	INDEX	218

LIST OF MAPS AND FIGURES

Map *Page*
1. North Island, New Zealand xii
2. North Island Tribes 8
3. Sample of *Hui* 1970–72 9
4. East Coast Rural Meeting–houses 58
5. City of Auckland – Urban *Marae* 1972 59
6. Distribution of *Whaikōrero* Patterns 154

Figure
1. *Marae* Plan: *Wairūrū Marae*, Raukokore, East Coast 30
2. Meeting-house – *Noa* and *Tapu* Sides 47
3. Structure of the Ritual of Encounter 178

PREFACE TO THE 2004 EDITION

Hui: A Study of Maori Ceremonial Gatherings was written in 1972–73, more than thirty years ago, but the experiences it describes remain remarkably fresh and vivid. During a recent visit to Raukokore, where Eruera and Amiria Stirling lie buried in a graveyard beside the sea, memories of our travels together came flooding back. It seems as if it all happened yesterday.

I was young then, newly married and in my late twenties. Eruera and Amiria had been my mentors and "grandparents" for some years, and when I enrolled in a PhD in Anthropology in 1968, Eruera suggested that I should accompany him and Amiria to *marae* to learn more about *tikanga Maori* (Maori ways of being).

For two years we travelled together to *hui* or gatherings, often in very remote parts of New Zealand. Sometimes my husband Jeremy came too, and acted as our photographer. There was usually little warning of these excursions – a phone call to say that someone had died, a wedding was being held, or a meeting had been summoned.

We would collect Eruera and Amiria from their house and set off, talking and singing as we drove. Those journeys were travelling seminars, listening to Eruera recounting tribal histories or chanting *waiata* (songs) as he prepared his whaikōrero (oration); or Amiria telling stories about family life on the East Coast in her inimitable fashion.

When we arrived at our destination, others were often waiting. Eruera was a well-known orator, and it was reassuring to enter a strange *marae* with such a person. As he introduced us to the elders, they gazed in bemusement at these young *Pākehā* companions, but were generous in their greetings. Many eventually befriended us, teaching me about tribal histories and *marae* rituals in different parts of New Zealand.

When the *karanga* finally came floating out from the meeting-house and we walked through the gate on to the *marae*, we entered another world. Here, Maori was the ruling language, tribal histories shaped the past, and ancestors were a living presence. Here, one became immersed in knowledge reaching back to the beginnings of the cosmos, the power of *tapu*, a different way of being. This book tries to distil those special, unrepeatable experiences.

Although *hui* are still held and *marae* continue to thrive in all parts of New Zealand, *Hui* remains a description of Maori ceremonial gatherings in the early 1970s. The experiences upon which the book is based were so particular and powerful that I have never been able to rewrite or update it. Perhaps the wisdom of hindsight might enrich the account, but it might also rob it of immediacy, and a sense of wonder. In any case, I will hold the memory of those years, and those who shared them with me, in my heart forever.

E koro mā, e kui mā, ka mau tonu te aroha mo ake tonu.

ACKNOWLEDGEMENTS

A great many people combined to make this study possible. First, my "grandparents" Mr and Mrs Eruera Stirling, to whom the book is dedicated. Both my debt of gratitude and my *aroha* for them are boundless.

Also our friends from the East Coast; Peggy Kaua, Ina Robb, George and Pare Marsden, and Mereaira Tawhai, who started it all; Mr and Mrs Bill Maxwell from Opotoki; Girlie Copeland of Whakatane, Roka Paora at Te Kaha, Hine and Paul Weka, and the late Pine Taiapa at Tikitiki, Henry and Lorna Ngata, and Louis Moeau in Gisborne, Tamati and Tilly Reedy and many others – *arohanui ki a koutou katoa.*

In the Tainui area, my thanks go to Queen Te Ata i Rangi Kahu and her council for their most generous co-operation, and our love to the kuia of Waikato and the Waiuku ladies.

In Auckland, Mrs Elsie Turnbull, Father Ryan, Clyde Tracey, students in Maori courses over 1970 and 1971, elders Bill and Connie Davis of Ngāti Whātua, and colleagues Bruce Biggs, Pat Hohepa, Sid Mead, Robert Mahuta, Mervyn McLean, Matiu te Hau and Mere Penfold acted as informants, mentors and an ever-present source of encouragement. Mrs Rangi Motu transcribed the tapes, and Eruera Stirling and Mere Penfold checked the translations – any errors still present do not belong to them. Cyril Schollum printed the photographs.

Dr Joan Metge and Koro Dewes at Victoria University in Wellington, and the Hon. Duncan MacIntyre, former Minster of Maori and Island Affairs, and his staff, also extended generous help.

I am indebted to Professors Ward Goodenough, Dell Hymes, William Labov and Erving Goffman at the University of Pennsylvania. Both in their own writings and in personal discussions they inspired each step of the research and their contribution is incalculable. My gratitude also to the National Science Foundation for the financial support that made the study possible.

Within my own family, my husband Jeremy worked closely with me on *Hui*, and his photographs capture much of the life of the *marae* that I found impossible to put down on paper. He knows the depth of my gratitude. My parents showed their interest and support every step of the way. And my love to my great-aunt Margerie McDonald, who first kindled my interest in *Maoritanga* when I was still a little girl.

Finally I greet the meeting-houses that gave us hospitable shelter on so many *marae* throughout the North Island, and the people who keep them warm. E kui mā, e koro mā, kaua e warewaretia. Research is supposed to be a business for the head, but our hearts have been deeply involved, and that *aroha* has been the best part of it all. *Tēnā koutou katoa.*

A NOTE ABOUT CORRECTIONS TO THE SECOND EDITION

Since the first edition of *Hui* was published in May 1975, I have had many enlightening conversations with and letters from those who had read the book, and I can now make some corrections and additions to the original text. My grateful thanks to those who shared their especial expertise and insights with me, in particular Reverend Maori Marsden for some illuminating material on the symbolic structure of the meeting-house (see pp. 40–7); Michael King for corrections on Māhinārangi meeting-house (pp. 61, 76) and the *kāhui ariki* (pp. 203–4); Joy Stevenson for revisions to the story on p. 152 about Te Arawa at King Koroki's tangi; Sir Bernard Fergusson for corrections to the same story; and Matiu te Hau for material on Ōrākei. I hope that other readers who detect remaining errors or misunderstanding in the text will get in touch with me, so that the account may finally be fully correct.

I also owe apologies to both Sir Bernard Fergusson and Te Arawa, for the incorrect story (on p. 152) about a Te Arawa filibuster at King Koroki's tangi. The story came to me from several different sources, but had obviously been dramatised on the way. I apologise most sincerely for any embarrassment that it may have caused.

A NOTE ABOUT THE THIRD PRINTING

In this reprinting of *Hui*, some minor corrections have been made to the text and to the map of East Coast meeting-houses, but the text remains essentially as it was written in 1972. *Te Ao Maori* (The Maori World) has not stood still in the past ten years, however – a spirit of determined pride has grown out of the struggles to retain Maori lands and language, and in every part of the country *marae* are being built and renovated and gatherings are held to plan for a Maori future. This book, then, has become a historical document, and I am glad that this is so. *Hui* was written to celebrate the creative diversity of tribal gatherings, not as a book of rules, and it is entirely proper that changing conditions and new practices should pass by it. Still, it stands as a memory to the elders – those makers and breakers of ritual regulations – whose practical wisdom it records.

Mauri tū, mauri ora   Act, and live
Mauri noho, mauri mate   Stay still, and die

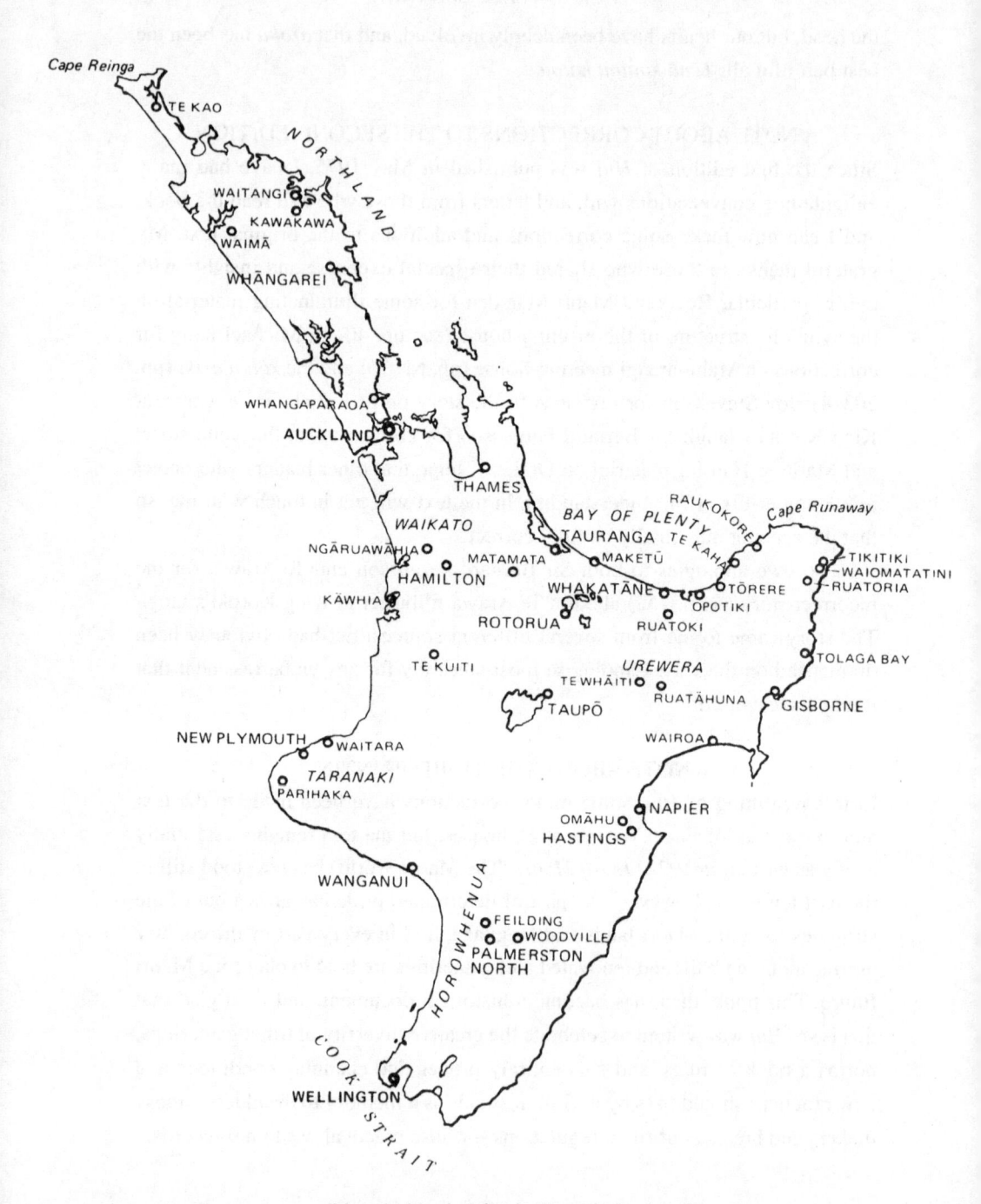

Map 1: North Island, New Zealand

CHAPTER ONE

INTRODUCTION

Over two hundred years of European contact, the Maori people of New Zealand have held on to their *Maoritanga* (Maori-ness, Maori culture) and expressed it most vividly through the *hui*. *Hui* is a general term in Maori for any kind of meeting, but when people say they have been to a *hui*, they are nearly always referring to a ceremonial gathering on a *marae*. The *marae* is a local centre, typically owned by a descent-group, with a meeting-house, dining-hall and forecourt for orators *(marae ātea)** set on about an acre of land. There are about a thousand *marae* throughout New Zealand, though they have never been precisely counted, and from time to time on every *marae* gatherings are held to celebrate the life crises of local people or major events in the life of the group. *Hui* include twenty-first birthdays, weddings, funerals, unveilings of memorial tombstones, tribal gatherings and the meetings of Maori organisations.

Hui (or huihuinga) are staged by the local people, and the hundreds or even thousands of visitors are accommodated and fed throughout their stay. As each group of visitors arrive on the *marae*, they are separately welcomed in a ritual that includes calling, wailing, chanting and oratory. This might be called the "ritual of encounter", because it is repeated for every group that attends the *hui*, and is structured as a balanced exchange between the local people *(tāngata whenua)* and the visitors *(manuhiri)*. On the "big day" of the *hui*, when all the visitors have arrived, the major ceremonial takes place. This depends on the type of *hui*, and it might be a wedding, a funeral, the opening of a new meeting-house or a religious ceremony. The rituals of encounter, however, are broadly the same for any *hui*, and it is they that define the *hui* as a class of occasion.

The *hui* is important to the study of contemporary Maori society, because it is in this context that *Maoritanga* is most deeply expressed.

---

*Throughout the text of this book, long vowels are represented by macrons over the vowel, except where direct quotes are given from other sources. This choice was made in deference to the wishes of those elders who contributed most to this study.

Throughout the *hui* Maori is the ceremonial language, Maori people dominate, Maori food is eaten, and Maori rituals are practised. On the *marae*, a distinctively Maori vision of New Zealand comes into play, a mythological landscape which includes places like Hawaiki the homeland, and the Underworld or *Pō*. Time stretches back in genealogical stages to the gods, the migrations to New Zealand, and the ancestors. People are aligned into tribes and sub-tribes, each with its own territory bounded by rivers and mountains. In the rituals, incantations are chanted that were once used for tree-felling, carving or paddling canoes, and the rituals themselves are not much different from those described by the earliest travellers. In the *hui* and on the *marae*, *Maoritanga* comes into its sharpest focus.

In everyday life, on the other hand, even in the most isolated Maori communities, European institutions and patterns of behaviour are a natural part of the scheme of things. English, not Maori, is becoming the daily language, and traditional values such as Maori *aroha* (love) mingle with newer enthusiasms for "rugby, racing and beer". The main social machinery of the country is European, and those parts of it that are set aside for Maori uses—the Department of Maori and Island Affairs, the four Maori seats in Parliament, the Maori Land Court, the New Zealand Maori Council, the Maori Women's Welfare League, the Maori Synods of the main churches and the Maori schools—are basically structures built from European blueprints. The chief indigenous structure that still operates is the descent-group system of tribes, sub-tribes, and extended families, and even this system is best expressed on the *marae*. Descent-group territories are now symbolic in many places, because the land has been sold or confiscated, and their remaining major corporate property is the *marae*. Descent-groups act as units in *marae* rituals, and recall their common history in genealogy and legend. The *marae* is becoming a place where people, particularly if they are city-dwellers, go to live for a time in a Maori way, and the *hui* is the gathering that calls them there. Maori people themselves see the *marae* as a last outpost of their traditional culture. "Without it," said one old man, "We are nothing."

Previous research on Maori culture has followed two main strategies. Early ethnologists such as Elsdon Best and Percy Smith, and professional anthropologists including Sir Peter Buck, Andrew Vayda and Bruce Biggs[1], have tried to reconstruct Maori society as it was before contact. Navigational routes, genealogies, legends, and the accounts of early travellers have all been used to suggest the outlines of the prehistoric period in New Zealand, and over the past forty years there has been a thriving archaeological tradition as well. Other scholars, the Beagleholes,

---

1. Buck (1962). Vayda (1960). Biggs (1960).

the Ritchies, Joan Metge and Patrick Hohepa,[2] have studied Maori communities in the field. Their accounts of the life of these communities form the basis of our knowledge of contemporary Maori society.

This study follows a different strategy from either reconstructive anthropology or community fieldwork. It is an exercise in what one might call the "anthropology of occasions", and it tries to capture Maori culture from the standpoint of its gatherings. As a result, both the field techniques and the theoretical perspective used are rather different from those of earlier accounts.

The main theoretical influences are threefold. Firstly there is the approach known as "emic anthropology". This broadly means that material collected in the field is analysed into those categories most commonly used by the people themselves. *Hui* and *marae*, for example, are pivotal concepts in this study, and the structure of each is expressed in categories whose validity and relative ordering are widely agreed upon by Maori informants. So the *hui* is distinguished into its various types, and its activities are described under their Maori names in the order they occur, as clearly and vividly as possible. The second influence, sociolinguistics, gives deep interest to the ways that verbal and other types of behaviour interact on the *marae*. Tapes were collected and analysed with a view to discovering how verbal behaviour varied at different parts of the ritual, and a paper was eventually written to show the structuring of on-stage verbal behaviour.[3] The final influence is a type of analysis pioneered by Erving Goffman, which recognizes the significance of situations as frames for human action. This gave validity to the original idea that Maori gatherings might be a valuable field for study. Plays for prestige, spatial behaviour and types of demeanour are investigated as part of a social drama, played out by actors who base their behaviour upon a set of ground rules and practise various types of manipulation. The ground rules are formally depicted in the paper cited above, and manipulations have become the topic for a separate paper on the political aspects of *marae* behaviour.[4] Theoretical discussion, however, is deliberately kept in the background in this account. The emphasis has been laid upon accurate, naturalistic description, not upon the theoretical ideas which informed the fieldwork. An acquaintance with the long tradition of Maori studies gives one a modest assessment of the values of theoretical argument in descriptive ethnography, because clear factual accounts date far better than those whose preoccupation rests with current thinking. I have therefore chosen to keep the full discussion of any theoretical insights arising out of the *hui* material for a separate series of papers. This

2. Beaglehole (1946). Metge (1964). Hohepa (1964). Ritchie (1963).
3. Salmond, A. In press (a)
4. Ibid. In press (b)

account, then, is not so much directed at the professional anthropologist, as those people in New Zealand, many of them Maori, who are deeply interested in *marae* activities and procedures.

Fieldwork

The study is based on two years of fieldwork in the North Island of New Zealand, from May 1970 to April 1972. During this time I was based at the Anthropology Department of the University of Auckland, and travelled from there to various *hui*, most often in the company of Mr and Mrs Eruera Stirling, respected elders of the Whānau-ā-Apanui tribe. I attended sixty-one *hui* in all, and of these twelve were taped with the permission of the local people, using a long-range microphone and a Nagra recorder. Eight other *hui* were photographed in detail by my husband to complete a photographic survey of *hui* activities. The total sample of *hui* was increased by eleven when students in the Traditional Maori Society course at the University of Auckland filed reports on *hui* they had attended in different parts of the North Island. Their accounts are listed in the bibliography, and are available in the University of Auckland and the Alexander Turnbull libraries.

The field strategy of this research was to gain a wide coverage of the North Island, partly because regional variation is an important aspect of *marae* rituals, and also because the *hui* forms an inter-tribal network (or set of networks), where people travel to each other's gatherings. Almost every *hui* attracts visitors from a distance, and some of the old people spend nearly all their time travelling on the network from one *hui* to another. The geographic distribution of the sample is given in Map 3. Coverage is lacking for the Tūwharetoa, Whanganui and Southern districts, and any statements about their rituals are based on interview material. The South Island was left out of the sample altogether because of distance, and the relatively small number of *hui* that are held there. (Only 6% of the Maori people live in the South Island.) Within the North Island, I aimed to become thoroughly familiar with one area, and chose the East Coast because it is both my own home district and that of my main informants. The other concentration of *hui*, in the Waikato area, happened as a result of its proximity to Auckland and the large number of *hui* that are staged there by the King Movement.

Urban as well as rural *hui* were studied, because the *hui* is undergoing some interesting changes in its adaptation to the towns, and of the total sample, forty-six were rural *hui* and twenty-six were urban. In the towns, gatherings are sometimes staged outside the *marae*, and of the sample, fifty-six *hui* were staged on *marae*, and sixteen in halls, schools, or private homes.

The seventy-two *hui* in the sample fall into the following types:

INTRODUCTION 5

Tangi (funeral)	18
Kawe mate (carry the death)	2
Hurahanga kōhatu (unveiling)	6
Weddings and twenty-firsts	3
Opening of a new *marae* building	4
Ministerial visits (Minister of Maori and Island Affairs)	5
Religious gatherings	8
King Movement gatherings	13
Semi-*hui*: conferences, meetings of Maori organisations, socials, etc.	13
	72

A continuing study might well have been made of *hui* staged at one *marae* throughout the research period, but this would really have been a separate project, and practical difficulties ruled it out. Studies of this type are included in field reports on Maori communities, although their perspective is the role of the *marae* in the community, rather than the life of the *marae* itself. The greatest number of *hui* attended at any one *marae* was six, at Māngere *marae* in Auckland.

The method of study for each *hui* was participant observation, backed by photographs and tapes. I heard of *hui* from contacts in other areas, at other *hui*, from the news media or, most efficiently of all, through the Auckland grapevine; and attended them with friends. Most *hui* were visited as a *manuhiri* (guest), but on East Coast *marae*, particularly in the Whānau-ā-Apanui district, I sometimes joined the Stirlings on the *tāngata whenua* (local) side. My knowledge of Maori was fluent, although by no means native, and I could understand most of what was being said on the *marae*, although it was difficult if the orator had a soft voice, or if there was loud background noise. People were most helpful about explaining what was happening, and some of my best information was gained in this way. After each *hui*, I wrote a full report of the activities from notes jotted down on the spot, or from memory, then cross-filed the notes by topic. Mrs Rangi Motu transcribed the tapes, and these provided detailed records of verbal behaviour for each *hui*. Photographs were valuable aids in working out spatial and movement patterns in the rituals, and the *hui* would make an excellent topic for an ethnographic film.

Field studies of *hui* were supplemented by extensive interviewing in people's homes and on the *marae*. The best results came from random conversations while the *hui* was actually in progress, or afterwards when people were discussing what had happened. Interviews were informal, and conducted in Maori, English or a mixture of both, whatever seemed most natural at the time. Informants were mostly selected for their expertise in different sections of *marae* procedure, but a number of people outside the *hui* network or only marginally involved in it were also interviewed, to gain a wider perspective. An excellent independent check on this material was provided by interviews conducted by about seventy members of the 1971 Contemporary Maori Society course at the University of Auckland, and of these reports fifteen were particularly valuable and are listed in the bibliography. These student papers are cited in chapter notes wherever they are the original source of data included in the account, and are also available in the University of Auckland and the Alexander Turnbull libraries.

Other valuable unpublished material included a series of talks, *Te Kawa o te Marae (Marae* etiquette), by the elders of different tribes, broadcast by the NZBC on the weekly Maori programme; a series of lectures entitled *Te Kawa o te Marae,* by Peter Awatere and Koro Dewes, written in Maori and cyclostyled by the Anthropology Department of the Victoria University of Wellington; and a series of newspaper articles written by Harry Dansey on Maori customs, printed in the *Auckland Star* during 1971 and 1972.

One major difficulty encountered in writing up the fieldwork was the decision whether or not to include detailed case studies of particular *hui*. In the end, no such material was included, because it proved impossible to preserve the anonymity of groups and individuals concerned. The ethnographer of a community can ask for local approval of any account to be published, but in the case of the *hui,* people from too many different areas are involved for this to be possible, and I feel that much of the data is unpublishable without proper permission.

Outline of Contents
This study was originally intended to be an account of the socio-linguistic patterns in *marae* behaviour, or to put it more plainly, how social and linguistic patterns interact on the *marae*. There is a great deal of this information to be discovered in *marae* rituals, for example the rules that govern turns of talk in oratory, the series of prescribed topics in a speech and the regulations about who may speak on the *marae,* who may *karanga* (call), who shall wail and who may sing. Verbal activity on the *marae ātea* is highly structured, and follows a definite sequence of ritual stages. It soon became apparent, however, that it would be partial and misleading to restrict the study to these sorts of patterns. The *hui* itself is a structured whole, and one cannot explain any of its parts in isolation. Many sections of the ritual include no verbal behaviour at all, for example the challenge *(wero),* but they are still clearly part of the whole and cannot be left out. The topic had to be defined on its own grounds, not according to some arbitrary theoretical perspective, and so the *hui* itself became the unit of analysis.

The aim of this study is to give a full portrait of the *hui;* not only of its rituals, but its background, setting, and staging as well. Because the topic is broad, the depth of coverage will inevitably vary. Some aspects of the *hui* have already been researched by specialists *(waiata*—ancient songs; *whaikōrero*—oratory),[5] and many other of its aspects are potential topics for full-scale study (e.g. the *hui* circuit; *hui* on one *marae* over a period; ethnographic film; the *karanga* or call). In this respect, the study might be regarded as a survey of a topic whose complexity invites a great deal of further investigation.

The account begins with the historical background of the *hui*. The *hui* is steeped in the past, and its rituals abound with mythological and historical allusions. This is a Maori past, however, reaching back through genealogy to a time before creation, and its account of the historical period differs considerably from those given in New Zealand history books.

Chapter 2 briefly describes this past, and outlines changes in *marae* rituals since contact.

Chapter 3 is a description of the *marae*. It discusses the physical and symbolic structure of *marae*, how they are established and opened, and their historical development from contact times to the present.

Chapter 4 is an account of how *hui* are staged. The *marae* has to be cleaned and made ready, visitors are contacted, and once they arrive at the *marae* they have to be fed, housed and entertained. This chapter describes how these tasks are carried out.

Chapters 5 and 6 give an account of the actual ritual performances on the *marae*. Chapter 5 describes the rituals of encounter stage by stage and all the rules that govern them. Chapter 6 on the other hand, is concerned with the main ceremonies on the "big day", and discusses how these vary for different types of *hui*.

Finally, Chapter 7 is conclusion and epilogue, a last statement about the research and the *hui*.

The one thing that must be remembered about this study is that it is an attempt to comprehend, from an unavoidably *pakeha* viewpoint, some matters that are deeply Maori. It is questionable whether the mystique of another culture can ever be truly experienced by an outsider; and more questionable still whether such experience could be captured in an academic account of this kind. It now seems to me that there are aspects of *hui* that can be understood only after a lifetime of participation, and that although the elders who helped in this study undeniably had such understandings, the *mauri* of their knowledge is inalienable, and remains with them. It is probably better that way. Despite these difficulties, their motive for helping in the study, and mine for writing this account, is a hope that it may somehow help to make the lives and hearts of Maori and *pakeha* a little less alien to each other.

5. McLean, (1965). Mahuta, (1974).

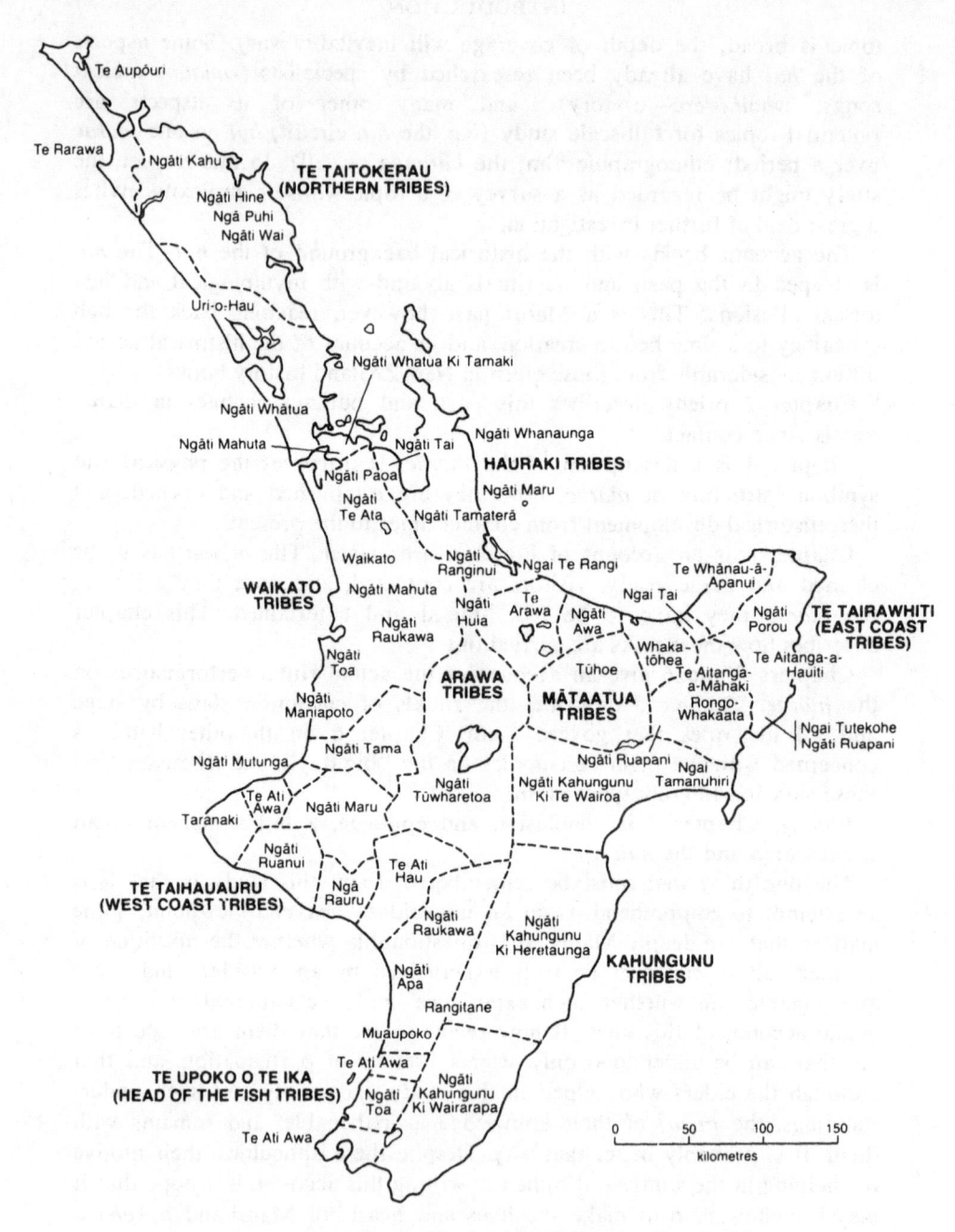

Map 2: North Island Tribes

The corrected North Island map in this fourth edition is derived from the map prepared for *Te Maori*, ed. Sidney Moko Mead, Heinemann Publishers (NZ) Ltd, 1984.

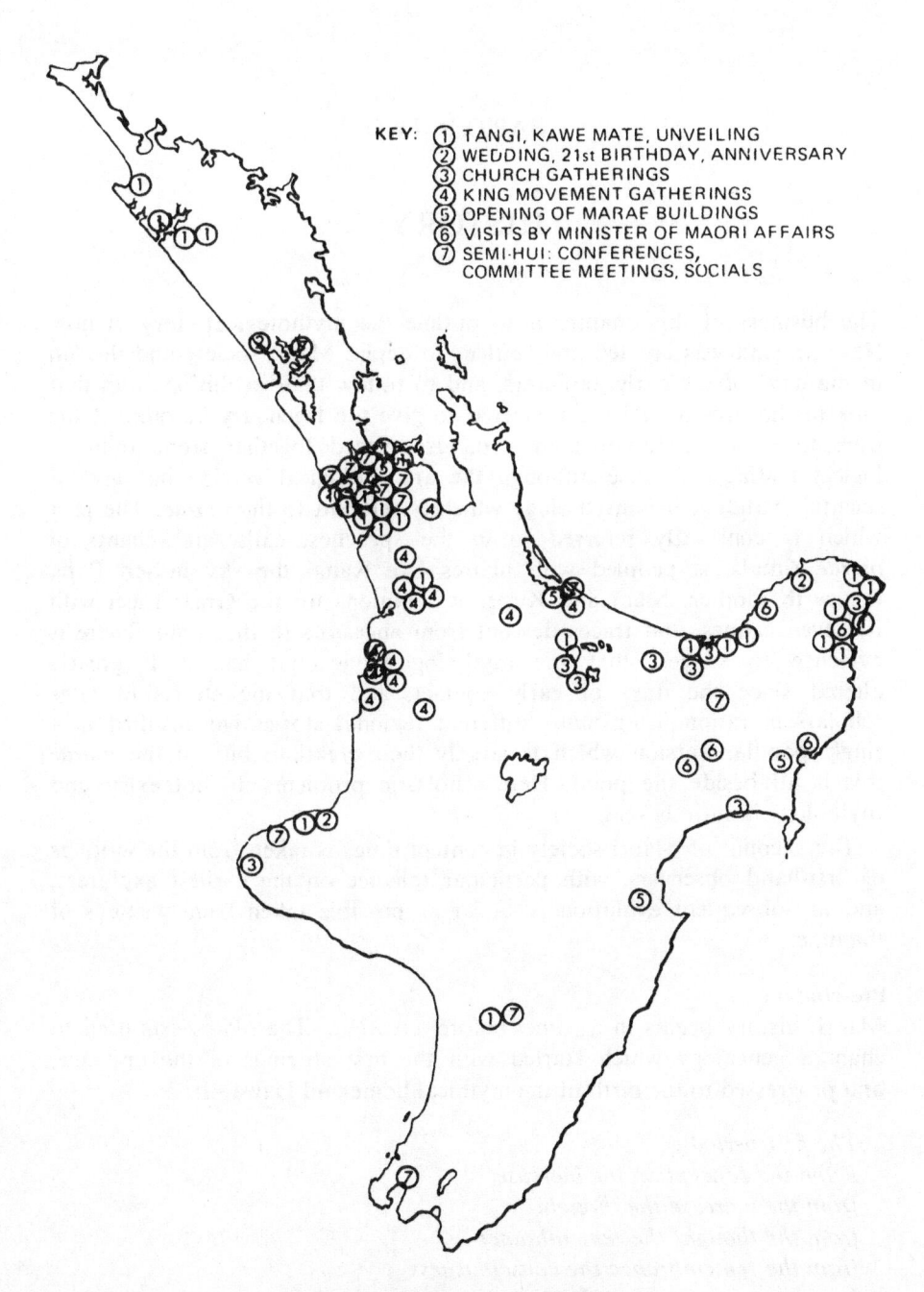

KEY: ① TANGI, KAWE MATE, UNVEILING
② WEDDING, 21st BIRTHDAY, ANNIVERSARY
③ CHURCH GATHERINGS
④ KING MOVEMENT GATHERINGS
⑤ OPENING OF MARAE BUILDINGS
⑥ VISITS BY MINISTER OF MAORI AFFAIRS
⑦ SEMI-HUI: CONFERENCES, COMMITTEE MEETINGS, SOCIALS

Map 3: Sample of *Hui* 1970-72

CHAPTER TWO

HISTORY

The business of this chapter is to outline the mythological story of how New Zealand was created and settled; to depict Maori society and the *hui* in the days of the early explorers, and to follow their evolution from that time to the present. I have preferred to give the legendary account of the prehistoric period rather than a picture pieced together from archaeological findings, because although the archaeological version has greater scientific validity, it is mythology which is relevent to the *marae*. The past which is constantly referred to in the speeches, calls, and chants of *marae* rituals, is peopled with figures like Rangi the sky father, Papa the earth mother, Māui and Kupe; it summons up the Great Fleet with its seven canoes, and traces descent from ancestors of that time. There is evidence to suggest that the mythological account has itself greatly altered since the days of early contact, and that the efforts of later scholars in rationalising many different regional stories has resulted in a single popular version which is largely their creation; but on the *marae* this is all beside the point. Here scholastic problems do not exist; and mythology is entirely real.

The account of Maori society in contact times is taken from the writings of first-hand observers, with particular reliance on the earliest explorers; and its subsequent evolution is as far as possible taken from writings of the times.

Pre-contact
Maori history begins in a time before creation. The old priests used to chant a genealogy which started with the first stirrings of the universe, and progressed to the birth of the mythical homeland Hawaiki:

The first period . . .
From the conception the increase
from the increase the thought
from the thought the remembrance
from the remembrance the consciousness
from the consciousness the desire.

The second period . . .
The world became fruitful
it dwelt with the feeble glimmering,
it brought forth night:
the great night, the long night,
the lowest night, the loftiest night,
the thick night, to be felt
the night to be touched
the night not to be seen
the night of death.

The third period. . .
From the nothing the begetting,
from the nothing the increase,
from the nothing the abundance,
the power of increasing,
the living breath:
it dwelt with the empty space and made the atmosphere which is above us
which floats above the earth,
the great firmament above us, dwelt with the early dawn,
And the moon sprang forth:
the atmosphere above us, dwelt with the heat
and thence proceeded the sun:
They were thrown up above as the chief eyes of heaven,
then the heavens became light,
the early dawn, the early day,
the mid-day. The blaze of day from the sky.

The fourth period . . .
The sky above dwelt with Hawaiki, and produced land . . . .[6]

Once the universe was created, and Hawaiki was born, then the gods were made. Rangi the sky father and Papa, the earth mother, were lovers, clasped in an age-long embrace. They had six sons who lived between them, the gods of the sea, winds, forest, wild foods, crops and mankind. The young gods lived in darkness, crushed by their parents, so they conspired to separate them and create a world of light. After several failures Tāne the god of the forests tore heaven from the earth, and the new world was made. The tears of the sky father rained upon his wife, and she returned his longing in soft mists which rose to greet him. Now the gods adorned their mother in trees and ferns, and their father with

---

6. Taylor (1855), pp. 109-10.

stars pinned to his cloak, and Tāne the male god made a woman from the earth and mated with her. From their mating mankind was born in Hawaiki, and a new era began.

One of the heroes of this time was Māui, last-born in a family of five sons. Māui was an outcast, scorned by his brothers, yet among other feats he tamed the sun, captured fire, tried to conquer death, and fished up New Zealand (afterwards called *Te Ika ā Māui*—Māui's fish) with his grandmother's magical jawbone. Once New Zealand was set in the ocean, it was only a matter of time before one of Māui's seafaring descendants from Hawaiki rediscovered it. This man was Kupe, and legend has it that he returned to Hawaiki from New Zealand and passed on his navigational instructions.

As time went on, Hawaiki became over-populated and war broke out. Those who were defeated had to find somewhere else to live, and some of them remembered Kupe's land to the south. Over a period a number of canoes, the *Tainui, Te Arawa, Mātātua, Kurahaupo, Aotea, Tākitimu* and *Tokomaru*, among others, left Hawaiki and navigated southward. Those canoes which made a successful landfall sailed round the coast until they found unclaimed territory, and there they settled. The crew members of each canoe cleared their land with stone adzes and fire, and began to cultivate it. As numbers multiplied and a settlement became overcrowded, some of its people moved out to pioneer a new tract of virgin bush. At first there was plenty of land for everyone, but after an initial period of expansion the best lands were taken, and boundary disputes became a common cause of fighting. By now the population was organised into descent-groups of different scale-tribes *(iwi)*, sub-tribes *(hapū)*, and extended families *(whānau)*. Each tribe occupied a large territory, and co-operated in large-scale gatherings and warfare. The sub-tribe was the main fighting unit, mustering about 150 fighting-men from its villages, a good number for the guerilla warfare tactics used; and the extended family was the living unit, sharing a cluster of huts and carrying out the everyday tasks. Men usually gave allegiance to their father's group, as a male link meant stronger claims to land and leadership in the group; but on occasion they might choose their mother's or some other group where prospects seemed more promising. Thus the descent continuity of a group, although it was predominantly patrilineal, sometimes included a female link as well.

The main themes in this society were *mana* (prestige), *tapu* (sacredness) and *utu* (the principle of equal return, often expressed in revenge). *Mana* was inherited at birth, and the more senior the descent, the greater the *mana*. From then on, despite an unequal start, men were engaged in a contest for relative *mana*, and according to performances in war, marriage, feasting and on the *marae, mana* rose and fell. *Tapu* (sacredness) invariably accompanied *mana*. The more prestigeous the event, person or object, the more it was surrounded by the supernatural protection of *tapu*. If a slave stole from a chief's hut, the gods protecting the chief's *tapu* would strike him down and kill him, but if a chief stole from a chief's hut, presumably their gods would match and nothing much would happen on that level. Politically, however, such an offence would demand *utu* (equal return). *Utu* was a human way of protecting *mana*, and it operated on the principle that for every slight on a person's *mana*, equal return should be taken. Sometimes *utu* was taken by the exercise of black magic, or *mākutu*, and the priests dealing in this art *(tohunga mākutu)* were greatly feared. Usually, however, *utu* was exacted on the battlefield, where it was difficult to mete out precisely the right amount of punishment, and after every such encounter, new *utu* accounts were established. As a consequence groups were forever skirmishing; villages had to be fortified and in the more embattled areas people lived in constant expectation of attack. It was such a society, based on hot pride and highly tuned to warfare, that was described by the earliest explorers. "No people can have a quicker sense of injury done to them," said Anderson in 1769, "and none are more ready to resent it."[7] Every man except the slave, who by definition had no *mana* at all, was entered in this touchy contest for prestige. Some by their descent started off with a considerable advantage, and were more likely to become chiefs than others, but ability in battle and on the *marae* could make a great chief out of moderate descent and a minor chief out of no descent at all. The *ariki* was a high chief at the tribal level who carried out important ceremonial functions, but although senior descent was a prerequisite for this position, the title-holder's ability largely determined whether he remained a figurehead or came to exercise real power. The *rangatira* was an executive chief, chosen for his ability in warfare and oratory, and senior descent was not essential for this role. The elders or *kaumātua* also wielded great influence, and age was a primary qualification for leadership.

Title-holders were revered in theory, but often disobeyed in fact. The Maori chief has frequently been depicted as an autocrat, but the earliest sources give rather a different picture: "The head of each tribe, or family, seems to be respected, and that respect may, on some occasions, command obedience; but I doubt if any amongst them have either a right or power to enforce it. The day we were with Tringo-boohee, the people came from all parts to see us, which he endeavoured to prevent. But though he went so far as to throw stones at some, I observed that very few paid any regard either to his words or actions; yet this chief was spoken of as a chief of some note."[8] (Cook 1769.)

7. Reed ed. (1951), p. 251.
8. Reed ed. (1951), p. 219.

Frederick Maning, a settler who lived among a Northern tribe for many years, gave a similar account in 1863: "The warriors . . . many of whom counted themselves to be very much about as good as the chief . . . were his nearest relations, without whose support he could do nothing, and were entirely beyond his control. I found out afterwards that it was only during actual war that this chief was perfectly absolute, which arose from the confidence the tribe had in him, both as a general and as a fighting man . . . The natives are so self-possessed, opinionated and republican that the chiefs have at ordinary times but little control over them, except in very rare cases, where the chief happens to possess a singular vigour of character, or some unusual advantage, to enable him to keep them under."[9]

Tribal and sub-tribal policy was forged by consensus, with all the chiefs and elders having a say. Whenever the group gathered, matters of policy were discussed, and the best orators commanded great influence. So it was that oratory became crucial to the exercise of leadership, and among the Maori it developed into an art. Chiefs took their small sons with them to meetings to watch the great orators perform, and in adolescence, highborn boys attended the night-time sessions of the *Whare Kura* ("Red" House, red being the sacred colour) to learn incantations, legends and genealogy. At any gathering the chiefs sat round in a circle, then one of their number stood to speak, as in this eyewitness account:

"Rising from old Kanini's side a chief with a glistening *kaitaka* mat . . . paces quietly and sedately forward, then he suddenly stops, faces about, and with slightly-quickened step paces back towards Kanini and delivers a sentence of his oration, arresting his further advance close to the chief. He now again turns round and walks deliberately back in silence to the starting-point, when again he suddenly faces Kanini, and, advancing this time more quickly than the last, he delivers a short sentence—never more than eight or ten words. Gradually, as he warms to his theme, he makes his advance and delivers his sentence at an increased rapidity. And soon the dignified orator begins to look a little wild; the flax mat now flies loosely about him, for he almost runs forward, and ends with a jump in the air almost at Kanini's feet, and looking rather as if he had intended to go clean over him! But the turning around and pacing back is always most sedately performed to give due breath and composing time to arrange his next sentence."[10]

Each chief spoke in turn, using proverbs, genealogy and argument to win over his audience, and for every fine performance, a man won extra *mana*. These gatherings were sometimes held in the village courtyard or *marae*, sometimes out on the beach or wherever two groups happened to

9. Maning (1863), p. 36.
10. Campbell (1881), p. 176.

meet. The initial encounter of hosts and visitors was ceremonious and formal because in those uneasy days it was difficult to tell friends from enemies, and as the groups approached they sent out challengers, performed the *haka* and enacted a sham battle that sometimes turned into warfare in earnest. This caution was well-founded, for there are many stories of visitors welcomed on to a host *marae*, only to be despatched into the *hāngi* (earth oven), and of guests who in the very act of greeting produced their weapons and slaughtered the local people. If peaceful intentions were established, the visitors were welcomed in, and speech-making began. To capture the atmosphere of these early gatherings *(hui)*, it is best to go back to a first-hand account:

"The path by which these doubtful friends were coming led through a dense forest and came out on the clear plain about half-a-mile from the *pa* (fortified village) . . . Morning came and an early breakfast was cooked and devoured hurriedly. Then groups of the younger men might be seen here and there fully armed, and "getting up steam" by dancing the war-dance, in anticipation of the grand dance of the whole warrior force of the tribe, which, as a matter of course, must be performed in honour of the visitors when they arrived. In honour, but quite as much in intimidation, though no-one said so. Noon arrived at last. Anxious glances are turning from all quarters towards the wood, from which a path is plainly seen winding down the sloping ground towards the *pa*. The outpost is on the alert. Straggling scouts are out in every direction. All is expectation. Now there is a movement at the outpost. They suddenly spread out in an open line, ten yards between each man. One man comes at full speed, running towards the *pa*, jumping and bounding over every impediment. Now something moves in the border of the forest—it is a mass of black heads. Now the men are plainly visible. The whole *taua* (party) has emerged upon the plain. 'Here they come! here they come!' is heard in all directions. Then men of the outpost cross the line of march in pretended resistance; they present their guns, make horrid grimaces, dance about like mad baboons, and then fall back with headlong speed to the next advantageous position for making a stand . . . No one can possibly tell what this peaceful meeting may end in, so all are ready for action at a second's notice. The *taua* still comes steadily on . . . They are now half way across the plain; they keep their formation, a solid oblong, admirably as they advance, but they do not keep step; this causes a very singular appearance when distant . . . this mass seems to progress towards you with the creeping motion of some great reptile . . . .

"The mimic opposition is now discontinued; the outpost rushes in at full speed . . . '*Takini! takini!*" is the cry, and out spring three young men, the best runners of our tribe, to perform the ceremony of the *taki* [challenge] . . . At this moment a tremendous fire of *ball* cartridges opens from the fort; the balls whistle in every direction, over and around the advancing party, who steadily and gravely come on, not seeming to know that a gun has been fired . . . Now, from the whole female population arises the shrill *'Haere mai! Haere mai!'* [welcome!]. Mats are waving, guns firing, dogs barking, the chief roaring to 'fall in' and form for the war dance . . . In the midst of this horrible uproar off dart three runners. They are not unexpected. Three young men of the *taua* are seen to tighten their waist belts and hand their muskets to their comrades. On go the three young men from the fort. They approach the front of the advancing column; they dance and caper about like mad monkeys, twisting their faces about in the most extraordinary manner, shewing the whites of their eyes and lolling out their tongues. At last, after several feints, they boldly advance within twenty yards of the supposed enemy, and send the reed darts flying full in their faces; then they turn and fly as if for life. Instantly, from the stranger ranks, three young men dart forth in eager pursuit; and behind them comes the solid column, rushing on at full speed. Run now, O 'Sounding Sea' . . . for the swiftest of the Rarawa, is at your back; run now, for the honour of your tribe and your own name, run! run! It was an exciting scene. The two famous runners came on at a tremendous pace . . . The pursuer gains upon his man; but they are fast nearing the goal, where, according to Maori custom, the chase must end . . . On came the headlong race. When within about thirty yards of the place where our tribe was now formed in a solid oblong . . . the pursuing native caught at the shoulder of our man, touched it, but could do no more. Here he must stop; to go farther would not be 'correct' . . . Our man has not, however, been caught, which would have been a bad omen. At this moment the charging column comes thundering up to where their man is standing; instantly they all kneel upon one knee . . . The *elite* of the two tribes are now opposite to each other, all armed, all kneeling . . . Only thirty yards divide them . . . All is silence; you might have heard a pin drop . . . Suddenly from the extreme rear of the strangers' column is heard a scream—a horrid yell. A savage of herculean stature, comes, *mere* in hand, and rushing madly to the front. He seems hunted by all the furies . . . he shouts the first word of the war song, and instantly his tribe spring from the ground." [Now the wardance is performed, the local people reply, then all is silence again.]

"Immediately a man from the new arrivals comes to the front of his own party; he runs to and fro; he speaks for his tribe; these are his words.—'Peace is made! peace is made! peace is firm! peace is secure! peace! peace! peace! . . . Some three or four others 'follow on the same side'. [Then a man from our side] 'Welcome! Welcome! Welcome! Peace is made! Not till now has there been true peace! I have seen you, and peace is made!' Here he broke out into a song, the chorus of which was taken up by hundreds of voices, and when it ended he made a sudden and very expressive gesture of scattering something with his hands, which was a signal to all present that the ceremonial was at an end for the time. Our tribe at once disappeared into the *pa* . . ." [and the visitors go to a long shed that has been prepared for them. Soon after the hosts bring out about seventy large pigs and heap up potatoes and kumara, about ten tons in all, then the younger women of the tribe bring hot food to the visitors.]

"They advanced with a half-dancing, half-hopping sort of step, to the time of a wild but not unmusical chant, each woman holding high in both hands a smoking dish of some kind or other of Maori delicacy, hot from the oven. The groundwork of this feast appeared to be sweet potatoes and *taro*, but on the top of each smoking mess was placed either dried shark, eels, mullet, or pork, all 'piping hot' . . .

"Next day, pretty early in the morning, I saw our chief . . . with a few of the principal men of the tribe, dressed in their best Maori costume, making their way towards the shed of the visitors. When they got pretty near, a cry of '*Haere mai!*' hailed them. They went on gravely, and observing where the principal chief was seated, our chief advanced towards him, fell upon his neck, embracing him in the most affectionate manner, and commenced a *tangi*, or melancholy sort of ditty, which lasted a full half hour, during which, both parties, as in duty bound and in compliance with custom, shed floods of tears . . . While the *tangi* was going on between the two principals, the companions of our chief each selected one of the visitors, and rushing into his arms, went through a similar scene . . .

"After the *tangi* was ended, the two tribes seated themselves in a large irregular circle on the plain, and into this circle strode an orator, who, having said his say, was followed by another, and so the greater part of the day was consumed . . . . Next day, at daylight, they disappeared: canoes from their own tribe had come to meet them . . . and they departed *sans cérémonie*, taking with them all that was left of the pigs and potatoes . . . Their departure was felt as a great relief, and though it was satisfactory to know peace was made, it was even more so to be well rid of the peacemakers."[11]

Maori gatherings have apparently long been called *hui*; in 1846 George French Angas mentioned that this was their label,[12] and although the rituals of encounter have changed in detail, they are not so very different from the ceremonies practised on modern *marae*. Sham warfare is no longer practised, in keeping with the general pacification of Maori society, but the challenge (now called *wero*), dances of welcome, calling, wailing, oratory, nose-pressing and feasting described by the early observers are still with us today. The *hui* included a wide range of gatherings, from life crises to policy meetings, and the

11. Maning (1863), pp. 41-56.
12. Angas (1847), Plate 36.

larger ones attracted thousands of visitors, many of whom had travelled 200 miles or more by foot and by canoe. In the early literature, the different types of *hui* were mostly referred to by their specific names e.g. *rūnanga* (policy meeting), *tangi* (funeral) or *hāhunga* (exhumation). One early type of *hui* which has now gone out of currency was the *hākari*, or feast for the sake of winning prestige. Today a feast is held at the end of every *hui*, but it is never the sole reason for gathering. In early contact times, however, magnificent feasts were staged by chiefs and later returned by their visitors as a visible display of wealth and a way of winning further *mana*. At one feast described by Angas, the pile of gifts, baskets of potatoes and dried fish was over a mile long;[13] and at another there were 11,000 baskets of potatoes, 100 large pigs, 9,000 sharks, and sacks of flour, sugar, rice and tobacco for about 4,000 guests.[14] It is still a matter of pride for the hosts at a *hui* to feed their visitors lavishly, but catering is no longer on such a grandiose scale. Despite these changes in emphasis and detail, however, the *hui* described by early observers is recognisably the forerunner of the *hui* today.

Post-contact

Since early contact times, the bases of Maori society have shifted profoundly. From an original subsistence economy, a peasant mode of livelihood developed, where flax, timber, food and kauri gum were sold to European traders; and later the industrial society was introduced to New Zealand, with Maori people mostly operating as wage-earners in the labouring echelons. From being an undisputed majority in the country, the Maori were brought near to extinction at the end of the nineteenth century by military clashes with the settlers, disease, and tribal warfare with the musket. Today they are an 8% minority in the population. Intensive missionary effort took much of the supernatural force from *tapu*, and pacification made the warlike settlement of *utu* accounts impossible. The indigenous political system based on territorial descent groups, with its checks and balances of continual skirmishing, has been replaced by a parliamentary system in which the Maori people are represented by four MPs. English has become the everyday language in all but a few rural communities, and perhaps 10% at most of those who are born Maori now speak Maori fluently. All these changes have had their effects on the *hui*, and can best be understood if we consider them chronologically and in greater detail.

The first contacts between Maori and European took place in 1642, when Abel Tasman and his party arrived at Golden Bay. A cock boat was rammed by the Maoris and four Dutchmen were killed. As always,

13. Angas (1850), Vol. I, p. 319.
14. Buller (1878), p. 91.

strangers who failed to engage in the proper rituals were treated as enemies, and attacked. In 1769 this pattern became clearer, when Captain James Cook circumnavigated the country. Time and again the local Maoris charged out in their canoes, brandishing weapons and chanting the war dance. On land, "they rose up and every man produced either a long pike or a small Weapon of polished stone . . . ; with these they threatened us and signed us to Depart."[15] These displays were indeed intended to intimidate, but they were part of the traditional rituals of encounter and not necessarily hostile. The explorers weren't to know this however, and they retaliated with musket-fire whose effects were anything but ritual. To do Cook justice, he fired on people only as a last resort, but others who followed him were not as circumspect.

After initial exploration came trade; the whalers and sealers found New Zealand a profitable hunting-ground and traded nails and cloth for women and food. These transactions were not always satisfactory, and fighting between Maori and European became common. The next visitors made an even greater and more lasting impact. The missionaries, headed by the Rev. Samuel Marsden, began to arrive in New Zealand from 1814 onwards. Dedicated to peace, and to the souls of the Maori people, the missionaries travelled to many *hui*, learned the Maori language, and preached on the *marae*. Marsden described the rituals of encounter in detail, and was present at many sham battles and war dances performed for his entertainment. It is to these early missionaries that we owe the first full accounts of *marae* custom. Mission stations were established, special church *hui* were held, and no doubt Christian doctrine became a favourite talking point on *marae* all over New Zealand. As more and more Maoris were converted, prayers for the first time played an important part in their gatherings.

After the missionaries, came the established commercial interests, and it was only now that the Maori economy really started to change. Guns were introduced to New Zealand, wholesale, and as a matter of survival many tribes left their cultivations and worked furiously to gather enough dressed flax or timber to equip their fighting men. Once they had traded an adequate arsenal, they went on the warpath. Fighting during this period was on a scale unrivalled in pre-contact times; guns were far more lethal weapons than stone *mere* or wooden *taiaha* had ever been, and some tribes were virtually exterminated. Old *utu* accounts began to run wild, and new causes for vengeance were established every day. The Northern Maoris, close to the European trading centres, were the first to be armed. Their leader, Hongi Hika, made a state visit to England in 1821, and returned laden with gifts which he traded in Sydney for 300 muskets. Clad in a suit of armour given to him by George IV, he led his warriors on a ram-

---

15. Morrell ed. (1958), p. 42.

page over the North Island, killing off old enemies in their thousands. At Rotorua the Arawa retreated to Mokoia Island in the middle of Lake Rotorua, believing themselves safe from attack. Hongi had canoes hauled overland and massacred them all. From Rotorua Hongi proceeded down the East Coast by canoe, stopping periodically to attack coastal *pā*. After a devastatingly successful attack on Whetumatarau Pā at Te Araroa, Hongi went on to Whareponga. Garbled accounts of the new weaponry had reached the people there, and according to contemporary legend, they concluded that these sticks which popped and shot off projectiles must be a new version of their familiar toy, the *whāmamaku* gun. They went into the bush, collected straight branches from the *patete* trees, hollowed out the pith, and manufactured *kūmara* projectiles. Soon they had a sizeable armoury of these 'pop-guns', which they took along with their more trusted weapons up into Kōkai Pā. Soon Hongi's canoes appeared around the point, and his war-party landed on the beach below the *pā*, armed with muskets. Now the story takes a twist which shows a wry humour characteristic of much of Maori history. The Ngāti Porou warriors were still far from taking these new weapons seriously, and as Hongi's men came up the beach, the defenders stood on the ramparts of their *pā*, waving their home-made guns and calling out *"Enā whāmamaku ki ēnei whāmamaku!"* (Your pop-guns against ours!) Hongi let them cavort around, and then dared them to carry their insults to the ultimate point of contempt—*"Whakarewa tō papatū, e mara!"* (Alright then, lift up your legs at me, you lot!) Ngāti Porou, unable to resist such a challenge, stood on the ramparts, turned round and exposed their bare bottoms to the Northern invader. There was a rattle of musket fire, and many of the Ngāti Porou toppled over, never again to jeer at firearms.[16]

Hongi's attacks set off further chain reactions of fighting, notably in the Waikato area, where the chief Te Rauparaha was expelled from Kāwhia and went on to invade and conquer land on both sides of the Cook Strait.

On his way south, Te Rauparaha made one last attack on the Waikato, and surrounded the camp of his kinsman Pōtatau, Waikato's paramount chief. It was nightfall, and the camp was entirely at his mercy. As his men moved in take *utu* for their expulsion from Kāwhia, Pōtatau called out *"E Raha, he aha tō koha māku?"* (Raha, what is your gift to me?) The nickname and the appeal reminded Rauparaha that they were kinsmen, and he let Waikato go. To illustrate how long these events are remembered, we can refer to an event 100 years later, when a descendant of Te Rauparaha was campaigning for the Western Maori seat in Parliament. He and his opponent had about equal support, and the Waikato votes hung in the balance. His opponent stood and traced

---

16. Eruera Stirling, personal communication (1973).

his kinship with the Waikato royal line, and called for their support. Then it was the turn of Te Rauparaha's descendant. For a long time he sat silent. When everything was absolutely quiet, he stood, and said simply, "I heard a voice crying in the night '*E Raha, he aha tō koha māku?*' " The Waikato people knew instantly what he meant and they knew that the old debt had never been repaid. That cry in the night won him the election, and he held the Western Maori seat to the end of his days.[17]

In the tribal fighting of those days the missionaries frequently acted as mediators, and they swore their converts to peace. Self-supporting mission stations were run on the lines of English farming villages, schools were established, and the mission Maoris were taught to read and write as well as to cultivate the land. The activities of the missions, however, were hampered by their own incessant squabbling and the general lawlessness of the European population. Kororareka, the "capital" in the Bay of Islands, was dominated by runaway sailors, escaped convicts and beachcombers, who ridiculed the missionaries, gave the Maoris liquor and acted as their fighting advisers. In 1825 a New Zealand Company was formed in London with the aim of promoting colonial settlement, and it united with the missionaries, merchants and shipping companies to form a powerful lobby for British intervention. In 1833 James Busby was sent out from Sydney as a British Resident, but his activities were ineffectual. Pressure mounted for more decisive British action, and in 1839 Captain Hobson was issued with instructions to enter into treaty with the Maori chiefs. They were to cede sovereignty and the sole right of land purchase to Queen Victoria, in return for the rights of British subjects and protection of their lands, forests and fisheries. In 1840 the Treaty of Waitangi was signed at a *hui* in the Bay of Islands, then the document was circulated around New Zealand for further signatures.

Maning, the "Pākeha-Maori" quoted earlier, has given a wry account of how one of his Northland friends viewed Captain Hobson's activities: "The next thing we heard was that the Governor was travelling all over the country with a large piece of paper, asking all the chiefs to write their names or else make marks on it. We heard also that the Ngapuhi chiefs, who had made marks or written on that paper, had been given tobacco, and flour, and sugar, and many other things for having done so. We all tried to find out the reason why the Governor was so anxious to get us to make these marks. Some of us thought the Governor wanted to bewitch all the chiefs, but our *pakeha* friends laughed at this, and told us that the people of Europe did not know how to bewitch people. Some said the Governor only wanted our consent to remain, to be a chief over the *pakeha* people; others said he wanted to be chief over both *pakeha* and Maori. We did not know what to think, but were all anxious he might come

17. Cowan (1934), pp. 119-24.

to us soon; for we were afraid that all his blankets and tobacco and other things would be gone before he came to our part of the country, and that he would have nothing left to pay us for making our marks on his paper.

"Well, it was not long before the Governor came, and with him came other *pakeha* chiefs, and also people who could speak Maori; so we all gathered together . . . and went to meet him; and when we met the Governor, the speaker of Maori told us that if we put our names, or even put any sort of mark on that paper, the Governor would then protect us, and prevent us from being robbed of our cultivated land, and our timber land, and everything else that belonged to us. Some of the people were very much alarmed when they heard this, for they thought that perhaps a great war expedition was coming against us from some distant country, to destroy us all; others said he was only trying to frighten us. The speaker of Maori then went on to tell us certain things, but the meaning of what he said was so closely concealed we never have found it out. One thing we understood well, however, for he told us plainly that if we wrote on the Governor's paper, one of the consequences would be that great numbers of *pakeha* would come to this country to trade with us, and that we should have abundance of valuable goods . . . we were very glad to hear this, for we never could, up to this time, get half muskets or gunpowder enough, or blankets, or tobacco, or axes, or anything . . . After Te Tao Nui and other chiefs had made marks and written on the Governor's paper, the Governor did not give them anything. We did not like this, so some of the other chiefs went forward, and said to the Governor 'Pay us first, and we will write afterwards!' A chief from Omanaia said 'Put money in my left hand, and I will write my name with my right' . . . but the Governor shook his head and looked displeased, and said he would not pay them for writing on the paper.

"Now, when the people saw this they were very much vexed, and began to say one to another 'It is wasting our labour coming here to see this Governor,' and the chiefs began to get up and make speeches. One said 'Come here, Governor; go back to England,' and Paapahia said 'Remain here and be Governor of this Island, and I will go to England and be King of England, and if the people of England accept me for their King it will be quite just; otherwise you do not remain here.' Then many other chiefs began to speak, and there was a great noise and confusion, and the people began to go away, and the paper was lying there, but there was no one to write on it. The Governor looked vexed, and his face was very red. At this time some *pakeha* went amongst the crowd and said to them 'You are foolish; the Governor intends to pay you when all the writing is done, but it is not proper that he should promise to do so; it would be said that you only wrote your names for pay; this, according to our ideas, would be a very wrong thing.' When we heard this we all began to write as fast as we could, for we were all very hungry with listening and talking so long . . .

and we were also in a hurry to see what the Governor was going to give us...

"Next morning the things came with which the Governor intended to pay us for writing our names, but there was not much tobacco, and only a few blankets; and when they were divided some of the chiefs had nothing, others only got a few figs of tobacco, some one blanket, others two... I saw there was going to be a dispute about them, and said, 'Let us send them back.' So we went to the house of a *pakeha*, and got a pen and some paper, and my son, who could write, wrote a letter for us all to the Governor, telling him to take back all the blankets and to cut our names out of the paper, and then my two brothers and my sons went back and found the Governor in a boat about to go away. He would not take back the blankets, but he took the letter. I do not know to this day whether he took our names out of the paper. It is, however, no matter; what is there in a few black marks? Who cares anything about them?"[18]

As it happens, a great many people have cared a great deal about the Treaty of Waitangi since it was signed, and it has been a contentious topic ever since. Maori grievances centre on two points: that the full implications of the Treaty were not explained at the time, and its Maori translation was in some parts misleading; and that its promises have not been honoured. The clause about protection of land, forests and fisheries has caused particularly bitter resentment, because whether by intent or not, the Maori people have been progressively stripped of their real estate by legislation and confiscation as well as sale. The annual *hui* at Waitangi to commemorate the Treaty has in recent years been attended by young demonstrators who heckle in Maori, chant war songs in the background and have brought these grievances to the public eye. On the other hand, many elders believe that such tactics of dissent have no place on the *marae*, where speakers are traditionally immune to interruption, and young people should be seen but not heard.

Once the Treaty was signed, representatives of the New Zealand Company as well as private entrepreneurs travelled around New Zealand buying up land, and settlement began in earnest. Men such as John Logan Campbell and E. J. Wakefield, son of the founder of the New Zealand Company, wrote vivid accounts of *hui* called at this time to discuss land sales, and Wakefield in particular describes the rituals that were followed. The land sale system was wide open to abuse on both sides. In Maori terms land was inalienable, taken only by conquest and occasionally transferred by gift; and it was group property, held in trust by the chiefs. The chiefs had no traditional right of disposal, since this like everything else operated by consensus, nor was there any precedent for sale. In their hunger for European goods, especially muskets, unscrupulous chiefs sold off land

18. Maning (1863), pp. 216-20.

without consulting their people, or even land to which they had no claims at all. In their greed for land, settlers did not always examine the chief's credentials carefully, and paid the lowest possible prices. Some of the missionaries ended up claiming blocks of 10,000 and 20,000 acres, and Crown agents routinely bought up land for sixpence an acre and re-sold it for ten shillings.

Along with these abuses, the rum trade caused widespread drunkenness among Maoris, missionary teaching undermined *tapu* and the authority of chiefs, the wives and children of polygymous marriages were abandoned by converts, and Maoris were denied the vote. As increasing numbers of settlers entered New Zealand, the *pākehā*, and not other tribes, became the figure to contend with. In an effort to put their house in order and to deal with the European on equal terms, a great *hui* was called at Taupo in 1857 to appoint a Maori King. Attended by 6,000 people, it was the first of many gatherings to be sponsored by the King Movement. The Kingship was offered to a number of major chiefs, all of whom turned it down, and finally the choice settled on Te Wherowhero, an old fighting chief of the Waikato tribes. After some persuasion, Te Wherowhero accepted the position, and became King Pōtatau I. Under his guidance, policemen were appointed, laws were passed, and a series of village *rūnanga* (policy meetings) were instituted to ensure internal law and order.

Although its supporters claimed that the King Movement was aimed at controlling local anarchy, and was not in opposition to the Queen, European officials interpreted it as a hostile movement. Soon after it was established, troubles broke out in Taranaki. Great pressure had been put on the Maoris in Taranaki to sell their land, but most of them entered into a Land League under Wiremu Kingi, and steadfastly refused. In 1859 a dissident chief offered a block of land to Governor Gore-Browne, and although his right to sell the land was disputed, the Governor accepted. When he tried to take possession, the local Maoris resisted and war broke out. Some of the Taranaki tribes had given their allegiance to the King Movement, and now they called for Waikato support. Pōtatau had died, and the new King Tāwhiao was reluctant to become involved; but when his territory was invaded after he received an ultimatum from the Government to submit to the sovereignty of the Queen, and to pay damages for the destruction in Taranaki, the war spread to the Waikato.

Skirmishing continued for several years; and in 1865 the war became a religious crusade. In South Taranaki a leader called Te Ua Haumene founded the bitterly anti-*pākehā* "Hauhau" cult, which combined a belief in angels with witchcraft and spiritualist practices. Te Ua claimed to have been visited by the angel Gabriel, who told him that the Maori people were the Lost Tribes of Israel. On instructions from Gabriel, Te Ua and his men ambushed a party of soldiers, decapitated their officer and preserved his head. They believed that once the head had been carried throughout the North Island, legions of angels would exterminate the *Pākehā*, and the gifts of tongues and all knowledge would descend upon the faithful. The cult spread to the East Coast, where it influenced a local man called Te Kooti. Although he was serving with the Government troops in the Gisborne campaign, Te Kooti was arrested as a Hauhau in 1866 and deported to the Chatham Islands, where he was told in a vision to found a church for the salvation of the Maori people. In 1868 he escaped on the schooner *Rifleman*, and began a prolonged guerilla campaign which did not end until 1871, when he fled to take refuge with King Tāwhiao in the King Country, a territory closed to Europeans. Over the next twenty years, Te Kooti shaped the scriptures into Maori chants, issued prophetic statements, and travelled about the North Island setting up branches of his "Ringatū" church.

About the same period in Taranaki, the Hauhau cult gave way to a peaceful movement which advocated passive resistance to land confiscations and negative aspects of European culture. Their leader, Te Whiti o Rongomai, founded a settlement at Parihaka in 1866, and over the next twenty years he instituted a strict moral programme forbidding drunkenness, moral laxity, and economic greed; he founded his own school, laid down sealed roads, and made Parihaka a model village with outlying farms, its own bakery, abattoir, water supply and electricity. Te Whiti preached brotherly love, regularly attracting several thousand people to his gatherings at Parihaka, and by 1881 it was estimated that 10% of the Maori people were his followers. Unforgivably, however, Te Whiti refused to recognise European law, especially as applied to land confiscations, and when European settlers came to occupy confiscated land in Taranaki, he sent out his men to plough over the survey lines and pegs. In 1881 the Government decided that Te Whiti had to be removed, and troops were sent to the *marae* at Parihaka. Local legend has it that while Te Whiti assembled his people on the *marae*, exhorting them to prayer, the troops set up a cannon and threatened that if the group did not disperse by morning, they would fire into the *marae*. All that night the people prayed to avert the disaster. In the morning at the appointed hour, a torch was applied to the cannon but it refused to fire. It seems that during the night a dog, inspired by Te Whiti's pacifism, had urinated on the powder, and the people were saved. Despite this moral victory, Te Whiti and his lieutenant, Tohu, were detained without trial in the South Island until 1883.

Also in 1881, King Tāwhiao signed a peace treaty with the Government's representative, Captain Gilbert Mair, and the so-called "Maori" wars were officially over. In retribution for Maori stubbornness, 3 million acres of land from friendly tribes as well as hostile were subsequently confiscated. Apart from an abiding resentment of the confiscations, the conflict had a long-standing effect in the form of the movements that were consolidated during its time. The King Movement, for one, continued for many years as a separatist organisation, fuelled by the bitterness of particularly heavy confiscations in the Waikato area. In World War I the Waikato people refused conscription into the Armed Forces, and it was not until 1946 when Prime Minister Fraser arranged for £50,000 compensation to be paid to the Waikato tribes that reconciliation could begin. In recent years the Movement has become far less militant, and a number of tribes outside the Tainui confederation have offered it their allegiance. The present Queen, Te Ata-i-Rangi-Kāhu, the sixth of the Maori monarchs, presides over a movement with wide influence in Maori circles, and amicable relations with the European world. The King Movement sponsors an annual celebration of the Queen's Coronation, a regatta, and a cycle of almost thirty *poukai* (visits by the Queen and her council to loyal *marae*), and the Waikato is one of the most active areas for *hui* in New Zealand today.

The Ringatū church founded by Te Kooti also sponsors a regular series of *hui* to celebrate their faith. Currently about 3% of the Maori population claim to be Ringatū, and of these the great majority are to be found in Tūhoe country. The 12th of each month and the first day of the year are sacred festivals, when Ringatū people assemble at their local *marae* to share a two-day service. The Ringatū church is often characterised as "the real Maori" church, and its services include features such as the chanting from memory of long Biblical passages, cadenced to sound like traditional Maori music, the cleansing of sins in a sacred fire, and priestly experts called *tohunga* (the ancient term for "priest").

The final movement founded during this period, the Te Whiti cult in Taranaki, has gradually faded, but the *hui* are still held by a small group of the faithful on the 18th of each month, with a special day on 6 November to commemorate the siege of Parihaka. There are signs of a revival in Parihaka, and some of the young people are trying to recapture the legends, chants, poi dances and the songs of Te Whiti's drum and fife band before the last of his second-generation followers die.

After the worst of the fighting in the 1860s, legislation was passed to speed the assimilation of Maori people into an essentially European social structure. In 1865 a Native Land Court was established to search out titles on Maori land and to regulate sales. Although this legislation was, in part at least, well-meaning, it led to further land problems. In Maori land tenure, the only right to land was the right to use it, acquired by inheritance from either parent and ratified by residence. The court interpreted this custom as inheritance of total rights through both parents, and lifted the residence requirement. As a result, over a number of generations there has been a disastrous fractionation of shares in Maori land. Now a single small block may have 1,000 or more owners, and the question of administration is very difficult. Sittings of the Maori Land Court, yet another type of *hui*, are frequently marked by bitter family squabbles, and legislation to force the sale of uneconomic shares has aroused further suspicions of a Government plot to seize all Maori lands.

In 1867 the Maoris were given manhood suffrage and four Maori seats in Parliament. Candidates for these seats campaign in election year on *marae* all over their district, and these gatherings too, are a type of *hui*. Initially intended as a temporary expedient until Maori people could be phased into European electorates, these seats are now jealously guarded as a Maori voice in Parliament, and leaders are calling for seven Maori seats, not four—an increase proportionate to the rise in Maori population.

In 1867 "Native Schools" were established in Maori settlements. Unlike the early Mission Schools, all classes were conducted in English, and from this time one can date the progressive decline in Maori as an everyday language. For a long time children were strapped for speaking Maori at school, and many of them were taught to regard their language as inferior. This attitude was fostered by parents who tried not to speak to their children in anything but English, the language for successful adjustment to the European world. The trend has continued, until today perhaps 10% or less of the Maori population are fluent in their ancestral language, and the process is constantly accelerated by urbanisation. Maori is now spoken as an everyday language only in a few rural areas, and in other districts it functions mainly as a ceremonial language on the *marae*. In the last few years Maori has been offered as a subject in many secondary schools, training colleges and universities, but this trend is still too recent to show any widespread effects.

Towards the turn of the century Maoris were entering employment as unskilled labourers, working on roads and railways, scrub-cutting and shearing sheep, while their leaders agitated for greater control over Maori affairs and a check on land alienation. An unofficial Maori Parliament, the Kotahitanga, was established in 1892 and continued to operate for eleven years, petitioning against unfavourable legislation and striving to unite the tribes into a single lobby. It was not until early in the twentieth century, however, that effective political action was taken. In 1897 a group of young Maori men, educated at Te Aute College, founded the "Young Maori Party" and began to travel to *marae* all over the North Island, urging their people to resist land sales, to improve their living conditions, and to take pride in their identity as Maoris. These men became effective orators, and used their *marae* skills as well as their ideals to get themselves elected to Parliament. Here they proceeded to put their ideas into legislation, and it was during this time that a number of major reforms became law. Chief among these leaders were Apirana Ngata, who specialised in land reforms and in the revival of Maori arts; Maui Pomare, a medical doctor specialising in housing and sanitation; and Peter Buck, who later became a well-known anthropologist in Hawaii. Apirana Ngata was probably the most powerful personality of them all; he led his East Coast people into revolutionary land reforms, setting up land incorporations, arranging Government finance, and stocking the holdings with dairy cows. These he paid for by the ingenious expedient of putting the entire Ngāti Porou tribe under a two-year Prohibition, diverting funds from the pubs to pay off the cows. He was in league with the women to push Prohibition through, and one of the most memorable and certainly the most abusive *haka* performed on the East Coast today dates from this time, its composer being one of the infuriated menfolk of the Ngāti Porou. Ngata survived these and other onslaughts and went on to become Native Minister for a time. In 1926 the Maori Arts and Crafts Act was passed which provided funds to establish a school of carving; and in 1929 the Native Land Development Act authorised the application of public funds to the development of Maori lands. All these new policies were debated at length on *marae* all over the country, and special *hui* were called for Government officials to explain the legislation to the people.

Not everyone was inspired by this new brand of leadership however, and when in 1920 a man called Wiremu Rātana began having visions and healing people at his home near Whanganui, he attracted thousands of followers. An angel instructed Rātana to turn his people away from the old superstitions and to heal them by faith, and by 1920 after a series of large gatherings at Rātana Pā, 20,000 people had signed his covenant. Rātana enraged some of the more conservative tribes by desecrating their cemeteries in an attempt to discredit remaining beliefs in *tapu*, actively discouraged traditional arts such as carving, and asked his followers to hand over their family heirlooms (cloaks, *mere*, etc.) In 1925 Rātana registered his movement as a separate church, and moved into politics. Soon the Rātana Movement controlled all four Maori seats, and an alliance was forged with the Labour Party which repeatedly tipped the balance of power in their direction. Other secular enterprises were less successful, however, including a bank that went bankrupt and a wheat farm that went barren, and the Movement began to lose its prestige. People began to move away from Rātana Pā, and Rātana died in 1939, but annual gatherings continue to be held by the Movement, and an estimated 13% of the Maori population, concentrated particularly in Northland, still follow Rātana's teachings.

In 1939, when the Second World War broke out, young men in their hundreds joined the Maori Battalion for service overseas, where their valiant fighting spirit won the admiration of other New Zealanders. At home their elders farewelled each new contingent of recruits with a great *hui*, joined the Home Guards, composed action songs for "their boys" and waited for them to come home again. The Maori Battalion still conducts an annual *hui* of reunion, and the songs that were composed in its honour continue in wide currency on *marae* all over the country. When the war was over, some of the soldiers took over Maori farms, but most of them turned to the cities. During the war, rural people had shifted to the towns to work in munitions factories and other essential services, and after the war there began a steady stream of young Maori people towards the cities. With increasing urbanisation, many *marae* were almost deserted, and gradually more *hui* came to be held in the towns. Urbanisation also meant a closer participation in the European system; more people began to seek higher education, and increasing numbers of Maoris entered the universities and the professions. New organisations such as the New Zealand Maori Council and the Maori Women's Welfare League, each structured as a hierarchy of committees, were established, and they brought a new co-ordination to the expression of Maori opinion. Their annual conferences are attended by delegates from all over the country, and remits are forwarded to Government to express the opinions of their members on questions of policy and legislation. Although these gatherings are still called *hui*, the main part of their proceedings are regulated by a version of "Robert's rules" and not by *marae* etiquette. These organisations and the universities have produced a new generation of articulate leaders. People like Dr Patrick Hohepa, a University lecturer and Chairman of the Auckland District Council, and groups like Ngā Tamatoa, a student-based organisation, are using such techniques as television interviews, speeches to European organisations, conferences, and demonstrations to express their views of Maori grievances. Although these leaders frequently visit the *marae*, they are fundamentally outside the *marae* system of leadership, and are forging a new forum for the expression of Maori opinion.

From earliest times to the present, therefore, the *marae* and its gatherings have played a central role in Maori policy-making, often with powerful historical effects. It is a tribute to the vitality of the *hui* that of all pre-contact institutions it has best survived changing historical conditions, altering its functions without substantially losing its form.

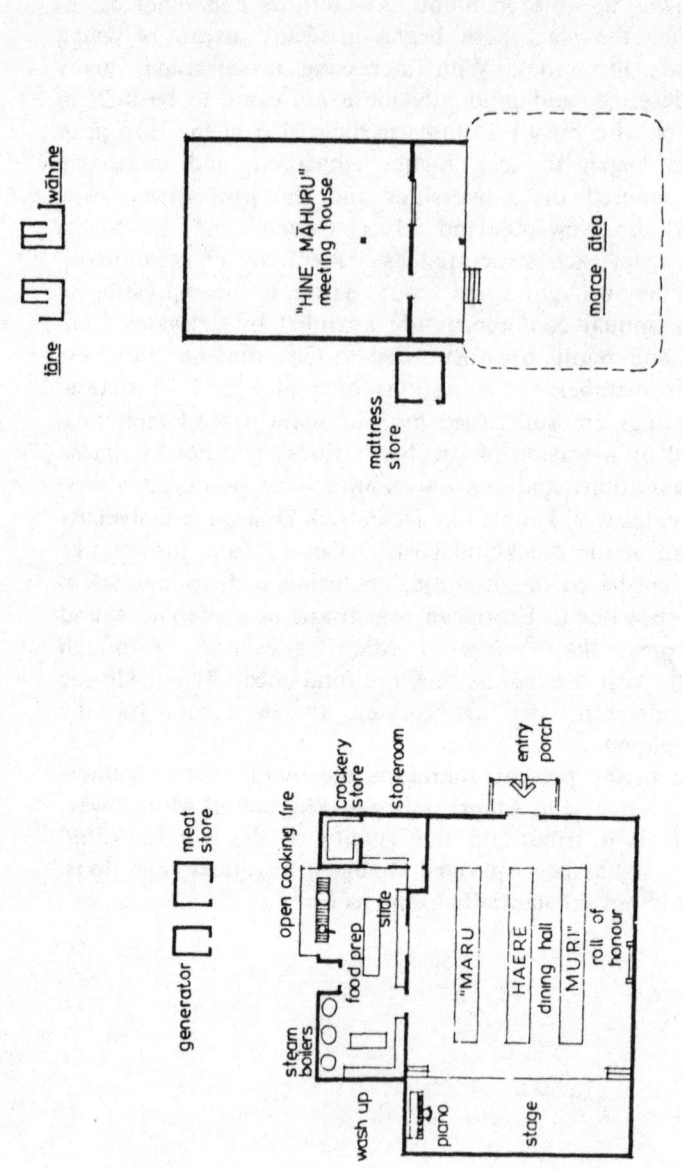

Figure 1: Marae Plan: Wairūrū marae, Raukokore, East Coast

CHAPTER THREE

THE SETTING: "A PLACE TO STAND"

The *Marae*
The *marae* is a local ceremonial centre, dedicated to the gatherings of Maori people and to the practice of traditional rituals. Each *marae* has a meeting-house, a dining-hall and other small buildings set in about an acre of land and fenced off from surrounding properties. Sometimes though, the total *marae* reserve can be thirty acres or more. Directly in front of the meeting-house lies an empty expanse of lawn, and this, although physically inconspicuous, is the focus of the complex—the *marae ātea* or ceremonial courtyard. These centres are a familiar feature of the New Zealand landscape, for there are several *marae* in most communities with a sizable Maori population, and about 1,000 *marae* in the country as a whole. Despite this familiarity, the *marae* retains a considerable aura of mystery for most New Zealanders, including increasing numbers of young Maori people; because their rituals are best understood only by those who frequent them.

The great majority of *marae* are found in rural districts, in areas of high Maori population such as Northland, Waikato, Urewera, and the East Coast. Each rural *marae* is owned either by the local community or by a local descent-group, usually a sub-tribe *(hapū)*, although a major *marae* might be vested in an entire tribe *(iwi)*, and a small one in an extended family *(whānau)*. For all members of the owner group, the *marae* is their "place to stand" or *tūrangawaewae*. They hold their weddings, twenty-first birthdays and funerals there; the meeting-house is carved with representations of their ancestors, hung with family portraits, and named after a major leader or event of the past. Their forebears are buried nearby, and they in their turn will be also. The *marae* symbolises group unity, and acts as a bridge to the past as well as a useful community centre in the present.

The term *"marae"* is ambiguous, since it denotes both the total complex and the ceremonial courtyard, so in some areas the complex is referred to as a *"Pā"* instead. The most common term however is *marae*, and it will be used throughout this study.

The *marae* often has a name of its own, e.g. Manukōrihi *marae* in

Waitara; but it may be referred to by the name of its meeting-house or its locality. In any case, each *marae* is a clearly-bounded and identifiable unit.

The business of this chapter, then, is to discuss the *marae*, its site and buildings, how a *marae* is established and opened, and its historical adaptation from pre-contact times to the present.

The site

A rural *marae* will be set on an acre or more of land, dedicated by the group or original donor to the communal use of all its members and their descendants. The land may be registered as a *marae* reserve (under Section 439 of the Maori Affairs Act 1953), in which case it is exempt from rates and cannot be sold unless the reservation is cancelled. If the land is freehold, its situation is more precarious; it is then liable to be rated, and some of the owners may even decide to sell out. This however, would be extremely unlikely, because once a *marae* site has been used over a period, it acquires sacred qualities which linger long after the *marae* is abandoned.

I have heard of one case where the *marae* site was never officially registered as a reserve, but remained by an oversight in the family of the original donor, a man from another tribe. Some fifty years after the meeting-house was built, the descendants of the donor discovered that the *marae* and its valuable buildings legally belonged to them, and planned to sell. It took a visit from a prominent local elder, and the barely veiled threat that "I might be the man to curse you," before they stopped counting the money they could make, and agreed for a reserve order to be passed through the Maori Land Court.

A more convincing example of *marae* sanctity is a former *marae* of the Ngāti Whātua people at Okāhu Bay in the city of Auckland. This was in use until 1950, when it was taken under the Public Works Act, and the meeting-house bulldozed and burned. Only a small church and its graveyard were preserved; the Ngāti Whātua community were relocated in a nearby hilltop site, and the *marae* area was declared a public domain. In recent years, however, the City Council has given permission for various large enterprises including the Moscow Circus (1970) and Disneyland (1971) to stage mass entertainments on the site. In 1970 the local Maori people looked down from their hilltop community to see elephants, monkeys and other strange creatures trampling over their old *marae*. Worse still, toilet facilities had been built adjoining the graveyard and church, where the *tapu* is traditionally most intense. The uproar was immediate and public. A deputation of local Maori leaders visited the City Council and asked for the removal of the toilets; one hot-headed warrior stated his intention of getting an axe and felling them to the ground. The Council had the toilets removed. In 1971, however, Disneyland promoters were given permission to use the site, and despite letters to the Editor, television programmes and anger at the commercialisation of the old *marae*, this permission was not withdrawn.

Presumably, the longer a *marae* has been in use the greater its *tapu* becomes, and some *marae* have functioned over long periods, with successive renovations, replacement and shifting of their buildings. Poho-o-Rāwiri meeting-house at Kaiti, Gisborne, for example, is thought to be at least the third house of that name in Kaiti, the first being erected (although not on the exact present site) around 1840.[19]

Usually the *marae* has been established well into historical times (1769 on), and many are as recent as the meeting-houses that still stand on them, perhaps 100 years old at the outside. This is partly because the *marae* as we know it has developed since European contact, and partly because original settlement patterns have thoroughly altered in this period. Soon after contact, changing economic patterns caused whole populations to shift from their cultivations to the flax swamps, timber stands and gumfields. Pacification rendered the old fortified *pā* sites obsolete, and ports and mission stations provided new magnets for settlement. Tribes that got the musket first threw other tribes off their land, and the Maori-European wars of the 1860s led to further massive relocations. Sales and confiscations of Maori lands and most recently, the drain of rural populations to the city, have shifted the Maori people about so thoroughly that long continuity of settlement is now likely only in the most remote areas. In all these cases, old *marae* have been abandoned or shifted, and new ones built.

Boundaries
In most country areas the *marae* is set in farmland and separated from it only by a post and wire fence. Privacy is no problem in such a setting—performers in a *hui* have only country noises to contend with, and the arrival of curious strangers is unlikely. Urban *marae* are different. Here, the area is likely to be smaller, the fence higher, and the complex will probably be surrounded by housing. Privacy is a major requirement, especially since the town is a place where European culture dominates, and onlookers are likely to be strangers. So high fences of tree-fern logs or some other material are erected, the ceremonial spaces are located as far away from the road as possible, and every effort is made to insulate the *marae* from outside interference. The adaptation of the *marae* to town conditions will be discussed in greater detail later in the chapter.

The fence marking the boundary of the *marae* has at least two gateways—one, usually towards the rear, for locals, and a more ceremonious entry for

19. Phillipps (1944), pp. 99-103.

visiting groups. During a *hui* the inflow of visitors is readily controlled by a local official, often a Maori Warden,[20] who reports their arrival, instructs those in doubt of local procedures, and tells them when to proceed on to the *marae*. At the large *marae* of Ngāruawāhia, centre of the King Movement, over 3-5,000 visitors may attend an important *hui*, and here entry control is correspondingly elaborate. One or two wardens dressed in navy blue uniform, tie and peaked hat handle traffic and parking, while several others, usually women, stay by the visitor's gateway and report the arrival of groups either directly or by walkie-talkie linked to a communications office.

Not only is the *marae* bounded physically by these techniques, but it is also culturally insulated to a remarkable degree. The *marae* in New Zealand is a Maori public place, and perhaps it is the last of these. In this setting Maori culture dominates. The *marae* is visually marked as Maori by its carvings and distinctive architecture: it is spiritually marked by its rituals and the use of Maori language. It is not that Europeans are forbidden access to *marae* or even deliberately excluded—if they come with friends and for good reason they are made very welcome—but the fact remains that most Europeans never attend a *hui*, nor do they have much idea of what happens on *marae*. In rural areas this is less likely to be the case, since close social contacts between Maori and European are more common, and the birthdays, weddings and funerals of friends may be attended. In the city however, such contacts are minimal, and *hui* attendance by most Europeans is an improbability. Part of the reason, no doubt, is that the *marae* is one major arena left in New Zealand where European culture stands at a disadvantage—the rituals are unknown and the speeches are unintelligible. An interesting fact of the current urban situation is that many young Maori people (70% of the total Maori urban population is under twenty-five) also share this disability. For most of them, not speaking Maori or even understanding it, *marae* procedures have become foreign.

So on the one hand the insulation works to the advantage of those who use the *marae*; because one of its most attractive features is that no concessions have to be made to European custom—you can wail, chant, orate, talk Maori and eat Maori food as much as you like, and everyone else will join you. This atmosphere would naturally be hampered if the dominant numbers at *hui* came to be European and not Maori.

On the other hand, it has its disadvantages in the loss of many of the young people, and in a lack of appreciation for Maori culture among Europeans who rarely see it in action in its most natural context, the *marae*.

20. An official appointed by the local Maori Committee, often uniformed, who has limited rights to supervise the social behaviour of Maori people.

Space and buildings

Perhaps the first thing to note about the layout of a *marae* is its tremendous variability. In rural situations a fundamental separation between ceremonial areas and those dedicated to eating and sanitation is observed. The meeting-house and its associated courtyard are *tapu* (sacred) to some degree and must be isolated from common *(noa)* activities like cooking and eating. In urban situations, however, for want of space, these areas may be merged despite the ritual violation.

Many *marae* have their burial ground nearby, e.g. The main *marae* at Tikitiki, where the burial ground is separated from the meeting-house only by the *marae* courtyard; yet the cemeteries of other *marae* may be hidden away, or they may even use European facilities.

In most *marae* the courtyard is grassed, but at Ohinemutu at Rotorua, for example, the main *marae* is asphalted to bear heavy tourist traffic; and at Judea Pā in Tauranga the *marae* doubles as basketball and sports courts.

Some meeting-houses are of wood-frame construction with a corrugated-iron roof, and have an interior decorated with traditional carvings, woven wall-panels *(tukutuku)* and painted rafters *(kōwhaiwhai);* while in others, concrete block, decramastic tiles and plastic *tukutuku* are the order of the day. Some houses have little or no traditional decoration, as in Northland, where many meeting-houses are absolutely plain—just small wood-frame halls with no sign of Maori craftwork to distinguish them from other buildings. The facilities for cooking also vary, ranging from large iron pots over an open fire to ultra-modern stoves and steamers.

Thus *marae* vary in size, location, the layout, construction and number of their buildings, and many other factors besides. Part of this variation is regional (e.g. halls in Northland; the central doorway in Whanganui meeting-houses; and regional "schools" of decoration); part is urban-rural, and much of it is the result of expediency and adaptation to particular circumstances. It is not part of the task of this account, however, to fully document such differences, so the following description will relate to a "typical" rural *marae*, abstracted from many such visited and sketched in the course of research. Urban *marae* will be considered in a separate section.

The meeting-house[21]

(a) Physical structure

The meeting-house, variously called *whare puni* (sleeping house), *whare whakairo* (carved house), *whare nui* (big house), *whare hui* (meeting house) and *whare rūnanga* (council house), is the dominant feature on

---

21. For special studies on this topic, see: Mead (1961); ed. (1969), (1970). Phillipps, W. J. (1944), (1955).

any *marae*. It is a large rectangular building (perhaps 80 ft long by 30 ft wide by 20 ft high), with a gabled roof and a frontal porch, marked by its rich embellishments of carving, painted designs, and interior wall panels.

Both the size and the degree of decoration of a house make some sort of statement about the *mana* or prestige of its owner group. Houses range from 40 ft long to over 100 ft. Porourangi at Waiomatitini, for example, measures 85 ft by 30 ft[22], Poho-o-Rāwiri in Gisborne is 93 ft by 40 ft; and Te Ikaroa-a-Māui at Waitara is 87 ft by 36 ft. All these are major houses.

There is legendary support for the idea that size in meeting-houses breeds success, in the story of Tūrongo and Whatihua, two brothers who lived at Kāwhia on the West Coast many generations ago. Tūrongo was the younger brother, and on his travels he met a high-born Taranaki woman called Ruapūtahanga, and fell in love with her. He returned to Kāwhia to prepare for her arrival and began to build a magnificent house. There had been some history of rivalry between the brothers, and Whatihua decided to settle it by winning his brother's intended wife. Tūrongo had cut a great *tōtara* ridgepole for his house; Whatihua inspected it and advised his brother to cut it much shorter, or the house would never be ready in time. Then he went off secretly and built a house of his own overlooking the Aotea Harbour. When Ruapūtahanga and her retinue arrived in Kāwhia, Tūrongo was ashamed to find that his house was much too small to accommodate them. Whatihua stepped into the breach and entertained the guests in his own spacious building. The outcome was that he won great *mana*, and the lady as well.

The size of a house also tends to vary with the scale of the group it serves, so that logically enough, a *whāmere* (extended family) house will tend to be smaller than that of a sub-tribe. The other feature mentioned is the degree of elaboration, and here, too, prestige is a vital concern.

Sir Peter Buck[23] tells the story of a chieftain named Taharākau who one day visited a rival at his roughly-constructed homestead in the bush. This man had a bunch of precious jade ornaments attached to the border of his cloak, and thinking to impress Taharākau, he jingled these and asked, "Taharākau, what are the signs of chieftainship?" The reply was immediate and contemptuous: *"He whare whakairo i tū ki roto i te pā tūwatawata."* (A carved house standing in a fortified village.)

Although carvings are normally a statement of prestige, there are exceptions to every rule. Early this century, plans were made for a great carved house to be erected in the Whānau-ā-Apanui district of the East Coast. A local chieftainess named Mihi Kotukutuku wanted it built near her home at Raukokore, as the only house nearby was plain. Sir Apirana Ngata, however, was in charge of the project, and he preferred a more

---

22. Firth (1959), p. 97.
23. Buck (1962), p. 374.

central location. He got his way by a most adroit piece of diplomacy. It happened that when Mihi was a girl, some Arawa experts came along the coast to give selected local maidens the facial tattoo *(moko)*. When Mihi was presented to them, however, they refused to tattoo her on the grounds that her ancestry was too high, and they dared not spill her blood. It was this circumstance that Ngata recalled in persuading the old lady to his way of thinking. "Mihi," he said, "it is only right that your house should be plain. Look at your face; it isn't carved; yet all the other women have the *moko*. Keep your plain house, and leave the houses of others to be decorated." His argument succeeded, and the house of Tūkāki was built at Te Kaha instead.[24]

The meeting-house is usually a timber construction with standard carpentry techniques employed. The exterior walls are weatherboard, the roof is corrugated iron, and the foundations are concrete. The back wall, these days, has a pair of windows cut into it for better ventilation, and the entire front of the house is occupied by a verandah perhaps 10 ft deep. The verandah *(māhau)* carries most of the exterior decoration of the house, with a carved figure *(tekoteko)* astride its apex, and almost every available wood surface intricately carved into ancestors, mythical monsters and historic motifs. These surfaces include the bargeboards and their supports, the door and window frames, the threshold plank, the underside of the ridgepole, and the supporting verandah pole. To add to this wealth of decoration, the underside of the porch rafters may be painted with the curvilinear *kowhaiwhai* patterns in red, white and black. The door is on the right side facing out of the house (except in such areas as Whanganui, where it is centrally placed), with the name of the house painted on a small sign fixed above it; and the single frontal window is to the left. The porch may have a couple of wood benches along its walls.

Entering the hall, the impression of decorative wealth is enhanced. The house is usually dimly-lit, since there are few windows, and dark carvings range along the walls alternating with decorated reed panels with geometric designs in yellow, black and white. Old portraits in square and oval frames are hung above, with bygone kinfolk dressed in Maori cloaks or Victorian costume. Wide rafters painted in *kowhaiwhai* rise from each panel to the ridgepole, and between each rafter on the roof are close-packed rows of *kākaho*, soft brown reed stalks sometimes imitated by fluted wood. The ridgepole is supported by one or two massive posts, carved at the base into full-length human figures, otherwise the floor is uninterrupted, except for a stage at the far end in some houses. If the house is in use, the wood floor is covered with fine-woven flax mats. Mattresses covered with sheets are rolled up against the walls, and rolled out again at night. Pillows are also provided for visitors, often with hand-embroidered pillow-

24. My thanks to Eruera Stirling for this story.

slips. All this bedding is either the property of the *marae* and brought from the storeroom for the occasion, or on loan from member households. A medium-sized *marae* will own perhaps fifty to seventy-five mattresses, and a corresponding number of pillows and sheets. All the linen is washed and stored away between each *hui*.

(b) Functions

The main pragmatic function of the meeting-house is a sheltering one. Normally, the ritual activities of a *hui* are staged outside on the *marae*, but if it rains, or if groups arrive on the *marae* at night, the ceremonial welcome can sometimes be given inside. It also acts as an accommodation facility, capable of sleeping about 100 people. Mattresses are rolled out from the walls and covered with sheets, and visitors bring their own blankets. Most *hui* last about three days, but it is increasingly common for visiting parties to attend *hui* for one day only as a minimum token of respect, and the turnover of guests accommodated in the meeting-house can be extremely high.

The activities of the *hui* usually shift into the meeting-house after the evening meal. A church service is held, then the evening passes in oratory, entertainment, and welcomes to incoming groups. It is said to be bad etiquette for a group to arrive on the *marae* after dark, as this is the time for "ghosts and lovers", but when people have been travelling all day to the *hui* their late arrival is excused. This does not always happen, though, and groups that break the rule may receive a frosty welcome or no welcome at all. Eruera Stirling tells of one occasion when a party of prominent Whānau-ā-Apanui people arrived after sunset at a Ngāti Porou *tangi*. Instead of being greeted with calls and speeches of welcome, they were ordered off the *marae* by an infuriated old man, who stood in the doorway of the meeting-house and showered them with insults and curses. They retired to their bus in some disorder, but returned properly contrite the next morning, humbled and very careful of their etiquette.

Apart from activities associated with the formal *hui*, the meeting-house is frequently used as a community centre for socials, the meetings of local associations and dances, but in larger towns, public halls may be preferred, because of the strict liquor restrictions which apply to most *marae*.

(c) Symbolic structure

The meeting-house symbolises the unity and distinctiveness of its owner group, and in the past it has often been used as a political counter. When a new sub-tribe emerges, when families squabble or community factions arise, a meeting-house may be built as a statement of the situation. In Ruātoki, for example, there are two meeting-houses right across the road from each other, built by two brothers to express their lasting rivalry. An even more dramatic example of factionalism expressing itself in this way occurred in the Northland community of Te Kao. It is reliably reported[25] that when the Rātana Movement first entered the community, the split between Rātana adherents and those of the established church was so bitter that a mob of angry men took up their axes, marched down to the meeting-house and literally chopped it in half. Meeting-houses have also been used in boundary disputes, as in the case of a house called Kupe at Horowhenua.[26] This was built by the Muaupoko people in 1870 on land claimed to have been conquered by their neighbours, Ngāti Raukawa. There was talk of burning the place down; but moderation prevailed and the boundary line was shifted after the opening ceremony to run through the house. Even the name of the house may have political overtones. In the Tūhoe settlement of Te Whāiti, there were two major groups living side by side. The latecomers had enjoyed a long period of dominance in the area, but when the local meeting-house was built the rightful people of Te Whāiti insisted that it be named after their ancestor, Wharepākau. They won the argument and have since regained their ascendancy.[27]

There are many such cases on record, not all of them historical. It is probably this desire to express group unity that is the main factor in the current construction of tribal rather than inter-tribal *marae* in cities like Auckland.

The meeting-house is peculiarly appropriate to express the state of community relations, because it is the most powerful symbol a group may possess. It represents reverence for the past and veneration for the ancestors, but more than this, it is an architectural history book of the people concerned. When the group gathers on its *marae*, the meeting-house is a statement that their ancestors are also present.

We can examine this symbolism on a series of three levels:[28]

(1) At the most general level, the house itself represents a specific ancestor or event of the past. Most often the house is named after a remote but famous male ancestor, who may have been an inhabitant of Hawaiki, the captain of the tribal canoe, or perhaps the founder of the group itself. There are important exceptions, though, as when houses are named after some event in their building (e.g. *Ngā Tau e Waru* (eight years) near Masterton, of which it was predicted it would take eight years to complete); an event in tribal history (e.g. *Te Whai ā te Motu* at Ruatāhuna (The chase of the Island), which refers to the feats of the outlaw hero Te Kooti in eluding Government troops); or the tribal canoe itself (e.g.) *Mātātua* in Rotorua). In some areas such as the East Coast, where

---

25. Henderson (1963), p. 81.
26. Phillipps (1955), p. 44.
27. Penfold, M. *Wharepaakau*, p. 4, in Mead, ed. (1970).
28. Many of the ideas presented in this section evolved during discussions with Dr Sidney Mead.

women have traditionally played an important role in tribal history, an ancestress may be commemorated (e.g. Hine Māhuru, at Raukokore). However, it remains true that the majority of house names can be traced to a male progenitor of the group.

The meeting-house does not symbolise the ancestor in name alone, for its structure represents the ancestor's body in quite a literal way. The carved head *(koruru)* between the bargeboards of the porch is said to be his head;* the bargeboards are his arms held out in welcome, and the carvings at their ends represent his fingers *(raparapa)*. The ridgepole *(tāhuhu)* represents the ancestral spine, also the main line of descent from the founder; the rafters *(heke)* are his ribs, also descent lines, and the interior is his belly —hence such house names as Te Poho-o-Rāwiri (Rāwiri's belly).* The concept of welcome is very important, and for this reason the door is always left open during a *hui*, and no-one must block it in any way.

Not only does the house represent the ancestor in name and structure, but it is often addressed by visiting orators in solemn greeting, and it is standard practice to begin a speech by honouring the house in this fashion.

(2) At the second level, each of the carved slabs within the house represents a slightly more recent figure in tribal history, or offshoots from the main descent-line. In effect, these are ancestors within the ancestor.

In most houses the ancestors represented in the carved slabs are directly related to the owner group, and so present a genealogy in wood around the walls. It is important to recognize the significance of genealogy or *whakapapa* in Maori society. In traditional times it was crucial to the assignment of status, and although nowadays it is often bypassed by achievement in the European world, genealogy is still of fundamental importance on the *marae*. At weddings, descent-lines are recited to link the bride and groom. At inter-tribal meetings they link the groups present; they may be used to display the learning of an orator or his superior descent to a critic. Above all, *whakapapa* presents continuity with the past. Many elders keep treasured *whakapapa* books in which this knowledge is recorded, and refresh their memories just before an important *hui;* for the elder with an expert knowledge of genealogy enjoys a great advantage in arguments on the *marae*.

In older houses the ancestor on each slab may be identified only by some distinguishing mark that portrays one of his feats or idiosyncracies, but nowadays hardly anyone knows enough history or mythology to interpret these with invariable success. A more recent practice of carving or painting the name of the ancestor on to the slab simplifies matters tremendously; and to go even further, Tūkāki house at Te Kaha, for example, carries a beautifully-printed genealogical chart on its back wall, which shows exactly how the carved ancestors were related.

* See notes at end of chapter (p. 90) for additional material.

In some major houses a wide selection of ancestors from many different tribes is made. This is said to reflect the concept of "ngā hau e whā" (the four winds), by making provision for all those visitors who come to the *marae*. It relates to a custom that is often discussed but rarely practised; that the visitor, on entering a strange meeting-house, should seek out his ancestor on the walls and make his bed beneath. This is said to give him confidence and protection from any evil influences that may be about.*

(3) The final presentation of ancestral figures in the house are the portraits hung about the walls, which represent the most recent kin of all. In earlier times, it is said, such portraits were given their position by the elders, and were arranged in family groups which could not be moved about. Only portraits of people of "some standing" could be hung in the house,[29] often including those of local boys who were killed in the First and Second World Wars. Normally a portrait is placed in the house for the first time shortly after the funeral. During the *tangi*, a photograph or painting of the deceased is propped against the end of the coffin, along with those of forebears and close kin who have predeceased him, and all of these are wept over. After the *tangi* they are returned to the house, and at the unveiling, perhaps a year or two later, they are taken out once more. On this occasion the portrait of the deceased serves as a substitute for the open coffin. It is placed on the porch of the house on flax mats, and visiting parties weep over the picture as they had done over the coffin a year or so before. The portrait can also "stand in" for a dead person if he died overseas, and the body could not be brought home for the *tangi*. A portrait of a living person is never used in any of these contexts as that would be a tremendous ill-omen, equivalent to a death curse. In any case, they should be there in person.

So we can see that the portraits, like the meeting-house and the carved slabs, can be regarded as "stand-ins" for the people they represent; and when the *marae* is in use, the full host of most remote, closer and recent kin are known to be present both in spirit and in some physical form.

One may wonder whether the other decorative forms in a meeting-house also have symbolic value. It appears that the geometric plaited wall patterns *(tukutuku)* and the curvilinear rafter paintings *(kowhaiwhai)* are largely decorative, and that their symbolic value is generalised. In the wall panels, for example, there is a repertoire of named patterns, each of which represents a broad theme such as strength *(kaokao*, "side", a row of chevrons which depict the fork between a warrior's fighting arm and his side), and abundance *(pātikitiki*, "flounder", presented as a series of diamonds); or a mythological reference e.g. *roimata toroa*, "albatross tears" (which refers to the legend of a man named Pou, who, on his return to Hawaiki,

---

29. Harper, J. *The portraits in Hine nui te Poo* p. 1; in Mead, ed. (1970).

* See notes at end of chapter (p. 90) for additional material.

forgot to give his two pet albatrosses travelling instructions so they could join him), or *niho taniwha*, "dragon's teeth".[30]

There are a number of named patterns for rafter paintings. Some of them are said to have been taken from tattoo motifs; others may depict a fern frond, a whale or a flounder; but like the wall panels, their symbolic content is generalised, and they recur in many houses. It is also important to note that only a limited number of experts know the names and significance of these patterns, and that for most of those who enter the meeting-house no symbolic message is apparent at all.

Cross-cutting the ancestor symbolism of the meeting-house is an entirely different type of distinction, which affects its use in many ways. This is the division of the house into its *noa* (common) and *tapu* (sacred) sides. The concepts of *tapu* and *noa*, however, are important to the understanding of many aspects of *marae* layout and usage, so before proceeding to discuss the meeting-house in particular, I shall try to establish the relevance of the distinction in general.

Let it be stated from the beginning that males, high descent, the dead, the elderly, and the history of the tribe all possess strong *tapu* qualities, as indeed does anything that enjoys great *mana*. The most sacred rituals, naturally enough, relate to this complex—they bear continual reference to the ancestors, they are practised by elderly male aristocrats, and they are invoked in the presence of death. On the other hand, women, the lowborn, cooked food, water and the young all have *noa* (common) qualities. Thus women, the lowborn and the young will be prohibited from carrying out sacred rituals; cooked food or water can be used to lift *tapu* contamination (as when returning from a cemetery or contact with a corpse); and the destructive *tapu* qualities of a newly-built meeting-house may be ritually neutralised by the entry of a high-born woman.

Tapu and *noa*, then, are opposite though complementary principles, and they must be kept separate. It is not argued here that every person who frequents the *marae* is aware of this distinction and its implications; in fact I have mostly heard it discussed by elders who are steeped in tradition, and some of the customs mentioned below are now practised only in the most conservative areas. One cannot ignore the great variation in traditional knowledge among different areas and age-groups. However, the *tapu-noa* concept provides a key that neatly and consistently explains a wide range of customs relating to the *marae;* and from the statements of experts in this field it is clear that they consider *tapu* and *noa* to be crucially involved.

Tapu qualities vary in intensity on different parts of the *marae*, and *noa* qualities are correspondingly strong or weak.

The cemetery is the most *tapu* place of all. It is kept separate from the

---

30. Taiapa, Pine; unpublished lecture at Tikitiki (1965).

marae complex and surrounded by a fence, and entry or exit are governed by strict rules. No food, cigarettes or liquor *(noa)* should be taken into a cemetery, and pockets should be emptied as well. No menstruating woman should enter. On exit any clinging *tapu* should be removed by sprinkling oneself with water from a bottle or basin left outside the gate or from a nearby stream. In some areas *tapu* is lifted by rubbing one's hands with bread. These forms of protection are no longer practised in some of the more acculturated communities, and in areas such as the Waikato it is not necessary, since the *tapu* has been ritually lifted from most cemeteries. The cleansing ritual (called *whakanoa*, "to make *noa"*) should especially be practised on visits to a strange area, where spiritual influences are likely to be hostile, and some of the older generation will even use it on entry to strange *marae*, before they proceed to eat.

The *marae* complex itself, though less *tapu* than the cemetery, is still more *tapu* than surrounding land. This is demonstrated by the *whakanoa* ritual mentioned above and also by the fact that liquor is prohibited on most *marae*. This prohibition reflects a general attitude that liquor is *noa*, desecrating and out of keeping with the dignity of *marae* rituals. *Marae* vary in their policies in this respect. On many *marae* liquor is allowed for occasions like twenty-firsts and weddings, providing a licence is obtained in advance from the local Maori committee; on others, liquor is prohibited at all times, while on a few no prohibition is observed at all. Such *marae* are regarded with some derision, however, and at one *marae* I heard of where "licensed" socials and dances were regularly held, the house had to be totally reconsecrated when the committee changed its policy, and liquor was banned. At strict *marae*, people repair just outside the gates or off to the pub for interim refreshments, and it is impossible totally to insulate the *hui* from the effects of drinking. Every now and then someone attends a *hui* the worse for liquor and may even stand to deliver a speech. On such occasions people react with tolerance and amusement up to a certain point, but if he starts violating *marae* etiquette by interrupting other speakers or making offensive remarks, he gets short shrift. People call out telling him to sit down or loudly mutter their disapproval. If all else fails, his wife or some other female relative may persuade him to leave the *marae*. This is a last resort, however, as the right of a male to speak uninterrupted on the *marae* is strongly protected under normal conditions.

The cooks for a *hui*, particularly the men, are customarily allowed some liquor for their efforts, so on some *marae* the cookshed is located just over the *marae* boundary to avoid violations. In any case, cooking is a *noa* activity, and drinking in this context is far less likely to constitute an offence.

Within the *marae* complex a strong division holds between the *noa* cooking-area, manned mainly by the middle-aged and young, and the *tapu* ceremonial area, where the elderly men and women are the chief performers. Women do have a role to play in the ceremonial area. They call, wail and chant ancient songs. But theirs is largely a supporting role and in most areas they are excluded from the central activity of speech-making *(whaikōrero)*.

None of these distinctions is absolutely watertight. In the cooking area, for example, one will commonly find old ladies peeling potatoes or making steamed puddings, and elderly men may help with the earth ovens; but it is still rare to find an orator there, and in earlier days this would have been unthinkable. To quote an observer in 1834[31] *"the kauta* [cookhouse] were also detached buildings, into which none but slaves or the meanest person in a tribe would choose to go, the chief hardly condescending so much as to cast a glance at what might be passing within." On the ceremonial courtyard, too, women of high rank are permitted to speak in East Coast districts and, it is said, in Northland; but they do so because their descent entitles them to act as honorary "men". A woman taking this role will often begin by declaring *"Kia whatatāne au i ahau"* (let me make myself a man), a saying that comes from the days when the famous ancestress Muriwai (some claim it was her niece Wairaka) saved the Mātātua canoe from drifting out to sea by playing a man's part and paddling it to safety. Even then, her rank must be impeccable if she is not to be challenged, and if she should stand on a *marae* outside her home territory the reaction is likely to be immediate and furious. Another exception is the case of young men or those of indifferent descent who have, however, attained high status through European channels (e.g. pastors, doctors, lawyers, university professors, welfare officers). Such men are almost universally acknowledged as honorary elders on the *marae* of today, and may be paid high ritual honours.

Despite these exceptions, efforts continue to be made to keep the activities of the cooking and ceremonial areas strictly separate. Food should not be taken into the meeting-house, nor should important speeches be made in the dining-hall. When the Minister of Maori and Island Affairs recently visited an East Coast *marae*, for example, it was found that the meeting-house was too small to accommodate his audience. Suggestions were made by the younger people that they might hear the evening speeches in the dining-hall, a larger building in this case, but the elders were outraged and spoke strongly against the idea. The minister moved to the meeting-house and many of the audience sat outside on the porch until late that night, peering in through window and door—an eloquent tribute to the power of custom.

Within the confines of the ceremonial area, the courtyard is perhaps more *tapu* than the meeting-house; for where the regulations forbid women

31. Marshall (1834), p. 211.

and certain categories of men (the young, the insignificant, younger brothers, or son of a living father) to speak on the *marae*, they are often permitted to speak inside the meeting-house. Another custom that formerly expressed the *tapu* qualities of the courtyard was the prohibition on smoking there, since smoking was regarded as a sort of eating. This is not often observed today, but at one *hui* I attended a visiting elder stood to express his scorn of the local women who apparently had lost all knowledge of the traditional chants. "All they are good for," he declared, "is to smoke on the *marae*." The double insult hit home, for the women looked very ashamed and stubbed out their cigarettes.

Finally, we come to the meeting-house itself. There are a number of practices that illustrate its sacred qualities. The meeting-house is most sacred of all while it is being built, and during this time both woman and food *(noa)* are most strictly forbidden entry. Even after the meeting-house is opened no food should be taken inside, and this is apparently an ancient prohibition that once applied to all buildings in which people slept. Nicholas in 1818 observed that "these people make it a rule never to take their meals in the huts appropriated for their residence, and this they not only religiously observe themselves, but enjoin strangers to do the same whenever they partake of their hospitality."[32] Food was eaten outside or in the cookshed, but in more recent times large dining-halls have been constructed on most *marae* to shelter people at their meals.

Within the meeting-house the first distinction that can be drawn is between the open-air porch and the interior. The porch is a transition area between the *marae ātea* and the house, and it has some noticeable differences in usage from both. At a *tangi* the coffin *(tapu)* used to be placed in a small shed to the left of the porch (facing out from the house) to avoid contaminating the building, but nowadays for convenience, the coffin is sometimes put on the porch under the window. In most areas, though, people are still reluctant to take the coffin inside, and this seems to indicate some fundamental difference between the porch and the interior. It may be that the porch is more *tapu*, and therefore less likely to be harmed by *tapu* contacts. This interpretation receives some support from an old custom reported from Tūhoe,[33] where women *(noa)* were forbidden to stand on the porch, as it was reserved for men of high standing; and from reports by Dr S. M. Mead[34] that in some houses at least the carvings of the porch represent mythological monsters and ancestors of greater antiquity (and *tapu?*) than those inside. In Northland, on the other hand, coffins are routinely taken inside the meeting-house.

The transition from porch to interior is made through the door by the

---

32. Nicholas (1817), Vol. II, p. 271.
33. Taipua, W. *Hine-nui-te-poo* p. 5; in Mead ed. (1970).
34. Dr S. M. Mead, Personal communication 1971.

living, and through the window (in conservative areas) by the dead. The window is thought to be *tapu*, and in areas such as the Tūhoe, if the coffin *(tapu)* is taken inside the house at all at a *tangi*, it is passed through the window. In most areas now, however, the door is used without comment. On the other hand, the door is said to be *noa*, and presents no dangers for the living who may pass through it freely. An interesting feature of the door is that the carving which surmounts it usually represents a female ancestress, often Hine-nui-te-Pō, the goddess of death. One old custom which is relevant here was practised when warriors returned from battle. The *tapu* of blood was lifted from them by a *whakanoa* ritual which involved crawling between the legs of an old woman. On most door *pare*[35] the female figure has her legs outstretched, and the door supports are named *waewae* or "legs". It could be that in entering the meeting-house from the *marae* or the porch any *tapu* from outside is being symbolically lifted. Also relevant is the myth of the founder hero Māui and the goddess of death, Hine-nui-te-Pō. Māui vowed to remove the threat of death to mankind forever by entering the body of Hine-nui-te-Pō and snatching out her heart. One day while she was sleeping on the ground, her legs stretched wide, Māui came across her with his companions, a flock of birds. He cautioned them to keep quiet, then put his vow into action by wriggling between her legs into her body. However the sight of his legs waggling about was too much for the irrepressible fantail, who got the giggles. The goddess awoke, clamped her legs together and Māui was killed. In those houses where Hine-nui-te-Pō is depicted over the door it is possible that this myth is being recalled.

One other custom which is practised on entry to the house is said to reflect its *tapu* qualities. This is the practice of taking off one's shoes at the doorway and entering barefoot. In the words of one informant, this is because "your boots have been walking outside, into the *whare kai* and all sorts". However, most attribute this to the destructive effect of European shoes on the flax mats inside, and it may have nothing to do with *tapu* at all.

Inside the house there is a very powerful *tapu-noa* distinction which discriminates the left side from the right; and this division explains quite a number of different customs.

There is some disagreement among informants over which side of the house is in fact the left side and which the right. This might be due to the difference in perspective between local people, who sit on the *marae* facing out from the house, and visitors, who sit facing towards it. According to whether the informant is visualising himself as host or guest, his attribution of left and right could change. The most expert and reliable informants, however, all of them elderly, consistently establish left and

---

35. Carved slab over the door.

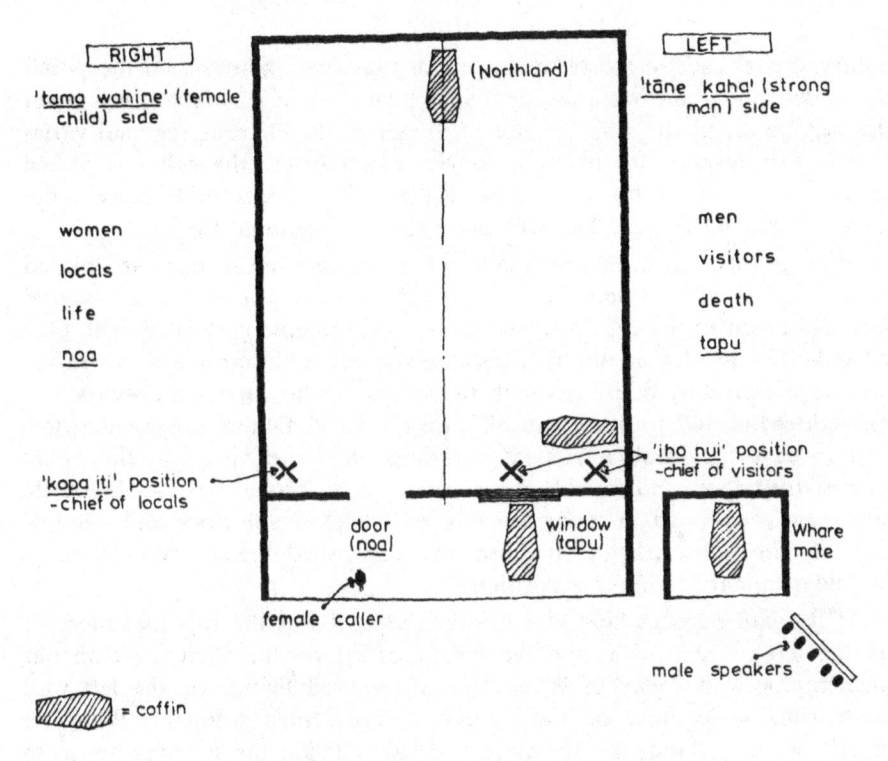

Figure 2: Meeting-house—*Noa* and *Tapu* Sides

right as though they were standing inside the meeting-house facing the door. The left side then is literally the left "side" of the ancestor, and similarly for the right. A large number of younger informants, interestingly enough, orient themselves quite differently, as though they were standing outside facing the house. The experts, moreover, claim that the left side of the house is *tapu,* and the right side *noa.* The left is associated with males, death and the setting sun; the right is associated with females, life and the rising sun. In earlier times the left was called the *tāne kaha* (strong man) side; while the right side was called *tama wahine* (female child).*

Of the entrances to the house the doorway on the right (facing out) is *noa,* with a female figure overhead, and it is dedicated to the use of the living; the window on the left is *tapu,* and dedicated to the use of the dead. Recently when a group of students visited a rural *marae* a cup of tea *(noa)* was served to them inside the house, and one of the party innocently placed her teacup on the window sill. When the local women noticed this, they made sure it was left there and later took the cup and saucer outside and broke them, as they had become *tapu.*

When a body is brought on to the *marae* it is either placed in a tem-

47

* See notes at end of chapter (p. 90) for additional material.

porary shelter *(whare mate)* to the left of the meeting-house, on the porch to the left under the window; or if it is taken inside it is laid down under the window or at the window end of the left wall. There is regional variation in this respect, for example in Northland where the coffin is placed at the far end of the house; but in Tūhoe, East Coast and many other areas the rule holds true. The *tapu* body stays on the *tapu* side.

When guests are accommodated in the meeting-house they are placed along the left wall. Because they are visitors *(waewae tapu* or "sacred feet") they go to the *tapu* side, while the local people go to the right. One informant claimed that this was because the left is the protective or safety arm of the meeting-house; as with the warrior, who carries the weapon in his right hand and protects himself with the left.[36] Others suggest that this custom gave the locals a tactical advantage in earlier times, as they were nearest the door and could escape if trouble broke out. A favourite stratagem mentioned in many legends was to close the door and window then set the house alight, so those who controlled the doorway were in an understandably fortunate position.

At Ringatū services held in meeting-houses, it was the rule that men sat on the left or *tapu* side, and women *(noa)* sat on the right.[37] At an old meeting-house at Tieke in Whanganui the carved figures on the left wall were men, while those on the right wall represented women.[38] When an elderly woman stands on the porch or just outside the meeting-house to give the call of welcome to a visiting group, she stands to the right in most areas. In Tūhoe, the male orators sit on a bench to the left of the house; although I have observed wide regional variation in this respect.

It is clear that the placement of a coffin, of visitors and locals, and of men and women in these contexts is no accident. They relate to a spatial scheme, now peculiar to the *marae*, which distinguishes left as *tapu* and right as *noa;* and from this principle the channelling of *tapu* objects to the left and *noa* objects to the right follows as a matter of course. The principle itself is now expressed only by a few expert elders, but the spatial patterns persist.

Another aspect of the spatial structure of the meeting-house are its places of honour. It is a well-known rule that the most prominent visitor to a *hui* (the *manuhiri tuārangi*, "visitor from afar") should sleep just under the front window inside the house, or at that end of the left wall. This position is called the *iho nui*, *iho* referring to an object of strength i.e. "the great strength". The most prominent local man should sleep by the door on the right wall, the *kopa iti* position.[39] *Kopa* has conotations of weak-

36. McManus (1971).
37. Cracknell, M. p. 14; in Mead ed. (1970).
38. Downes (1929), p. 153.
39. Jones (1945), p. 16.

ness or disability, while *iti* means small. These terms reflect the sentiment that to place the visitors along the left wall is to give them a position of advantage and honour, but as we have seen the advantages were not all one-sided. Only a visitor of accredited high status can occupy the place of honour; and anyone else would have to shift. Some generations ago a party from Maraenui on the East Coast attended a *tangi* at Tolaga Bay. Their chief, Kōpu, was ill, so a man named Tātāhare led the group instead. When they were taken into the meeting-house after their welcome, Tātāhare sat in the place of honour, under the front window. The local chief called out to him, "Kōpu!" Tātāhare made no reply. So the chief called out again, "Hey Kōpu!" Still there was no answer. Finally the chief called out a third time, "Kōpu, where are you sitting?" Everyone knew that this was no genuine mistake of identities, for the chief knew the Maraenui people well, and that a breach of etiquette was being pointed out. Tātāhare was unable to make any adequate reply, so in shame he stood, and left the meeting-house.

A final aspect of the symbolic structure of the meeting-house is its dedication to the god Tāne, or Tāne-whakapiripiri (Tāne the uniter).[40] Tāne in the old cosmology was the god of the forests, and it is from his domain that the timber fabric of the house is taken. He should be ritually appeased both when the timber is felled and when the house is opened; but the felling rituals are rarely performed today as most timber is cut commercially, and the correct opening rituals rest in the hands of a few remaining experts, mostly from the Waikato tribes.

The *tapu-noa* distinction, all in all, appears to be undergoing an interesting process of evolution. It is clearly of ancient origin, and was well-entrenched in pre-contact Maori society. It has long discriminated cooking from ceremonial areas in Maori settlements, and dictated differences in their usage. It has discriminated men from women, commoners from aristocrats, and the living from the dead. However, since contact, *tapu* observances have progressively been phased out of people's daily lives. The commoner-aristocrat distinction has less relevance as other channels to status are opened, and the role of women has considerably altered with the change in family structures, the possibility of wage-earning and the creation of powerful groups such as the Maori Women's Welfare League. People used to follow *tapu* rules in their homes—don't put your hat on the table (hat is *tapu* because it's been on your head; table is *noa* from food); don't leave toilet paper on the same shelf as food (toilet is *tapu*, food is *noa)*; keep genealogy books out of the kitchen; never wash the baby in a basin you've had dishwater in (baby is *tapu;* dishwater has *noa* food in it), and so on. However, these are no longer practised by most families.

40. Awatere and Dewes (1969), Lecture 2, p. 2.

Tapu and *noa*, like a great deal of *Maoritanga*, are increasingly relegated to the *marae*. The *marae* is the place where tradition is deliberately remembered, and old ways have virtue. Those people who have no time for the past keep away from the *marae*, while those who find in it a source of pride and identity go there whenever they can. All the same, many inconvenient *tapu* restrictions are being discarded from *marae* practice. The small "house of death" is rarely built today to receive a coffin and its mourners; and if it is too cold, mourners no longer stay outside all night with the body, but shift inside the meeting-house. *Tapu* restrictions on a number of cemeteries have been raised, and even where they remain many people forget them. People now take coffins through the door instead of the window. These examples are numerous, and informants are conscious that many of the old ways are being forgotten or discarded. *Tapu* and *noa* even as concepts are unknown to many of the young.

In other respects, however, the *marae* seems to be increasing in sanctity. Its earlier role seems to have been more matter-of-fact; a community centre for housing visitors and for staging a wide range of local activities. In the latter part of last century, though, there was a prolonged period of cultural depression when the extinction of the Maori people was regularly predicted, and activities such as *marae* building and large-scale *hui* partially lapsed. From early on this century to the present, a marked revival in population and also cultural activity has occurred, and leaders of the Maori people have fostered *marae* construction as a symbol of the renewed vitality of *Maoritanga*. Along with the revival of ancient customs has come a selfconscious interest in them, particularly among urban populations who are no longer raised in familiar contact with a *marae*, and *marae* etiquette has become the subject of school and university classes, newspaper articles, and "grass-roots" seminars held by the elders of many tribes to instruct their younger kinsmen, all in the past twenty or thirty years. If the *marae* is indeed becoming more sacred, it is natural enough, for as treasured parts of *Maoritanga* such as the language, respect for the ancestors and the recital of tradition, increasingly retreat there, its value to the people will rise.

Marae (ātea)

The next major area to consider is the ceremonial courtyard, usually called the *marae*, or *marae ātea* to distinguish it from the total complex. It lies directly before the meeting-house, an inconspicuous expanse of grass or asphalt—all the same, it is the place where most of the major ceremonies are enacted. One of the distinctive qualities of *marae* gatherings is a marked preference for outdoor staging. Once a ceremonial welcome is under way, people sit unmoving on their benches even in a heavy rain shower, with only umbrellas for protection. The true orator scorns even this small shelter, and when he strides on to the *marae* to address the gathering, he leaves his overcoat and hat behind him. It is quite common to see an elderly man pacing backwards and forwards across the *marae*, magnificently ignoring the rain for half an hour or more while he delivers his speech.

The main furniture on the *marae* are two groups of wood benches, one for locals and the other for the visiting party who are receiving the welcome. These are placed opposite each other, with the locals facing out from the meeting-house and usually to its left, and visitors facing towards it. This placement varies widely, though, and the only invariable factor seems to be that the groups are placed along the borders of the *marae* and facing each other. This leaves the courtyard free for the orators and other performers, and give both parties a good view of the ceremony as well as of each other. There may be other benches around the *marae* for the rest of the audience.

While the *marae ātea* is in use for a welcome, it is treated with great respect. No-one may wander across it or drive a vehicle over its borders. Often a temporary rope cordon is erected to fence it off securely. If a dog or a child moves on to the *marae ātea* they are chased off or someone carries them away. If anyone wants to move to another part of the *marae* they carefully walk right around the outskirts. None of these restrictions is observed at other times, and in this respect the *marae ātea* is very like a stage, where none but accredited actors may enter while the play is in progress. The *marae* is also the arena where the two groups size each other up, try their relative strengths in oratorical excellence, and together enact the stately rituals of encounter.

It is said that the gods of the *marae* are Tāne i te Wānanga (Knowledgable Tāne), the god of oratory; and Tū te Ihiihi (Tū, the powerful war god), the god of war dances and martial activity.[41] In earlier days the *marae* was the place where a chief won his allies and inflamed his warriors by oratory; but today more peaceful messages prevail.

Often associated with the courtyard and situated on one of its borders is the flagpole or *pou hāki*. This may be a memorial to a chief, and on many *marae* it is elaborately carved. It carries the *marae* flag while the complex is in use, commonly a Red Ensign with the name of the *marae* lettered onto it. There is a tradition, established by Sir George Grey in the early colonial days, that the Government should present such a flag to a new *marae*.

Flagpoles, though, have played a dramatic role in New Zealand's contact history. They have been a favourite symbol of Maori resistance and nationalism, for example the Governor's flagpole at Kororareka, three times chopped down by Hone Heke in 1844, or the *niu* flagpole of the Hauhau rebels in the 1860s. Each of the significant nationalistic movements such

---

41. Awatere and Dewes (1969), Lecture 2, p. 2.

as the King Movement, the Ringatū church, and others have their own array of flags; so it is understandable that a Government flag does not hang well on every *marae* flagpole. A recent widely reported case illustrates the sort of dilemma that may arise. A *marae* just out of Hastings was to be opened by the Governor-General late in 1970. One old lady had contributed heavily to its finance, and several days before the opening she hung a Ringatū flag from the flagpole in honour of the occasion. Local Maori Welfare Officers saw the flag, interpreted it as "a display of disloyalty to the Crown",[42] and hauled it down, replacing it with the Union Jack. There was talk of chopping down the flagpole on one side, and of placing a night patrol around it on the other; but the situation was soon settled by discussion, and nothing further was heard about it except in the papers. In this case the conflict was more verbal than anything else, but it does show that flags and flagpoles are still occasionally a touchy subject on the *marae*.

Apart from the flagpole, there may be one or more memorials placed about the fringes of the *marae ātea*. The leaders that they commemorate are always of great importance, and their history is intimately linked with the *marae*. At Manu-kōrihi *marae* in Waitara, for example, a dominant feature is the vault surmounted by a tall statue of Sir Māui Pōmare, which stands to the left of the house (facing out from it); and at Judea Pā in Tauranga it is the sculpture of Dr Maharaia Winiata—both of them famous local sons. All these monuments are treated with respect, and children are told not to climb on them, although on one *marae* I visited the local elder encourages children to play around the memorial, "so the old man won't feel lonely".

The cooking area
The facilities in this area are the most variable of all on the *marae*. Unlike the meeting-house, there is no strong traditional pattern to follow, so convenience and finance are the major guidelines.
(1) *Whare kai*
The main unit in the cooking-area is the *whare kai* or dining-hall. As the cooking-area is *noa*, it is only appropriate that this building should be named after a female ancestress, often the wife or sister of the man after whom the meeting-house is called. At Judea Pā in Tauranga, for example, the two levels of the double-storied *whare kai* are named for the two wives of the meeting-house ancestor. However, events in local history or even a male ancestor can be commemorated. The *whare kai* is typically a wood-frame building with a corrugated-iron roof, like the meeting-house; but it is unusual to find any carving, *tukutuku* or *kowhaiwhai* inside. Some examples do exist, though, e.g. Tāwhiwhirangi dining-hall at Tikitiki,

---
42. *Hawke's Bay Herald Tribune*, 12 June, 1970.

built during a prolific period of *marae* decoration under Sir Apirana Ngata along the East Coast. Ngata's policy was for the people to practise their skills on the dining-hall, so that their work in the meeting-house would be impeccable.

A small porch surmounts the doorway, which leads into the dining-area of the *whare kai*. This is in the form of a large hall, furnished with long trestle tables and benches. On the walls are hung photographs of past *hui*, or perhaps a Memorial Roll of local soldiers who died in the two World Wars. There is often a piano at one end of the hall on a stage, because people prefer to use the dining-hall rather than the meeting-house for socials and dances.

When the dining-hall is prepared for a feast, it is a tremendous sight. Streamers hang from the roof, the tables are laden with trifles, sweets and jellies; mounds of apples and oranges stand between plates of seafood and great round home-baked loaves; and by each setting stands a bright coloured bottle of "fizz". The local ladies put great effort into arranging the tables so that they look hospitable and plentiful. All sorts of rare delicacies are collected, and there are special signs of thought, like apples bristling with cigarettes on toothpicks, or piles of toffees for the children. Waitresses walk to and from the serveries with steaming plates of vegetables and meat, and schoolchildren serve cups of tea from large enamel teapots.

The other main part of the *whare kai* is the kitchen, connected to the dining-room by a door and several serveries. In an old *marae* there are often a couple of open fires in this area, with big iron pots hung above them or resting on a grate, in which stew or vegetables simmer. In more modern *marae* these are replaced by steam-cookers or electric stoves, though in general stoves are quite inadequate to cater for the crowds that come to a *hui*. An average-sized attendance would be 3-500, and it can reach 5,000 or more. At Tūrangawaewae *marae*, which regularly caters for such numbers, there are four dining-halls which can be supplemented by large marquees, and over 1,000 people can be fed in a single sitting.

Also in the kitchen are wood or formica benches, a number of sinks for dishwashing, and a series of cupboards where teatowels and cooking utensils are stored. Some *marae* have hot-water cylinders, and others have cold running water only. There may be a special storeroom at one end of the kitchen where all the crockery and silver is kept. Many *marae* have a set of crockery especially made, with a small seal bearing a picture of the meeting-house and the name of the *marae* stamped on each piece. A list is hung up in the storeroom with the numbers of each item recorded, and at the end of the *hui* the ladies carefully count everything. Breakages are replaced out of the hire fee if one is paid to the *marae*, or the person responsible meets the cost.

One small *marae* had a list as follows:

Knives	127	Cups	100	Jam Dishes	21
Basins	3	Saucers	183	Meat Dishes	6
Forks	132	China plates	132	Trays	2
Spoons	131	Fruitbowls	22	Teaspoons	19
Teapots	6	Sugar Basins	26	Large jug	1
Jugs	24	Butter Dishes	27		

A medium-sized *marae* might have 20 dozen of all the major items, and extras can always be borrowed from member households.

The kitchen has its own entrance, often with a couple of 44-gallon drums standing nearby for scraps. The final facility in the kitchen is a pantry or cool-store for meat and vegetables, or even a refrigerator.

Under most circumstances the kitchen is the province of the ladies. The women peel potatoes there, prepare puddings, wash and dry dishes and serve food. If the kitchen is supplied with copper steamers or more elaborate cooking equipment, these are managed by the men, who do most of the cooking, but usually they work outside in the cookhouse.

On many *marae* there is also a small shop in the *whare kai*. This is run by a local woman, who also orders supplies like jellies, custard, tinned fruit, salt, butter, pickles, jam, cheese, and sugar for the *whare kai*, and quantities of these goods may be stored in the shop between *hui*. Cigarettes, sweets, icecream and soft drinks are sold from the shop while the *hui* is in progress, and profits help to pay the bills for electricity and maintenance.

(2) *Outdoor cooking*

Cooking in the modern *marae* is increasingly indoors. Convenience, the installation of steamers and the less frequent use of earth ovens all support this trend. Most *marae*, however still have a *kāuta* or outdoor cookshed behind the *whare kai*. The *kāuta* is a shed contrived from timber, corrugated iron and tarpaulin whose construction varies with the fancy of the builder and materials available. Often it has a big corrugated-iron chimney to one side, which takes away the smoke from a large open fire. Water boils in 44-gallon drums or coppers for washing, steaming puddings and cooking vegetables, and a stack of firewood nearby is used to keep the fires going. The *kāuta* is a man's place. Men between about eighteen and fifty stand around in bush singlets, trousers and gumboots, tending the fires, telling jokes, and every now and then fending off the heat with a drink of beer. The meat is butchered here or in a special butchering shed, and hung in the meat store; and the earth ovens are dug nearby. When the *hāngi* is ready, it is dug up and the containers of food are carried to the kitchen for serving. There is usually at least one expert cook in the *kāuta* who regulates the open fire and manages the *hāngi*.

In parts of Rotorua food can be naturally steamed over hot pools, and this is perhaps the most streamlined outdoor cooking method of all.

Apart from cooking, other *marae* facilities include sanitation, water supply and electricity; sporting grounds; and the church and burial grounds associated with many *marae*.

Sanitation is provided for in separate toilet facilities for men and women, with washbasins, enclosed pit toilets, and often showers as well. In country areas the showers usually run cold water, and on *marae* without them, a nearby river or the ocean serves just as well. This kind of bathing area, however, has its dangers. At one *marae* I visited, a small stream ran behind the meeting-house, and there the ladies repaired late at night to wash. Just after prayers one evening, a great uproar of shrieks and guffaws arose from the creek-bed area. One of the local elders, something of a comic, had run his car quietly down to the water's edge, then switched on the headlights. The clamour came from twenty or more ladies, many of them portly, trying to efface themselves in six inches of running water.

Water supplies are plumbed into the kitchen and toilet areas from rainwater tanks, filled off the corrugated-iron roofs of the main *marae* buildings. The meeting-house is not supposed to be used for this purpose, as its roof represents the sacred back of the ancestor, but this prohibition is frequently ignored. Only *marae* in built-up areas are likely to be on a main supply, and water sometimes has to be brought to the *marae* in a water-truck when the tanks run low.

Electrical supplies also largely depend on the location of the *marae*. Many *marae* still operate off a generator housed somewhere in the grounds, but as power supplies are wired in to more rural areas this becomes no longer necessary. There are usually electric lights in all main buildings, and many *marae* have electrical kitchen equipment and wall-heaters in the meeting-house. Electricity bills after a *hui* can be high, especially as it is common practice to leave on the meeting-house lights all night, so that old people or mothers with children can make their way outside if necessary during the night.

Some *marae* have tennis and basketball courts in their grounds, and sporting competitions are a favourite element in the more lighthearted sorts of *hui*. At the King Movement's annual Coronation at Ngāruawāhia, for example, competitions in football and basketball as well as action songs and war dances are an important part of the celebrations. They attract the young people, who otherwise have little to do at a *hui* except watch and work.

A church may be sited near the *marae*, although not within its boundaries. Services are a main part of most *hui*, although it is only for weddings that people move to the church itself. Regular Sunday services are held in the church, and in many areas people return to the *marae* afterwards for a meal. Churches of this sort are often beautifully decorated with Maori craftwork, their altar furniture finely carved and the pulpit embellished with *tāniko* (red, white and black knotted geometrical patterns.)

The graveyard can be sited next to the church, or in some quite separate locality. Many of the tombstones are elaborate and costly, and reflect the status of those they commemorate. Carved angels imported from Italy and tall obelisks mingle with vaults and headstones. Messages of love and Biblical quotations are inscribed in Maori, and portraits in porcelain may be let into the stones. New graves are lovingly decorated with shells, stones and flowers, all displaying the devotion of the living for those who have "gone on". These are kin graveyards; people are buried in family groups among their more distant relatives, and all are linked in some way to the *marae*. Those who care for the *marae* also look after the graveyard. In communities such as Waimā, recorded by P. W. Hohepa,[43] the cemetery is tidied every Christmas by locals, and migrants who have come home for the holidays.

Establishing a *Marae*
A *marae* may be established for a wide variety of reasons. Former facilities fall derelict or are burnt down, new groups form by processes of expansion and fission or urban migration. Followers may wish to honour a great man, or an individual hopes to establish his *mana* with a lasting memorial. There have been waves of *marae* building in times of Maori nationalism and pride, and periods of stagnation when the people felt hopeless. But whatever the initial reason, a *marae* gets built only when there are a substantial group of people who feel they really need it. A great deal of time and money is involved in establishing any *marae*, and schemes which don't reflect a genuine need rarely get off the ground. Effective leadership is also crucial. Earlier figures such as Te Kooti, founder of the Ringatū Church, and Tāwhiao, the second Maori king, inspired the building of many *marae;* and in more recent years, Sir Apirana Ngata of the Ngāti Porou organised the construction of *marae* all over New Zealand, including many along the East Coast, and Princess Te Puea carried out a similar role among her Waikato people. A famous meeting-house which resulted from their collaboration is Mahinārangi, the main house at Tūrangawaewae *marae*.

Owner groups
In the rural situation, one *marae* typically serves a *hapū* or sub-tribe. This is a descent group of anything from a few hundred to several thousand people,[44] although with urbanisation numbers have been reduced over the

43. Hohepa (1964), pp. 85-88.
44. Metge (1967), p. 131.

THE SETTING: "A PLACE TO STAND"

past thirty years in many rural districts. Sometimes a *marae* might be built by a *whāmere*, an extended family descended from a common ancestor and numbering perhaps thirty to fifty people, but such a family would have to be strong and united, a possible candidate for the nucleus of a new *hapū*. A single country *marae* serves on average 100 to 200 people, so population increases in the area may provide the impetus for establishing a new *marae*. To give some concrete examples of *marae* to population ratios: in Waimā, studied by P. W. Hohepa in 1959,[45] there were four active *marae* serving a Maori population of 329. Two of the *marae* were sponsored by the community, and two were extended family *marae*. In "Kōtare", another Northland community studied by Joan Metge in 1955, there were three *marae* serving a Maori population of 537.[46] One was the community *marae*, and two belonged to extended families. In "Rākau" a Tūhoe community studied by the Ritchies, there were three *marae* serving a Maori population of 356.[47] Two were sub-tribal *marae*, and the other was the main community *marae*. At Ruātoki in the same general area, there are ten *marae* within 10 miles. In the Whānau-a-Apanui district of the East Coast, from Tōrere to Cape Runaway, there are thirteen *marae*, each associated with a sub-tribe. The total Maori population of the area is about 1,600 (1966 Census). For the total East Coast rural district between Opotiki and Gisborne, there are about seventy *marae* serving a Maori population of about 8,000 (Map 4). Some areas are far better supplied with *marae* than others, and these tend to be the remaining rural enclaves of Maori population, like Northland, the East Coast, Bay of Plenty, Urewera, Waikato, and Rotorua-Taupo districts. A rural *marae* in these areas might be used for a *hui* about once a month on average, but in seriously depopulated areas the number of *hui* could decrease to only one or two a year, and the *marae* is virtually abandoned.

Urban centres show far more unfavourable *marae*-to-population ratios. In Auckland, for example, there are currently six operating *marae* (not including the Maori Community Centre) which cater for a Maori population of 44,300 (1971 Census). (Map 5.) This suggests that in Auckland a single *marae* is required to serve about 7,000 people. The figure is in part misleading, since a great proportion of the urban Maori population rarely or never use a *marae*. The reasons for this are not simple, however. It is partly due to increased pressures for acculturation, so that people stay on the job, for example, rather than take time off for a *hui;* and also to the fact that 70% of this population are under twenty-five, an age when they are not especially active on the *marae* in any case. Residential nuclei of descent groups are fragmented in the city, and kin are no longer in

---

45. Hohepa (1964), p. 70.
46. Metge (1964), p. 30.
47. Ritchie (1963), pp. 8-9.

daily close contact. However, people still prefer to hold their *hui*, especially the *tangi*, on a *marae*, and one of the things that stops them is the scarcity of urban *marae* facilities. Those that do exist are heavily booked, and if a *tangi* arises, other *hui* have to be cancelled. This factor leads people to hold wedding receptions and twenty-first birthdays elsewhere. City *marae* are widely scattered, they sometimes lack privacy, and few

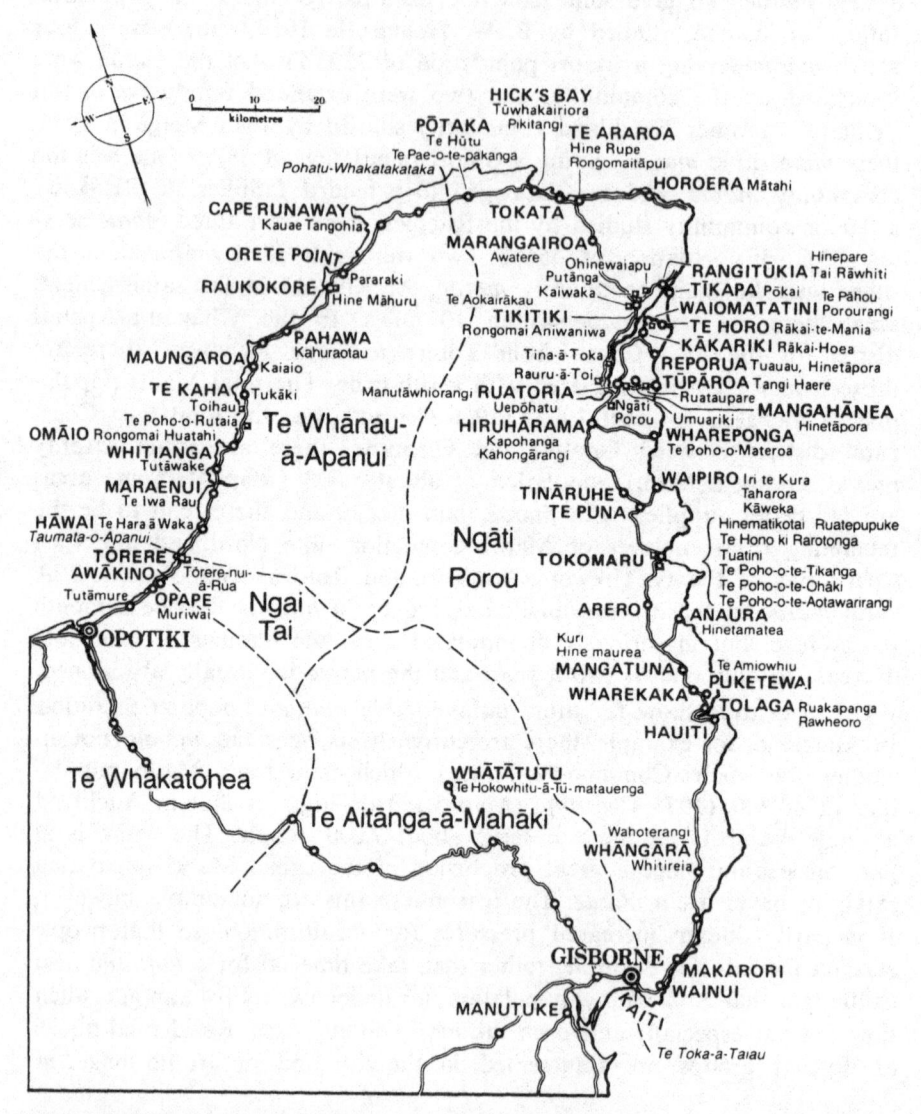

Map 4: East Coast Rural Meeting-houses as recorded by Eruera Stirling. This map has been corrected for the fourth edition. My sincere apologies to Ngai Tai for the previous erroneous version.

THE SETTING: "A PLACE TO STAND" 59

descent groups have a *marae* they can really call their own. Urban migrants can return to their original country homes to hold their *hui*, but often this involves travelling hundreds of miles, and the longer they stay in the city, the less free they feel to do so. This outlet is less available to second and third generation city dwellers, as ties with the home *marae* atrophy in time.

In addition to the six *marae* that have already been established in Auckland, there are at least seven others in the planning stage. However, if estab-

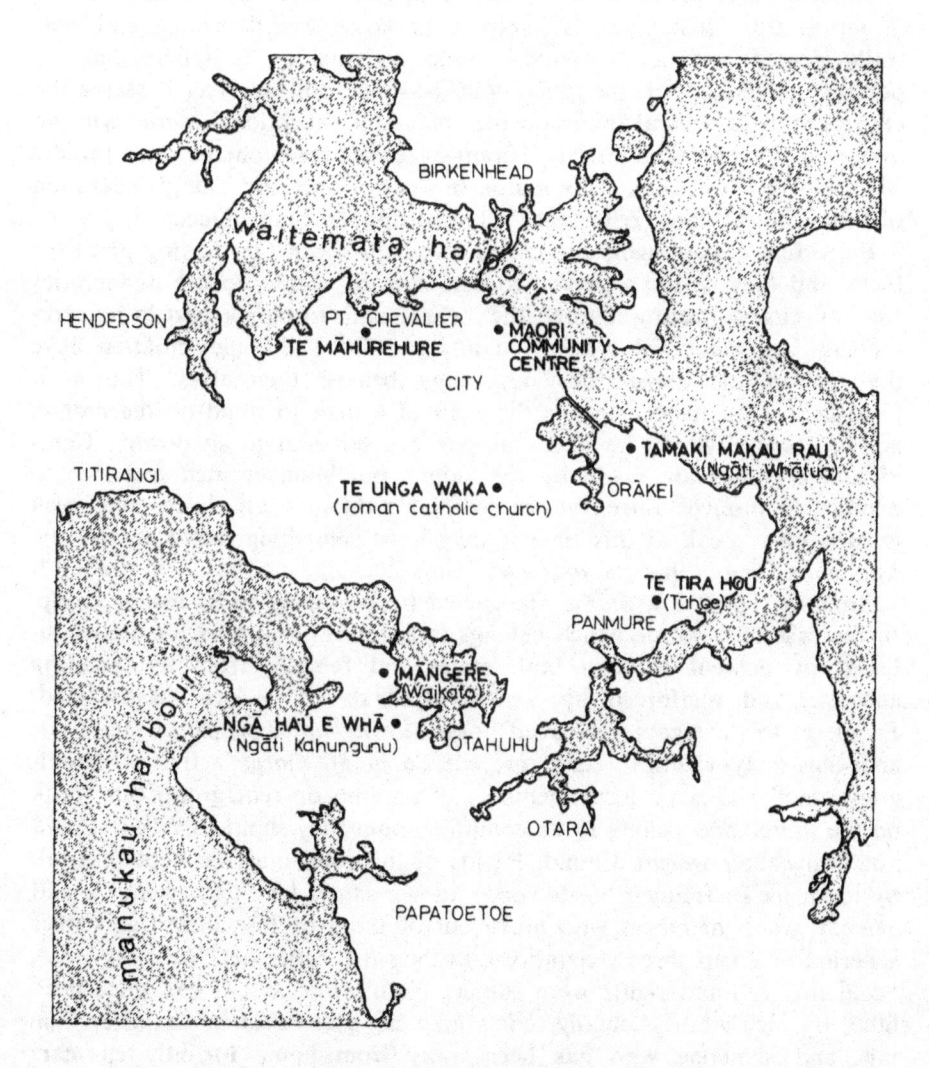

Map 5: City of Auckland—Urban *marae* 1972

lishing a *marae* in the country is expensive, it is doubly so in the city, where all materials and land have to be bought; and plans are often frustrated or delayed by financial problems. Sponsors must be convinced that urban *marae* are necessary and desirable, and in many cases this fails since they are persuaded that such *marae* will only hinder the rapid cultural assimilation of Maori populations. On the other hand, Maori leaders argue that the urban *marae* is essential to the successful adjustment of Maori people to city conditions, as it offers them a place of their own in alien surroundings, where they can "recharge their spiritual batteries".

In most rural districts one *marae* is singled out as the "main *marae*" of the group. This *marae* is likely to be large, well-decorated and centrally located, with an honourable name and history. It is here that important gatherings of the tribe will be held, and in effect it serves the entire group of several thousand members. An exceptional *marae* with an even wider scope than this is Tūrangawaewae, ceremonial centre for the Maori King Movement. This *marae* serves not only the Tainui federation of tribes, but all those tribes that acknowledge the Maori Queen.

Individual *marae* rights are called *tūrangawaewae* (a standing place for feet), and they entitle a person to help run the *marae*, to use its facilities free of charge during family life crises, and to play a part in its ceremonials. All these rights apply mainly to adults, although children have the run of the *marae* providing they behave themselves. The most cherished of all these rights is the right of a man to stand on the *marae*, and to "say anything he likes—no-one can tell him to sit down". Ceremonial speeches are made by the elders, but younger men feel free to express themselves once the ceremonial welcomes are over, and even women may speak at this time if they have something important to say. The main thing is that on your own *marae* "no-one can boss you around".

Primary rights to a *marae* are gained by belonging to its owner group. In the case of a *marae* which belongs to a descent group, rights are established by descent through both males and females from its founding ancestor, and reinforced by ownership of shares in local Maori land. People in this category are called *"tāngata whenua"* (people of the land), and they may rightfully take precedence in all *marae* activities. Immigrants to the area or local members of another descent group can speak on the *marae* and belong to its committee, but they should speak last, and not throw their weight around. Rights of this kind must be kept "warm" by residence or frequent visits (once known as *ahi kā*, "lighted fire"), and descent group members who move out of the area lose their rights over a period of about three generations, as their fire "goes out" *(ahi mātaotao,* "cold fire"). Land rights were subject to this rule, but it has since been lifted by legislation. Actually, one's fires can grow cold much faster than this, and someone who has been away from home for only ten years treads somewhat carefully when he returns to the home *marae*. In the case of a "community *marae*", anyone who lives in the area has *marae* rights, and everyone will co-operate when such a *marae* is being built. Several *hapū* may join in the task, and this could indicate that they are ripe for merger or simply that they are willing to co-operate on a joint project before building *marae* of their own. In the case of Wharepākau,[48] a Te Whāiti house studied by S. M. Mead and his students, a long-established sub-tribe worked with a group of later immigrants to build the *marae*, only to split from them at the last moment in a quarrel over the name. For a community *marae*, all local residents are *tāngata whenua* (people of the land), although early families in the area maintain priority.

Secondary rights to a *marae* are acquired by being formally welcomed there. Strangers visiting a *marae* for the first time are called *waewaetapu* (sacred feet), and they must move very carefully indeed. After the ceremonial welcome, however, the local people may call out *"Kua tāngata whenua koutou"* (you have been made "people of the land"), and one often sees prominent elders after their welcome speaking for the local side and acting as honorary locals in welcomes to later visitors. These honorary rights are tenuous, however, and are exercised only upon invitation.

Planning

The idea of building a new *marae* is usually first broached in public at a *hui*. There may have been discussion around the district or among local leaders first, or it could be the spontaneous suggestion of a single orator. Sometimes the inspiration comes in a vision or dream, and it is said of Waiwhetū *marae* in Lower Hutt that it was started in this way.

A young man called Ihaia Puketapu had a vision while he was visiting Taranaki in 1904, and saw "a great meeting-house at the head of the fish of Maori mythology [the North Island]—a meeting-house not for one tribe alone, but all the people".[50] The house was completed fifty-six years later.

Whatever the origins of the idea, it is likely to be presented to the people at a *hui* after the ceremonial welcomes are over, and matters of policy and business are being discussed. The orator must pick a moment when the right people are in a mood to listen, and if he speaks persuasively and the idea catches on, it is likely to be a major topic for discussion at a string of succeeding *hui*. The plan is progressively elaborated and examined from every angle; visiting speakers offer their expertise, flaws are eliminated, and consensus is reached on the broad outlines of the scheme. This could take years, but the initial publicity is valuable, be-

---

48. Penfold, M. *Wharepaakau*, p. 4, in Mead, ed. (1970).
50. Hutt Valley Tribal Committee (1960), p. 3.

cause planners gain from it a reliable idea of the degree of public support to be expected, both at home and in other tribal areas. Some initial capital can also be raised at this stage, as those who see the beauty of the scheme are likely to show their support by laying a ten-dollar note on the *marae* or by starting up a collection.

The next stage is to establish a committee. This might be done on the *marae*, or more likely a public meeting will be called. People are nominated, others stand to speak in support, and a voice vote decides the issue. Again the decisions are taken only when a consensus is reached, and the chairman must be sensitive to the feelings of the meeting, so he can call for a vote at the right moment. The *komiti marae* may have officials such as chairman, secretary and treasurer, or it might end up as all those who attended the meeting. Often a subsidiary *komiti wāhine* (woman's committee) is elected to help with the fund-raising and to organise female helpers. The *komiti marae* does not wind up when the *marae* is built, but continues functioning as an administrative and maintenance unit throughout the life of the *marae*.

Usually the first business of the *komiti marae* is to decide on the *marae* site and to start raising money. A rural *marae* site rarely has to be paid for. A local landowner donates a section, or land may already be set aside as a *marae* reserve. Only in urban situations does the land regularly have to be purchased. In any case, once the land has been obtained, a request is usually made to the Maori Land Court to have it legally declared a "Maori reserve" by an Order-in-Council. Under Section 439 of the Maori Affairs Act 1958, land can be set aside "for the common benefit of the owners" as "village site, meeting-place, church site, building site, burial ground, or place of historical interest, etc." There are at present 562 such reserves in New Zealand, many of them in use as *marae*.[51] Each *marae* reserve is vested in a group of trustees appointed by the Maori Land Court, who may not sell the land or lease it for more than seven years at a time.

"*Marae* which have not been legally reserved are 'private' *marae*, held on ordinary Maori title by one of several related owners. The latter own individualised shares in the land. In theory, they can dispose of them independently, subject only to the approval of the Maori Land Court. In practice, this is rarely either sought or given."[52]

The area of a site may vary between half an acre and ten acres or more, with one to two acres the norm. Where the *marae* site is large, part of it may be leased to a local farmer for an annual cash payment or perhaps for a continuing supply of firewood or some farm product whenever a *hui* is

---

51. My thanks to the Hon. Duncan MacIntyre, in his former capacity as Minister of Maori and Island Affairs, for this information.
52. Metge (1967), p. 175.

on. In quite recent times the extra land was cultivated for the *marae*, and crops were stored for the entertainment of guests.

Once the site is decided upon, the land may be ploughed and grassed, and a fence built around it if there isn't one already. Some *marae* are carefully planted as well.

The next task for the *komiti marae* is fund-raising. The treasurer opens a bank account, and activity begins in earnest. The locals hold gala days, raffles, bring-and-buys, dances, card evenings, and Queen Carnivals. They may place a weekly levy (say $2) on each family, hold sports days and bingo evenings. Rents from leased lands might be dedicated to the *marae* project, and earlier this century on the East Coast revenues from sales of maize and barrels of whale oil also financed the construction of meeting-houses. The people may form a concert party to tour the country, raising funds with their performances of action songs and war dances. The committee can apply to the Golden Kiwi (the Government lottery fund), the Maori Purposes Fund Board or the local tribal Trust Board for support. In these sophisticated days professional fund-raisers may be hired, with all the panoply of house-to-house appeals and intensive advertising. In short, the people tap funds from every source they can think of. Despite all this effort, it is still extremely difficult to finance a *marae*. A *marae* complex with half the carvings donated can cost $54,000 (Waiwhetū *marae*, opened 1960),[53] and a single meeting-house may cost $32,000 (Kahukuranui at Omāhu, opened 1970). Rural *marae* owners save money by using local timber and materials wherever possible, but the cost is still high. When one considers that approximately ten fully-decorated buildings were erected along the East Coast between the two World Wars, even allowing for Government subsidies, local materials, outside donations and lower prices, the amount of local investment from a Maori population of around 6,000 is astonishing.

Deficits are likely to be reduced or paid off on the day of the official opening, when visiting tribes and individuals place their donations on the *marae*. Official treasurers sit at a central table, write out receipts and keep a running total; the MC periodically announces the names of donors and the size of their gifts to rounds of applause, and visitors find themselves digging deep into their pockets to make their donation a generous one. Amounts of $3,000 and $4,000 are often raised in several hours of such activity.

Once some initial capital is raised, the *komiti marae* meet in one of their homes, and decide on the personnel to be hired. In pre-contact times, of course, the community handled the project from start to finish, although visiting carvers might be called in; and payments were made in feasting for the labourers, and valuable gifts of cloaks or greenstone to important

---

53. Hutt Valley Tribal Committee (1960), p. 27.

specialists. More recently, local people still handled all the work non-commercially. The head carver was likely to be the chief builder as well, and he and his team worked on a basis of voluntary reward. In 1878, for example, the house Hotunui at Thames was being built for the Ngāti Maru people by a team of about seventy Ngāti Awa from the Bay of Plenty. At the completion of their work the Ngāti Awa refused any extra reward and set off on their journey home. Ngāti Maru felt that their long-time reputation for generosity was about to be outdone, so the local chief despatched his daughter-in-law, Mereana Mokomoko, to overtake the builders on the road, and present them with a parting gift. As she said when she later told the story to Gilbert Mair,[54] "One thousand pounds in single bank-notes did I give them, and Ngāti Awa went on their way rejoicing." Today, however, commercial methods have infiltrated *marae* construction, and tradesmen and carvers are usually hired on contract. Builders are employed because local men can no longer afford to work on the job full-time, although they often devote their evenings, weekends and holidays to the *marae*. A *marae* built solely by part-time labour would take a very long time to complete, as even a *marae* constructed with full-time carvers and a building team can take ten years or more to finish. It is not unusual for eight years to pass before a single meeting-house is fully decorated and finished; and the dining-hall may take several years more. For this reason these two main buildings are usually handled as two separate projects. Tenders are called for, and the lowest tenderer, Maori or European, gets the job. He takes on his own labourers, and gives out sub-contracts for wiring, plumbing, painting etc., although he receives expert voluntary help from local Maori tradesmen, and large parts of the job may be completed by local men working in their spare time.

The carvers today are also hired on contract. A local carver is preferred, but if there are no experts living in the area, an outsider will be called in. Carvers may gain a national reputation, and men such as Pine and John Taiapa from the East Coast, Henare Toka from Northland and Piri Poutapu from Waikato are well-known throughout New Zealand. Such experts make a profession of carving, and in the course of a lifetime handle a large number of carving projects. Pine Taiapa, for example, during forty-five years of carving worked on a total of 103 carving jobs all over New Zealand. In earlier times carvers were trained by attaching themselves to a well-known expert as an apprentice, in return for which they would present him with gifts. Today the great majority of carvers have been taught their skills either at the Rotorua School of Arts and Crafts, established in 1927 to promote Maori craftwork, or by one of its graduates. It is said that in the 1920s, outside the Rotorua district where carvers worked largely for the tourist trade, there were only two experienced

54. Mair (1897), p. 41.

carvers left in New Zealand.[55] Since then the school has produced many carvers, and they in their turn have trained many others by taking on local apprentices for each major carving project, and teaching them "on the job". Carvers are usually men, and I know of only two examples where women have worked on significant projects. In one case Princess te Puea dismissed a professional carver working on the house Waikato at Tūrangawaewae *marae*, and completed the door architrave herself,[56] and in the other case a Northland woman named Heni Topia carved the house Rangi Kurukuru at Dargaville in the 1930s, to fulfil a dream.[57]

There have been famous carving families and sub-tribes, but today trainee carvers are largely recruited by the interest they display in the craft. Also in the past there were marked regional "schools" of carving, but although carvers from different areas today display different styles, the isolation which fosters strong regional variation has largely disappeared.

Carvers work in teams, headed by one or more *tohunga whakairo* (expert carvers). An average team might be one expert and four or five trainees, although for a large project many more carvers may be employed. Te Ikaroa-a-Māui at Waitara, for example, was carved by a total of fifteen men, including three experts, all affiliated to the Rotorua School of Arts and Crafts.[58] Carvers specialise in different aspects of their task, and the master carver supplies co-ordination and quality control of the team's work.

The carvers can work independently of the construction team, since carvings are slotted into the building and are not part of its basic structure. They are housed in a temporary structure on the *marae* or in a house nearby, and the local people supply their food. Sometimes they operate from a central workshop, such as the Tainui Carving School at Ngāruawāhia, or the Rotorua School of Arts and Crafts, but in general a carver prefers to work on the *marae* itself. Their first task is to select the timber, to split and shape it. *Tōtara* is the preferred carving timber, and in earlier times the *tohunga* would select his material from trees standing in the bush. There was a special ritual to propitiate the forest god, Tāne, and those who neglected it would incur his displeasure. A well-known myth recounts the trials of a man named Rata, who felled a tree for a canoe without citing the correct incantations. Every day he worked at hewing out the hull, every night all the birds and insects put the tree back together again, and it was not until he finally learnt the proper ritual that the canoe was completed. The ritual is rarely performed today because most timber is milled commercially, but on occasion the Minister of Forests or some

---

55. Mead (1961), p. 25.
56. Phillipps (1955), p. 201.
57. Phillipps, *ibid;* p. 245.
58. Phillipps (1955), p. 127.

individual who owns suitable standing timber will donate the *tōtara* required, and the felling ceremonies may then be performed.

The other material required by the carvers is the irridescent *pāua* shell, from which the eyes of carved figures are fashioned. Special types of large and brilliant shells are obtained by divers under the instructions of the main carver.

The timber that comes to the carvers may already be partially treated and trimmed, but experienced carvers prefer to adze and season the wood themselves. Once the *tōtara* slabs are ready, the design is laid out on the wood, and the carvers set to work with steel chisels and gouges. Carving work is surrounded by *tapu*, and violations can bring dire results. A carver must not smoke or eat near his work, nor should he blow away the carving chips and let them lie. The chips should be collected and buried or thrown in a stream, in case someone should accidentally use them on a cooking fire. The carver should wash his hands before and after working, to lift the *tapu;* and he traditionally chants *karakia*[59] at every step of the carving, to breathe his own life spirit into the figures created. Women should not approach the work. Donne in *The Maori Past and Present* tells the story of an old carver whose *tapu* was threatened in this way: "As I watched the carver deftly using his mallet and chisel in transforming a huge log of *tōtara* timber into a work of art . . . I saw a middle-aged woman approaching the [meeting-] house with the apparent intention of entering it, I therefore said 'Here come a white woman.' The carver looked up, realized her intention, dropped his carving implements, jumped to his feet and rushed to the threshhold just as the stranger raised a foot to step over it. While she was in this unbalanced position he reached her, and placing his hands on her chest he gave her a vigorous push which was almost a blow; she disappeared down an embankment, tumbling head over heels more quickly than she had done anything else in her life."[60] This reprisal was not in fact extreme, for if the woman had entered the house, the building and all its carvings would have been desecrated and useless.

One *tapu* which has recently caused considerable public debate is the rule that the work of a carver who dies in harness should be left unfinished. A well-known Maori opera singer, Inia te Wiata, who had formerly trained as a carver, was commissioned in London to complete a large carving for New Zealand House. When he died in 1971, some unfinished sections of the work were flown back to New Zealand for completion. His widow protested, and claimed that such an action was in violation of Maori custom. A local expert stated that because the singer was not a master carver there was no violation, and that he would be willing to complete the work. A public debate arose, the matter was dis-

59. Incantations.
60. Donne (1927), pp. 72-73.

cussed in newspaper articles, television programmes, and on many *marae*. The consensus of Maori opinion seemed to be that if the carving must be completed, then either Te Wiata's son or his former master were the correct people to do the work, and in fact they collaborated to finish the carving in 1972.

A carver can pay with his life for an error or innovation, and a lasting curse may also fall upon a house for this reason. There are houses which have a history of death and misfortune for all who have worked on them. Phillipps tells of the house Uawhaki in Manakau, where the carver made an error so serious that he had to make a special visit to the Waikato to consult a *tohunga* and have the offence mitigated. "Mr D. Gardiner tells us that all who have had much to do with Uawhaki house have had trouble, so the house has always been more or less *tapu* and is now generally shunned."[61] Another such house was built at Paeroa, south of Rotorua, about the middle of last century, and its story was recently told by Harry Dansey. "A chief called Te Waru commissioned the house in honour of his young wife . . . , but when the carvers were working he broke the *tapu* by entering the partly-built house smoking his pipe. He was warned that the building would have to stop, but he disregarded the advice and his wife died. The carving stopped and the fern grew round the uncompleted house for many years. Later he had the carvers take up the work again. Then his second wife died. The carvings were left again for many years, but when he was an old man he had the work begun again. His third wife died, and a son too. So the carvings were taken away and considered highly dangerous. One would think that no other carver would ever put his chisel to such wood again, but it happened. The first carvers, Tara and Poroa of the Ngāti Tarawhai sub-tribe of Te Arawa were long dead when Anaha, Neke Kapua and Tene Waitere agreed to complete the house. They did so, and no carver ever felt the breath of ancient evil things. No doubt they took the spiritual precautions their culture demanded. Nevertheless, death did intervene. Both the *tohunga* who performed the opening ceremony of the house died within days of carrying out the ritual."[62] Another such meeting-house is a *tapu* house in Te Whāiti, where the carver accidentally inverted a carving motif. It is said that when the prophet Te Kooti came to open the house, his horse shied. He noticed the error (known as a *hapa*), and prophesied that "There will come a day that the people of Te Whāiti will lose everything, their land, their timber, and all that will be left to call their own will be their meeting-houses."[63] All these stories show the virulence of the *tapu* powers that can be unleashed by a careless mistake in meeting-house construction. Carvers are in general

61. Phillipps (1952), pp. 36-37.
62. Dansey, H. *Auckland Star*.
63. Spragg, E. *Eripitana*, in Mead, ed. (1970).

conservative about such rituals, but today many of the rules are relaxed or even ignored altogether.

Once the builder is hired, work on the building frame begins. The contractor in consultation with local elders and the head carver lays out plans for the *marae* facilities. The locals decide whether they want to build the dining-hall or the meeting-house first—quite commonly the dining-hall is built then used to accommodate the carvers, but traditionally the meeting-house had priority, and the carvings were completed under its roof. The locals also decide on the size, names and orientation of the buildings. In the East Coast meeting-houses are faced east to the rising sun, and in Northland it is said they are faced north to Cape Reinga, the mythological jumping-off place of spirits. Other factors such as orientation to the road are also important today, however, and often receive priority. The size of the buildings largely determines their cost, as it dictates the amount of decorative work required. The meeting-house at Waiwhetu *marae* in Lower Hutt, for example, measures 98 ft by 58 ft and contains 10,000 super feet of *tōtara* carving plus 600 square feet of *tukutuku* panelling.[64] Old carvings from previous buildings can be used, and represent a substantial saving.

If the contractor is new to this type of building, he works in close consultation with the head carver, who advises him on architectural detail and layout. It was traditionally important, for example, that there be an odd number of rafters in both the porch and interior of a meeting-house,[65] and that the ridgepole should go up before the foundations were laid. Even if these customs are ignored, as they mostly are today, the builder should be advised about acceptable style and detailing for the building, since deviations from traditional patterns can be regarded with some misgiving. When young Maori leaders earlier this century mounted a campaign for more windows, no sunken floors in meeting-houses, and proper sanitary facilities outside, they met with formidable opposition from their elders. Today conservatism is not so entrenched, and urban *marae* in particular display quite startling innovations in form and materials. Architects are employed on many of these projects, and A-form meeting-houses, houses with exterior carvings and other stylish adaptations are among the results. The difficulty and expense of obtaining traditional materials has led to the production of painted copies of "carvings" and *"tukutuku"*, the use of plastic or raffia fibres in *tukutuku* weaving, and suggestions that plaster replicas of carvings or wallpaper copies of fully-decorated interior walls might be used. All these substitutes, however, are regarded as second-best and are used only when expense prohibits their originals.

Apart from carvings, the main decorative elements in the house are the

---

64. Hutt Valley Tribal Committee (1960), p. 17.
65. Buck (1962), p. 124.

rafter paintings or *kōwhaiwhai*, and decorative reed panels or *tukutuku*. Rafter patterns are usually painted on before the rafters go into place, and though this was traditionally the task of male experts, women today often fill in the designs. The rafters are laid outside on trestles, the master carver or some expert chalks the designs on to them, and teams of women with pots of red, white and black paint complete the product. In one house recently built, however, all the rafter panels were painted by a local sign-writing firm.

Tukutuku panels are made by teams of women supervised by a female expert or the head carver. Strands of natural fibre in yellow, black and white are woven in a cross-stitch pattern around each reed in the panel to produce strong geometric designs. At the slightest error, sections of the work are slashed out by the supervisor and must be repeated. Preparation for this craft is laborious. *Kākaho* reeds are gathered, sorted, and lashed together, then attached to a wooden frame. Yellow strands of *pīngao* are collected from a plant that grows in sand dunes in certain areas of New Zealand, then dried and trimmed. *Kiekie* fibres come from a plant which grows deep in the bush. They are gathered, sorted and boiled, and if black fibres are required, they are then steeped in specially-prepared mud pools for a period of three days. Women helping in this work should avoid all sex relations for several days beforehand, nor should a menstruating woman enter the pool. If these *tapu* are broken, it is said the dye will not take. Once I was present when *tukutuku* work was being carried out. A batch of *kiekie* went into the mud, and came out several days later blotchy and uneven in colour. The women immediately began to try and track down the offender in a ribald and hilarious investigation, during which allegations of impropriety were freely exchanged. No one could be made to confess, however and the precise nature of the *tapu* violation remained a mystery. When panels and fibres are ready, work days may be called on the *marae*, and special tents are set up to shelter the frames, or each family may be alloted one or two frames for its womenfolk to complete at home. *Tukutuku* work is not supposed to be done in an unfinished meeting-house, because of the *tapu* against women entering the building, but there are occasional exceptions. When the house Parewahawaha was being built at Bulls, for example, no other *marae* buildings were available, so the director Henare Toka performed special ceremonies to raise this prohibition.[66] The art of *tukutuku* weaving was all but extinct in the 1920s, but when the Rotorua School of Arts and Crafts was established in 1927 Sir Apirana Ngata had East Coast experts instruct teams of women in this skill. These teams subsequently worked on many meeting-houses under his supervision. In the past ten years several *tukutuku* schools have been held on the East Coast under the guidance of

---

66. My thanks to Joan Metge for this information.

Pine Taiapa, and groups who are planning to build their own *marae* have been instructed in the art.

Once the main buildings and their decorations are nearing completion, the *Komiti Wāhine* get to work and plait the fine flax mats or *whāriki* for the meeting-house floor, embroider pillowcases, purchase mattresses, order linen, crockery and cooking utensils. The men build wooden benches for the *marae*, dig latrines, check the fences and paint the buildings. In these last months there are working bees (traditionally called *ohu*) almost every weekend, and people work on the *marae* late at night. The *komiti marae* have frequent meetings and keep in touch by telephone as they plan the details of the grand opening, make final decisions on the names of buildings, and reckon up their financial position. One of their number may be delegated to produce a commemorative booklet complete with photographs, diagrams of *marae* facilities, ancestral names of carvings, genealogies, and the history of the *marae*, and this is printed and sold on the opening day. Supplies are ordered, invitations are sent out, and everything on the *marae* is brought to a high pitch of perfection as the opening day approaches.

Opening the *Marae*

The opening ceremony for a new *marae* is itself a type of *hui* and one of the most infrequent. There might be perhaps two *marae* openings in the North Island in a good year, although the reconsecration of renovated buildings and the opening of dining-hall facilities can add to this number. A total of three "openings" were attended in the course of this research. The opening of a new *marae* is surrounded with pomp and circumstance. Larger tribal delegations from many areas and distinguished visitors attend in force. Among the dignitaries who are likely to declare a *marae* officially open one may list the Governor-General, the Prime Minister, the Minister of Maori and Island Affairs and the Maori Queen. Publicity for such events is wide, and they often rate national news items on both television and radio. Although the opening of a major *marae* is comparable in scale to an important *tangi*, which may also be widely reported and attract several thousand visitors, its atmosphere is one of joy and celebration, quite different from the sombre dignity of a *tangi*.

Invitations are printed and sent to leading elders throughout the country. An invitation or *pōwhiri* is typically structured like the oration of an elder welcoming visitors to his *marae*. It begins with a traditional incantation, followed by formal words of welcome which summon the seven canoes, the four winds, the chiefs and orators of New Zealand to the new *marae*. Any important matters to be raised at the hui are mentioned, and a detailed programme is attached. Pei te Hurinui Jones in his booklet *Mahinārangi* gives a translated version of the invitation that was sent out for the opening of that famous house:

TE POWHIRI
  [The invitation]
  Uea! Uea!
  Uea te pou o to whare kia tu tangatanga!
  He kapua whakairi naku ki runga o Moehau!
  Taku kiri ka tokia e te anu matao
  E tau e!
  Nau mai, e waha i taku tua . . .

  TRANSLATION:
  Shake! Shake!
  Shake thine house to its very foundation
  Until it stands quite loosened!
  Like unto that cloud suspended o'er Moehau
  My skin is pierced by the cold winds;
  O thou whom I cherish
  Come up unto me!
  And place thine arms around mine shoulders . . . [67]

  Come all ye chiefs, all ye tribes and all ye orators!
  Come from the many courtyards of our ancestors;
  Come! Come! Come!
  Come to the Tainga o te kawa, the Dedication; to the Kawanga, the Solemn Dedication of Mahinarangi House at Ngāruawāhia.
  The official opening will be performed by the Right Honourable Coates.[68]

Openings are usually held on a weekend, with Friday evening and sometimes all day Saturday set aside for the ceremonial reception of visiting groups. (These rituals of welcome are discussed in detail in Chapter 5.) Tribal groups arrive by bus or car, and are greeted, fed, and shown to their accommodation. In the evenings there are church services, followed by discussions and entertainment in the marquee where visitors are housed until the meeting-house is opened. Sunday is usually the "big day", and all the cooks are up at dawn. More tribal groups arrive and are welcomed, and some time during the morning representatives of every group formally lay their gifts or *aroha* (love) on the new *marae*. A treasurer's table is set up amid great excitement, donations and progressive totals are announced, receipts are distributed, and small children are sent running to the treasurer's table with fistfuls of banknotes. Later in the morning there is a massed church service with all denominations represented, and each

---

67. This incantation was traditionally used by heralds inviting visitors to a feast—Taylor (1855), p. 343.
68. Jones (1945), p. 34.

minister lays his blessings on the *marae*, and all its buildings. Then comes the reception of the official party. At one opening I witnessed, this was heralded by the arrival of the Vice-Regal Rolls Royce, its black paint gleaming in the sun. The Governor-General stepped out in full ceremonial uniform, accompanied by his *aide de camp*, and was joined by Members of Parliament, the local mayor and councillors and their wives at the entry to the *marae*. A warrior rushed out to the gate of the *marae*, jumping, grimacing and whirling his *taiaha*,[69] and laid a carved baton before the Governor-General, who stopped and picked it up as a sign of peace. A party of local women in front of the meeting-house started up the chant of greeting, while two old ladies gave the high and melancholy cry of welcome. The challenger whirled around, raised the *taiaha* over his head with its blade pointing to the meeting-house, and stepped stiffly into the *marae*, followed at a distance by the official party. When they were seated on a dais, speeches followed in full formality, most of them in English. The Governor-General spoke last, and the time of the official opening had finally arrived.

At this point the ceremony varies according to whether the ritual known as *kawanga whare, whai-kawa or tāinga o te kawa*[70] is performed. Today the major remaining experts for this ritual come from the Waikato tribes, and if they are unable to be present, the buildings may be consecrated by a church service instead. The purpose of the *kawanga whare* is to remove the *tapu* attaching to a newly-carved meeting-house, "because the trees which have been felled to build the house are the sacred children of Tane-Mahuta, God of the forest, and because they have been carved into the semblance of revered ancestors, and into representations of natural and tribal deities. The *tapu* must be laid, its dangerous powers averted, before the house can be occupied safely."[71] In all three openings that I attended, a church service was given in place of this ritual, but fortunately there are several detailed accounts of the *kawanga whare* ceremonial in print, and it has been described to me by informants as well.

The first of these accounts was written in 1930 by James Cowan, a very reliable observer of Maori custom. He describes the Arawa version of the ritual as he observed it in 1908 at the opening of Wahiao meeting-house in Whakarewarewa, Rotorua.[72] The incantations were dictated to him privately by the officiating priest, Taua Tutānekai Haerehuka, after the ceremony. First, the priest moved to the left of the house, and recited an incantation to propitiate the Forest God, Tāne Māhuta, for felling his trees.

69. A wooden weapon about 5 ft long, with polished staff and carved blade.
70. *Kawa* is a term referring to the leafy twig that was originally used in ceremonies to raise *tapu*.
71. Cowan (1930), p. 129.
72. Cowan (1930), pp. 131-5.

THE SETTING: "A PLACE TO STAND"

Ko te tuanga o te rakau ki raro;
Kakariki powhaitere
I te Wao-nui-a-Tane
I te urunga tapu
Kua ara, kua ara
A Tane ki runga;
Kua kotia nga putake
O te rakau o te whare nei;
Kua waiho atu
I te urunga tapu;
Kua kotia nga kauru
O te rakau o te whare nei;
Kua waiho atu
I te Wao-nui-a-Tane
Kua tae au
Ki nga pukenga
Ki nga wananga
Ki nga tauira
Patua kuru
Patua whao
Patua te toki a Tai-haruru.
Kua piki hoki nei
Ki te maro-hukahuka-nui
A Tangaroa
Te ngaru ai e whati ai.
E Nuku-tai-maroro
Kaore ko au
E kimi ana, e hahau ana
I nga uri o te whanau a Rata
Hai pokapoka ia Tane
E tui-i-i
Kaore i kitea
Kua mate noa atu
I te awa i Pikopiko-i-whiti
Ma te maranga mai ai
Ko hiki-nuku e!
Ta taua rangi!

Cowan includes an excellent free translation of the invocation:

   For the felling of the tree.

"King of the Forest Birds, chief of the parakeets that guard Tane's mighty woods, Tane's sacred resting place (listen to my prayer!) Tane (the tree) stood erect, stood erect, amidst the forest shades, but now he's fallen. The trunk of Tane has been severed from the butt; the stump of the tree felled to build this house stands yonder in the sacred resting-place. The branchy tree-top, the leafy head has been cut off; it lies yonder in the Vast-Forest-of-Tane. I have performed my ceremonies of propitiation; I have appealed to the spirits of our priestly ancestors and to the sacred ones. I have struck these timbers with mallet and chisel; I have struck them with the axe of the Sounding-Seas. I have mounted upon the great foaming girdle of the sea-god Tangaroa, the waves beaten down and divided by the canoe *Nuku-tai-maroro*. I am seeking, searching for the descendants of the children of Rata, to carve these timbers for me. I found them not; they were slain at the river Pikopiko-i-Whiti. O ancient ones; return and aid me on this our sacred day."

The second incantation is not given in full by Cowan, but it can be identified as one that is still used by Arawa elders. Its purpose was to lift the *tapu* from the carving tools that had been hung from the porch bargeboards, and to raise the *tapu* from the carvings themselves. It is said to have first been used by the priest Ngātoro-i-rangi, when he saved the Arawa canoe from a whirlpool on its voyage to New Zealand:

Takina te kawa ko te kawa tuatahi
Takina te kawa ko te kawa tuarua, ko te kawa tuatoru,
Ko te kawa tuawhā, ko te kawa tuarima
Takina te kawa ko te kawa tuaono, ko te kawa tuawhitu,
Ko te kawa tuawaru, ko te kawa tuaiwa, ko te kawa tuangāhuru
Takina te kawa ko te kawa mā wai?
Ko te kawa mā Maru-te-whare-aitu
Mā Maru-whakawhiwhiā
Mā te whare Hau-te-ananui
Whano, whano
Haramai te toki
Haumi e!
Hui e,
[All] *Tai ki e!*

"Recite the sacred ritual, the first ritual,
Recite the sacred ritual, the second, the third, the fourth, the fifth
Recite the sacred ritual, the sixth, the seventh, the eighth, the ninth, the tenth ritual
Recite the ritual for whom?
The ritual for Maru-te-whare-aitu, and Maru-whakawhiwhia
[two great Arawa ancestors]
For the house Hau-te-ananui
[an ancient house of instruction which stood on Mokoia Island]

Go, go
Bring me the adze
Join it, unite it, it is done!"

As the chant proceeded the priest entered the porch, and struck each carved slab and post in turn with his *taiaha*. The third and final incantation, a house-warming prayer, is also still known in the Arawa district:

*Rukutia
Rukutia nga pou tahuhu
O te whare nei
Rukutia nga poupou
O te whare nei
Rukutia nga tukutuku
O te whare nei ...
Rukutia, rukutia
Kia u, kia mau
Kai tae mai
A te Anu matao
Ki roto i a koe-e!
Kai ninihi atu ai
A Ua-whatu, a Ua-nganga
Kai whakamai hoki
A Hau-nui, a Hau-roa
A Tawhiri-matea
Taku hiki i pai ai
Mo roto ia Tane
E tu nei-i
Ko Mahana
Ko Pu-mahana
Ko Werawera
Ko Kohakoha
Nga tangata mo roto
I a Tane e tu nei
Whano, whano
Haramai te toki
Haumi e!
Ui e!* [all] *Taiki e!*

TRANSLATION:
"Bind fast the ridgepole supports of this house; bind fast the carved slabs and reed panels [other parts of the house are then enumerated]; bind, bind together that all may be firm and steadfast, so that into thee, o Tane, may not enter the cold and stormy elements, the Frost-wind,

the Great Rain, the Long rain, the Cold Sleety rain, the Hailstones; that you may stand against the assault of the Mighty Wind, the Long-prevailing wind, the tempests of the wind-god Tawhirimatea! May all be warm and safe within your walls! These shall dwell therein—Warmth, Heaped-up warmth, and Glowing heat, Joy and Gladness, these are the people who shall dwell in Tane standing here! Now it is done! Bring me the axe and bind it on! Our work is o'er!"

At this point in the ceremony in some areas, the *tohunga* climbs to the ridgepole of the house, recites a further incantation, then asks of the people assembled:

Ko wai te ingoa o tēnei whare?
What is the name of this house?

and all the people in unison call out the new name. This practice is followed by the Waikato tribes, but is not included in Cowan's account.

Finally, the house is entered by a woman for the first time, an act called *takahi paepae* (treading the threshhold). A chieftainess of the tribe accompanied by the priest and carving experts steps across the threshhold of the house and enters it, carrying a cooked *kūmara* to remove any last traces of *tapu*. The *noa* qualities of the woman and the cooked food complete the task of rendering the house safe for all to enter and everyone can now go into the house and admire the skill of its builders.

The main source for the contemporary Waikato version of the *kawanga whare* are two booklets written by Pei te Hurinui Jones, one for the opening of Mahinārangi meeting-house at Ngāruawāhia in 1929, and the other for the opening of Auau-ki-te-rangi meeting-house at Kāwhia in 1962.[73] In these booklets Dr Jones gives a description of the ritual and texts of the incantations used, which differ substantially from their Arawa counterparts. For Mahinārangi house, interestingly enough, the entire ritual was repeated three times: First the Arawa *tohunga* Tutānekai, Cowan's informant, chanted his incantations, and the threshhold was crossed by the daughter of Te Heuheu, chief of the affiliated Tūwharetoa people. Secondly, elders descended from the *Mātātua* canoe performed their dedication. And on the final day, the Waikato ritual was performed, and the threshhold was crossed by Koroki, male heir to the Maori throne. This repetition of the ritual symbolised the dedication of Mahinārangi, the major house of the King Movement, to all the tribes of New Zealand, not just to the Waikato people.

The Waikato ritual, like the Arawa one, has three main incantations. The first refers to Tāne the forest god, and Rata, the legendary figure

73. Jones (1945), (1962).

who forgot to ask Tāne's pardon for felling a tree; and it proclaims the name of the house. The second incantation dedicates the house to the Maori Queen, and carries the priest and his assistants over the threshhold. The third and final incantation is performed inside as the priests, followed by the people, walk round the house from right to left, touching the carved slabs in turn and finally lifting the *tapu*. In the Waikato area this ritual is followed by a church service with the Queen's brass band accompanying the hymns, and this brings the proceedings to an end.

The *kawanga whare* ritual, however, as I have mentioned, is not always performed at the opening of a new building. A new but uncarved meeting-house or dining-hall, while they still call for formal celebration, do not really require the *tapu*-raising ceremony; and knowledgeable elders are not always available. On such occasions the church service which normally supplements the ritual may replace it entirely, although elders speaking on the *marae* prior to the service may give parts of the old ritual in their speeches. The opening in this case is performed by the guest of honour, when he unveils the nameplate of the house or an inscribed foundation stone, and the custom of having a high-born woman tread over the threshhold may be left out altogether. As the nameplate is unveiled, one old woman or several give the *karanga* of welcome, greeting the house by name for the first time, and welcoming it into existence. Visitors may enter the house on a tour of inspection and view its interior. Sometimes other minor ceremonies accompany the opening, and the honoured guest may be asked to unveil a new memorial stone or something similar. Afterwards the guests are entertained with action songs and war dances performed by a party that has been training for weeks or months in advance, songs that may have been especially composed for this day. Backstage, the earth ovens are opened and cooks add last-minute decorative touches to the dining table. Finally, the feast is ready and the guests are summoned. The official party is seated at a special table, then the visiting tribes are called in one by one in order of prestige or distance travelled to the *hui*. A Minister stands to bless the food, and the feast begins. Waitresses move round the tables with plates of meat and vegetables, every now and then starting up a song. The first twenty minutes or so are almost silent, then people begin to laugh and chatter and stand to give speeches or to sing a song of thanks. In about an hour the feast and the *hui* are almost over. Guests begin to leave the *marae*, and the locals start to think about clearing up. Although some visitors may stay overnight and leave after breakfast, the real business of the *hui* is now at an end.

Historical Development of the *Marae*

The *marae* as a complex of meeting-house, courtyard and dining-hall is a recent innovation in Maori society, the end product of a long series of changes in settlement patterns since European contact. Upon contact, the explorers found the Maori living in several types of settlement. The first of these was the fortified hilltop *pā*, with its elaborate trenchworks and palisades. Some *pā* were permanently inhabited, and their defences enclosed small "towns", like that described by John Nicholas in 1814: "Passing this fortification, we entered the town itself, which consisted of huts built on each side of several little lanes, or rather pathways, for they were made barely wide enough for one person to pass through at a time. Before each hut was an enclosed space, resembling a courtyard, in which there was a shed . . . employed by the inhabitants for various purposes of domestic convenience. The entrance to these enclosures was by stiles ingeniously contrived, and fancifully embellished; and I observed some on which there was a rude carving of the human form."[74]

In areas less prone to attack, people lived in scattered houses or undefended villages, and retreated to their nearby fortifications only in times of emergency; and on the coasts, there were seasonal settlements for gathering shellfish or fishing, with shelters rapidly thrown together, or in some cases, no shelters at all.

The *marae* was an ancient and widespread component of Polynesian settlements, usually an area dedicated to religious performances, with an earthen courtyard and a raised stone platform. Early explorers, however, failed to find comparable structures in New Zealand, and in 1769 Captain Cook observed "they have no such thing as *morais*, or other places of public worship; nor do they assemble together with this view".[75] Probably Cook was looking for the raised stone platforms or *ahu* to be found on *marae* elsewhere in Polynesia, but in New Zealand the *tūāhu* was just a few unworked rocks set in the ground, still a sacred place but physically inconspicuous and set apart from the village. The other component of the ancient *marae*, the earthen courtyard, had become secularised, and now functioned as a sort of village plaza. Crozet described such a courtyard in a Bay of Islands settlement in 1772: "The space which divided the two rows of houses, and which was more or less roomy . . . served as a sort of parade ground, and extended the whole length of the village. This parade ground was raised about a foot higher than the surrounding ground on which the houses stood. It was raised by means of soil brought there and beaten down; no grass was to be seen on it and the whole place was kept extremely clean."[76] This secularised *marae* was the centre of village activities, including ceremonial gatherings but not devoted to them exclusively. In the village described by Crozet and mapped by Roux[77] the

74. Nicholas (1817), Vol. I, p. 174-5.
75. Reed ed. (1951), p. 237.
76. Kelly ed. (1951), p. 32.
77. Kelly, *ibid*, p. 72.

chief's house, by far the largest there, was sited on the courtyard; and it is here we find the probable forerunner of a second element in the modern *marae* complex, the carved meeting-house.

Cook and Banks in 1769 both observed that apart from the commonly small and roughly-constructed huts, there were some distinctly superior houses. "The best I ever saw," says Cook, "was about 30 ft long, 15 ft broad, and 6 high, built exactly in the manner of one of our country barns. The inside was both strong and regularly made of supporters at the sides, alternately large and small, well-fastened by means of withes, and painted red and black. The ridgepole was strong, and large bulrushes, which composed the inner part of the thatching, were laid out with great exactness . . . This, however, ought to be considered as one of the best, and the residence of some principal person; for the greatest part of them are not half the above size, and seldom exceed 4 ft in height."[78] Of a similar house, Banks said, "the woodwork of it was squared so even and smooth, that we could not doubt of their having among them very sharp tools; all the side posts were carved in a masterly stile of their whimsical taste, which seems confined to the making of Spirals and distorted human faces."[79]

These houses were strikingly similar to the modern meeting-house in form and decoration, despite their smaller scale. They had a gabled frontal porch surmounted by a carved figure, a ceiling lining of reeds; the "supporters at the sides, well-fastened by means of withes and painted red and black" probably foreshadowed modern *tukutuku* wall panels; and later houses painted by Angas in the 1840s show rafter paintings almost identical to those used today. Almost all early sources agree in claiming that these houses were the residences of chiefs.

Other houses in the village might have "either over the door, or fixed somewhere in the house a piece of Plank covered with their carving, which they seem to value as much as we do a Picture, placing it always as conspicuously as possible."[80] but the chief's house was distinctive by its size and amount of decoration. As the most impressive residence in the village, it served to house visitors as well as the chief's own family; and in some communities it was apparently also used to store valuable weapons, as the chief's *tapu* extended to his home and made it safe from thieves. Chiefs usually had a number of wives, and their families were correspondingly large, so the size of their houses was not purely motivated by prestige factors.

Very shortly after contact, however, with the arrival of missionaries, whalers, then permanent settlers, the construction and functions of these

78. Reed ed. (1951), p. 249.
79. Morrell ed. (1958), pp. 63-4.
80. Morrell ed. (1958), p. 134.

buildings began to alter. The missionaries built their own houses using European tools and methods, then started to teach their converts carpentry. As early as 1814 Nicholas observed a storehouse with a mortised door frame, "a curious specimen of their . . . attempts in carpenter's work",[81] and similar techniques were used on the houses built by chiefs. Steel tools including adzes and pitsaws made it much easier to fell and shape timber, and subsequently to carve it, so houses were built larger. Chiefs hoping to attract traders to their settlements built special guesthouses for Europeans, like one observed by Cruise in 1820: "Tippooi's house was one of the largest . . . in the country; it was quite new, and when he showed us into it, he remarked 'that he had built it for the white men who might be sent to work in the woods' "[82]; or Wakefield in 1840: "E Kuru signed to me to follow him, and led the way to a very large *ware*, about 20 yards from the bank. 'This house is yours,' said he, 'tell your White men to go in.' On entering, I found it indeed a noble present. The house was 50 ft long, and 28 ft broad. Slabs of *tōtara* wood . . . neatly smoothed with the adze, formed the framework of the walls . . . ."[83] These houses were a new development, for like the modern meeting-house, they had no permanent residents, and were devoted purely to the accommodation of visitors.

After an initial burst of enthusiasm in using steel tools to improve the scale and precision of prestige constructions, it was soon discovered that carved houses would no longer ensure respect. The musket was introduced to New Zealand, and tribes who were not armed had to bend all their efforts to buying guns, or they were eradicated. In 1847, Angas observed that "the natives have now ceased to construct works of so much labour and ingenuity, and content themselves with building a *raupo* hut to dwell in. The consequence is, that in a few years not a single aboriginal edifice, displaying that skill in carving and ornament for which the New Zealanders have been so pre-eminently distinguished among savage nations, will exist throughout the whole country: even at the present hour, they are rarely to be met with . . . I have found houses splendidly carved, in ruins, amidst the decay and overgrown vegetation of their long-since deserted *pahs*."[84]

In the tribal skirmishes which increased in scope and deadliness as more guns came into the country, many carved houses were burnt, and settlements were abandoned or laid waste. In the 1850s and 1860s, however, when land sales provoked Maori military resistance, a number of large houses were built by leaders of land leagues in token of their earnest not to sell, and inter-tribal meetings were held there to deliberate

81. Nicholas (1817), Vol. I, p. 340.
82. Cruise (1823), p. 116.
83. Wakefield (1845), Vol. I, p. 380.
84. Angas (1850), Vol. I, pp. 266-7.

the great questions of the day. These houses were known as *whare rūnanga* or council houses, and they came to symbolise Maori resistance to European encroachment. Movements such as the Kingitanga and the Ringatū church also built houses where their members could assemble, and gradually the concept of a distinctively Maori meeting-house evolved. All this time, the village of which the chief's house and courtyard had once been the core had gradually been altering in character. In remote areas the *raupo* hut and the '*pā*' as a settlement type lingered well on into the twentieth century, but in most places, changes were more rapid. Houses were built European style, shops were established, with streets and services, and Europeans moved in. In larger communities Maoris were soon outnumbered and lived scattered in suburban neighbourhoods, while in country areas they shifted out on to farms. The focus of these settlements was now the shopping centre, where people met and gossiped, no longer the village courtyard. The meeting-house and *marae* were now built on the outskirts of the settlement, as a stage for the intermittent gatherings of the local Maori people. Village cooking facilities were no longer available, so the cookshed and later the dining-hall and kitchen were built as final additions to the complex. The *marae* was becoming a special place, deliberately set apart; a symbolic place which visibly stated the survival of *Maoritanga*.

In the late nineteenth century *marae* building largely lapsed as the Maori population declined. Inter-tribal fighting, the land wars and European diseases had almost put paid to the Maori people, and their extinction was predicted. Early in the twentieth century, however, a number of young leaders set out to re-establish their people, and along with a programme for material betterment went a plan to awaken pride in Maori culture once again. Sir Apirana Ngata in particular, who went on to become Native Minister in 1928, dedicated himself to the building of meeting-houses all over New Zealand, and it is from this period that one can regard the contemporary form of the *marae* as established.

Ngata was interested in building fully-decorated meeting-houses, and he sponsored teams of carvers, *tukutuku* workers and *kowhaiwhai* painters who travelled all over the country as the competitive house-building spirit took fire. The decorative arts which had been almost dead at the turn of the century now flourished with a new vigour. Ngata was interested not only in reviving the old arts but in adapting to new conditions as well, and these *marae* were built with stages, wood on concrete floors, and the most modern facilities. There are at least fifteen houses in New Zealand in which Ngata took part, and although at the time his people grumbled that while he was building meeting-houses they still lived in *raupo* huts, they have lived to be proud of his efforts.

The other great movement in this century has been the shift of Maori population to the towns and cities. Maori urbanisation gained momentum after World War II, and since then the rural areas have been steadily drained of young people. Country *marae* in many cases have only a few old men and women left to look after them, and although they are sometimes renovated, few new *marae* are being built in these areas. As always, the *marae* follows the people, and increasingly the location for new *marae* is in the towns.

Urban *Marae* in Auckland

In 1936, only 6% of the Maori population were city dwellers, but in 1971 the figure had risen to 51%. The implications of this exodus for the future of the *marae* are still far from clear. It is popularly thought that rural *marae* are being deserted as people leave for the cities, and in many rural areas there does appear to have been a decline in *marae* activities over the past thirty years; but according to Census figures, natural increase has more than compensated for urban migration over this period. In 1939, for example, there were 77,500 Maoris living in rural areas; by 1971, this figure had risen to 111,400. The process also holds true for the older people (fifty-five years and over), who are the stalwarts of any *marae*. In 1936, before the urban drift really began, there were 6,400 people of this age group in New Zealand; by 1966, the latest figures available, there were 7,100 elders in country areas alone, and 3,164 more in the cities. If *marae* activities have decreased in many rural areas over this period, therefore, it means that either the local people have become less active on their *marae*, or that they have shifted away from their *marae* to small country towns in a mini-process of urbanisation. Only in quite recent years have the absolute numbers of rural Maori people begun to fall from a peak reached in 1966.

In the cities, where the surplus rural population ends up, *marae* are being built, but they vary greatly in owner groups and physical structure, and appear to represent a trial-and-error period of adaptation to urban conditions. It is difficult to make any predictions about the future of the *marae* in the cities, because the most radical changes are probably yet to come. The current urban leaders are mostly rural-born, basing their lines of action at least in part on rural precedents and values. The real effects of urbanisation on the *marae* will not be felt until urban-born generations come into positions of influence. They have no rural background to draw on, and one might expect their activities to be governed by different priorities. It could even be that this generation will find the *marae* no longer relevant to their lives.

The country *marae* is closely attuned to the rhythms of a rural economy. *Hui* are held when crops and sea food are in season, and workers can let their livelihood look after itself for a few days. *Marae* buildings are constructed largely from local materials by local labour; and beasts are slaughtered, vegetables and sea-food are collected to feed the guests at a *hui*. Cash is relatively unimportant to the life of a rural *marae*, and because most of the local population are Maori in any case, closely linked by descent, the values of the *marae* can be taken for granted. The great majority of *marae* fall into this category, because there are only about twenty urban *marae* in New Zealand, out of an estimated 1,000 total. Urban values are, however, pervasive, and when urban expatriates return home from a *hui* they bring some of the constraints of urban life with them. Their visits are usually brief, as they have to hurry back to their jobs in the city, much to the disgust of their rural kin. Country *hui* are increasingly timed for their convenience, in weekends and public holidays. Not only does urban life affect the rural *marae*, but it would seem in the light of current population movements that if the *marae* is to have a significant future, it will be in the towns and cities.

Here the situation is very different. Descent groups are no longer local units, except as they relate to their rural origins, and Maoris live scattered among a majority European population. *Marae* in the cities are run by churches, inter-tribal or even inter-racial groups. In recent times, however, descent-groups have tried to preserve their identity in the city by building their own *marae*, and most of the theoretically inter-tribal or inter-racial *marae* are in fact identified with a single tribe. People work for wages, and everything costs money, including time. *Hui* are shorter, and fewer people attend them, except in weekends and after work. Building materials, provisions, firewood and other goods essential to the *marae* have to be paid for in cash. *Marae* facilities are extremely expensive to build, and the land on which they are sited adds to the capital cost. One suspects that this is why many urban *marae* begin with inter-tribal or inter-racial committees, to extend as far as possible the range of potential donors. Hui catering becomes a major investment, and some *hui* are run by invitation only to save expense. Wage earners find it difficult to get leave to attend *hui*, and those who regularly travel to family funerals are labelled unreliable workers. *Hui* have to be held at weekends and public holidays, so urban *marae* are overloaded at these times. Often there are several *hui* on the same day at the *marae;* the tail-end of a funeral in the morning, a wedding in the afternoon and a twenty-first birthday in the evening, in total contradiction to the rural rule that the *marae* should be left free for several days after a *tangi*. Many people use halls or their own homes instead, to save expense and to be safe from a cancellation. Some *marae* also double as community centres, where dances and club meetings can be held, and people get angry if they are refused the use of the *marae* for a *tangi* because it has been booked for a bingo evening instead. Space is at a premium in the city, and *marae* facilities are telescoped, with cooking, eating, sleeping and toilet facilities under a single roof, in violation of ancient spatial restrictions. The *marae ātea* may be reduced or left out altogether, so that rituals are enacted indoors or in an inadequate space which distorts the proper spatial arrangements. Because the *marae* is often in a residential area or on a busy city street, some of the more audible ritual activities like wailing may be left out altogether, in case an unsympathetic audience should hear them.

The city is in many ways a hostile environment for the *marae*, but it is where many Maori people are now living, and as long as they value their *Maoritanga* they will continue to build *marae*. To understand how the *marae* has adapted to city conditions so far, we can examine the case histories of seven urban *"marae"* in one major city, Auckland.[85]

Orākei Marae[86]

The first *marae* to be considered belongs to Ngāti Whātua, the *tāngata whenua* of the Auckland isthmus, who conquered the area in the eighteenth century. After most of their land had been sold, or gifted to schools and churches, they were left with a village and a *marae* on the waterfront in Okahu Bay. Some Aucklanders complained that the village was an "eyesore"; in 1950 the meeting-house was destroyed, the last few acres of the original 700-acre "inalienable domain" were taken under the Public Works Act, and the people were relocated in rented houses in Kitemoana Street on a hill overlooking the bay. Ngāti Whātua were given £2,000 compensation for their *marae*, which was then made into a park; and an £800 *marae* improvement fund. All this money was spent on rebuilding the chapel by the tribal graveyard in the domain. Once this task was completed, Ngāti Whātua began to consider building a new *marae* on a Crown reserve that had been set aside "for the use of all Maoris" behind Kitemoana Street. A Board of Trustees was elected, including four local representatives, four representatives of the Waitemata Tribal Executive, the four Maori Members of Parliament, and one member each from the Auckland Rotary Club, the Department of Maori Affairs, and the Okahu Bay Progressive Association. It was hoped that this Board would ensure a wide base of support for the new *marae*, but in fact it has been universally regarded by Auckland Maoris as a Ngāti Whātua *marae*, in a Ngāti Whātua residential area, and one that they would feel diffident about using. Fund-raising went ahead, and several buildings including a play school, a homework centre, a *whare puni* and a carving centre have already been erected on the site, and are in regular use by the community. Architects have drawn up plans for the *marae* project which include a $57,000 meeting-house, a dining-hall and a cultural centre, to the estimated total cost of $650,000. In 1965 Ngāti Whātua travelled to Tikitiki on the East Coast to study the arts of carving, and since then they have been pre-

85. See Map 5.
86. Kawharu, H. "Urban Immigrants and Tangata Whenua", in Schwimmer ed. (1968), pp. 174-86.

paring decorations for their meeting-house. The foundations of the house were unveiled in April 1971. Ngāti Whātau lost much of their *mana* as *tāngata whenua* when their original meeting-house was burned and they may regain it when the new house, Tāmaki Makau Rau (lit. "Tāmaki of a hundred lovers", the traditional name for Auckland) is completed. In the meanwhile they stage their *hui* on the unfinished *marae*, housing visitors in the existing buildings or in their homes, and erecting a hired marquee to serve as a *whare kai*.

Māngere Marae
The Ngāti Māhuta section of the Waikato federation was established in Auckland in 1849, when eighty selected warriors with their families were brought to settle in Māngere to defend the city against possible attack from the North. Each family was given one acre of land for a dwelling, and five acres for cultivation. In 1863 they left Auckland to join their kinsmen in the Waikato wars, and the land was confiscated, but some of it was subsequently returned when peace was signed. In the 1960s the descendants of Ngāti Māhuta decided to build a *marae* in the area, on about an acre of land that had been set aside for the purpose by Mrs Te Paea Rewha in 1933. Mrs Mere Nutana bequeathed her estate to the project, King Koroki donated £4,000 in Government compensation monies, and other funds were raised under the leadership of Mrs Tura Hira, the daughter of the original owner of the site. The Akarana Marae Society donated more than £3,000 worth of carvings, and other carvings and *tukutuku* panels were fashioned by the local people. Craftsmen from Ngāruawāhia carved the *pou tokomanawa* (centre-pole) of the meeting-house and the exterior carvings; and *punga* logs were collected from Port Waikato to make a palisade around the boundaries of the site. The *marae* complex is valued at well over $60,000, and it includes a large meeting-house, connected to dining, cooking and toilet facilities under a single roof. The meeting-house is named Te Puea in memory of the well-loved Waikato princess, and it looks out over the Manukau Harbour towards Auckland city. The *marae* was opened on 13 November, 1965 by Sir Bernard Fergusson, then Governor-General, at a *hui* attended by 4,000 visitors.

Māngere is one of the busiest *marae* in New Zealand. It is used by people of all tribes living in Auckland, who favour it because of its excellent facilities, its privacy, and its relatively traditional layout. Mrs Hira acts as the caretaker, and a constant stream of bookings pass through her hands. Weddings, twenty-first birthdays, funerals, conferences of Maori organisations. Maori language schools and unveilings are all staged there. There are a number of local elders who can preside as *tāngata whenua* if required, but in general the group who are sponsoring the *hui* act as hosts, cooks and workers. No set hiring fee is paid for the use of the *marae*, and people are simply asked to give what they can afford. A board of three trustees supervise the *marae*—Mrs Hira, a close kinsman, and Queen Te Ata-i-Rangi-Kahu. Although Māngere is tacitly regarded as a "Waikato" *marae*, other tribes use it quite freely, and there appear to be no special difficulties in the running of the *marae*. Māngere is a particularly successful adaptation to city conditions, because it closely replicates familiar rural patterns, and because the local people have succeeded in making other tribes feel comfortable about borrowing the *marae* for their own gatherings.

The Maori Community Centre

The Maori Community Centre is not a true *marae*, because it has no open space *(marae ātea)*, no proper owner group, and because *tangi* are hardly ever held there. The Fire Department has prohibited the use of the building as sleeping quarters, so guests cannot be housed there during a *hui*. For almost twenty years, though, from its opening in 1948 until Māngere *marae* was opened in 1965, the Centre was the main facility for non-*tāngata whenua* gatherings in Auckland. The Centre has had a chequered history. It started life as an American bulk warehouse during the war, then the Government bought it and leased it at a nominal rent to an intertribal, inter-racial Trust Board, for the use of those 10,000 Maoris who had come to the city during the war. Four trustees were nominated by the Department of Maori Affairs, four by Auckland Rotary Clubs, six by the Waitemata Tribal Executive, four by the Maori Women's Welfare League, and one by the 28th Maori Battalion Association. The warehouse was a large rambling structure on the corner of Fanshawe and Halsey Streets, on the fringes of the downtown commercial area. It was unlined inside, with a rough concrete floor, and it took £11,000 to convert the building into a community centre with a hall, dining-room and kitchen. The local Maoris had little part in the choice or conversion of the building, and most of the cost was met by Maori Land Board grants, a Government subsidy, funds from the Maori Trustee and an appeal run by the Auckland Rotary Clubs. The local Maori investment was about £460, a trifling sum compared with the large amounts of capital enthusiastically donated to rural *marae* in the same period. Its setting could scarcely be more different from a traditional *marae*. The building extends along the footpaths of two busy city streets, with a park and a gasworks on one side, and a view to the wharves on the other.

The Centre has no proper *tāngata whenua* group, and its leadership has been a succession of managers, executives and committees, who have often departed in acrimony, leaving a trail of bad debts behind them. It is questionable whether Auckland Maoris have ever regarded the Community Centre as a truly "Maori" place, and it has never functioned as a serious *marae*. It has been a focus for in-fighting and scandal, not a symbol of Maori pride. One has only to contrast its perfunctory decorations with the elaborate craftsmanship displayed say, at Māngere, to recognise this difference. Although the Centre has not succeeded as a ceremonial centre, it has been extremely popular with the young people, particularly in the 1950s and 1960s. During this time Maoris living in the nearby residential areas of Ponsonby and Freeman's Bay used the Centre on most weekends for dances, talent quests, and *haka* club practices. Weddings and twenty-firsts were held there, as well as the meetings of many Maori organisations. Today, however, the Maori Community Centre has passed its heyday, and people find it convenient to stage their gatherings elsewhere, either in modern halls or on proper *marae*. Many of its former patrons have moved out to the suburbs, and the Centre is no longer a vital element in the Auckland Maori scene.

Te Unga Waka (The canoe landing-place)
Te Unga Waka is an attractive building in modern style, sited on Manukau Road, an arterial highway that runs between the suburbs of Epsom and Greenlane. Formerly a large bakery, the building was bought in 1965 by the Auckland Maori Catholic Society, and redesigned by a local firm of architects. The total investment of $100,000 was met by the Maori Catholic Society under the leadership of Mrs Whina Cooper, by Catholic and local groups, and with the help of grants from the Golden Kiwi Lottery Fund and the Logan Campbell Trust Board. The Centre includes a large kitchen and dining-room, a hall, an entrance courtyard decorated with *tukutuku* and *kōwhaiwhai*, and a chapel downstairs. It also has offices and a large room where visitors can sleep overnight on the first floor. All these facilities are under a single roof. When the Centre was opened in March 1966 each member household of the Maori Catholic Society donated a set of bed-linen, and the Society donated mattresses and kitchen equipment.

The Centre is run by a *marae* committee for the benefit of all Maoris in Auckland, but it is tacitly regarded as a Catholic *"marae"*. Because the Centre has no open space or *marae ātea*, and because its architecture bears little resemblance to a traditional *marae*, it cannot be considered a *marae* in the strict sense of the term, but a wide range of *hui* including *tangi* are staged there, and guests can be housed overnight. Traditional decorative elements are included in the decor to mark Te Unga Waka as a Maori place, and the Catholic Society functions as an adapted form of *tāngata whenua*. The key personnel are a priest, a female caretaker and a female warden, all of whom are members of Northern tribes, and Te Unga Waka has Northern as well as Catholic associations. The *"marae"* is fully-used, and as well as *tangi*, dances, receptions, twenty-first birthdays, weddings, conferences, acclimatisation courses for newcomers to the city and the meetings of many clubs are held there.

When Te Unga Waka is booked for a *hui*, the members of its *komiti* show the sponsors of the gathering where everything is and how to use it, but otherwise the sponsors run the *hui* by themselves, and do all the cooking and cleaning-up. Many people find it inhibiting to hold a *tangi* at Te Unga Waka, because the approach to the *marae* is right next to a busy street, and even from inside wailing and *karanga* are clearly audible to passers-by. Because the senior dignitary of the *marae* is the priest, the role of visiting *kaumātua* (elders) is sometimes uncertain, and for many ceremonious occasions, Auckland elders of different tribes are invited in instead to act as *tāngata whenua*. Despite these minor difficulties, Te Unga Waka functions successfully as a *marae*, because it provides all the facilities of a traditional *marae* except the open speaking-ground, and *hui* can be staged there without too many radical changes from the rural pattern.

Te Tira Hou (The New Company of Travellers)
In recent years the Tūhoe Benevolent Society rented office space, cooking facilities and a room for meetings in an inner city arcade. These facilities however, were not really suitable for tribal activities—the rent was high, no funerals could be held there, and Tūhoe people in Auckland had to take their dead back to the Urewera country for proper burial. In 1970 the Presbyterian Church offered a disused church hall in Panmure to the Presbyterian Maori Synod for the use of all Maoris in Auckland, and the Synod in turn offered the building to the Tūhoe community in Auckland. Later that year the hall was ceremonially opened as Te Tira Hou, a new urban *marae*. The *marae* is set in a half-acre section near the Tamaki River, and it includes two connected halls and a storeroom. At first the hall nearest the road functioned as a *whare kai* and kitchen, and the back hall acted as a *whare nui*, where ceremonial gatherings could be held. This arrangement was not altogether convenient, because guests often approached the *whare kai* mistaking it for the ceremonial hall, and extensive alterations have now been effected to the buildings, to convert them to a closer approximation of a traditional *marae*. A traditional carved porch has been added to the side of the main building, and a *marae ātea* cleared before it. This building was opened in November 1973 as a *whare nui*, "Te Tatau Pounamu" (The Greenstone Door). Tūhoe act as *tāngata whenua* for the *marae*, and stage their own life crises there, including funerals; but the facility is open to all tribes resident in Auckland.

Ngā Hau e Whā (The Four Winds)
Over a period of ten years the "Tātou, Tātou" society of Ngāti Kahungunu residents in Auckland raised funds to buy a large house in Māngere, set on a half-acre section. In 1971 the house was opened as Ngā Hau e Whā *marae*. It has a spacious front lawn which serves as a *marae ātea*, and the living-room can be used for small-scale meetings. In

the back yard a marquee is raised on important occasions as a *whare kai*, and both outdoor cooking facilities and the kitchen are used for catering. The house is called Parehuia, after the late Lady Carroll, wife of the Ngāti Kahungunu leader Sir Turi Carroll, and a great lady in her own right. Although the *marae* is owned and operated by Ngāti Kahungunu, it is open for all Auckland Maoris to use for their gatherings. The society had hoped to build a hall on the site, providing a permit was forthcoming from the Manukau City Council, but it now seems their *marae* is located on a scheduled motorway and they may lose it altogether.

Te Māhurehure Community Centre
In 1970 Te Māhurehure residents financed the purchase of a football club and grounds in Point Chevalier. The centre includes a hall with cooking and toilet facilities, and sports grounds. *Hui* including *tangi* are staged there, but its most popular use at present is as a sporting centre for Māhurehure members and their friends.

In addition to these seven urban *marae*, at least seven more are in the planning stages, mostly in the outer suburbs. In the meantime, however, many Auckland Maoris either have no access to a *marae* or cannot afford the hiring fee and the expense of catering for large crowds. Because the existing urban *marae* are often fully booked, people use public halls instead for dances, wedding receptions and twenty-first birthdays, and schools sometimes offer their assembly halls for the meetings of Maori organisations. In these situations a large open space is typically left at the front of the hall to serve as a *marae ātea*, and seating is shifted to the sides or the back of the hall. Funerals are sometimes held in the chapels of funeral parlours, or in churches such as the Holy Sepulchre, centre for the Anglican Maori Mission, which is presently in the process of being converted into a *marae*. Family *hui*, including funerals, are held at home, in the living-room, the garage, or under a marquee on the back lawn. Catering is managed by friends and relatives, and mattresses are laid around the walls of the living-room to create a "little *marae*" where guests can sleep overnight. These *hui* suffer from limited spaces and grave lack of privacy, guests approach the house across the front lawn, and are often too embarrassed to call or wail. All these makeshift facilities reflect the need for more *marae* in Auckland as well as the higher cost of living there.

Marae in Auckland, then, are a diverse collection. Expediency more than any other factor governs the choice of location, buildings and land. Although a traditional arrangement of meeting-house, *whare kai* and *marae ātea* is greatly preferred, people will manage with all sorts of deviations from the traditional pattern, providing that they own the *marae* outright and have complete control there. When they can raise extra funds the original structures are modified to look more like a traditional *marae*.

Urban *marae* are difficult to finance, not only because a large cash investment is required, but also because in many cases people are still helping to look after the rural *marae* back home, and the fact that seven "*marae*" already exist in Auckland is a tribute to the importance of the institution. The most successful urban *marae* are those where the initiative and most of the work have come from their Maori sponsors, and where there is a strongly-united owner group. This group is usually tribal, although in the case of Te Unga Waka a religious bond seems to work as well.

Marae with inter-tribal and inter-racial governing bodies do not appear to succeed. Factionalism and struggles for leadership mark their history, and it is dubious whether the ideal of integration should ever be applied to the *marae*. The *marae* requires some sort of a *tāngata whenua* group, which cannot be replaced by a European-style Board with diverse membership. Wherever *pākeha* are placed in positions of leadership in urban *marae*, resentment inevitably results. The *marae* is a Maori institution, and Europeans should have the grace to leave it that way.

* Page 40: The porch itself is named *roro* (brains); the doorway is called *kūwaha* (mouth). It is interesting to note that the human body as a metaphor also extends to the terms for the main social groups—*iwi* (tribe; also bones); *hapū* (sub-tribe; pregnant); *whānau* (extended family; to give birth).

* Page 41: Alternating with the carved slabs are the panels of plaited *tukutuku* work, and it is said that these represent and evoke the living, in contrast to the past ancestors of the carvings.

* Page 47: Given the uncertainties of the left-right distinction, one should perhaps argue that the fundamental (and most ancient?) way of discriminating one side of the meeting-house from the other is by the labels *tara* (or *pakitara*) *whāiti* "lesser wall"—the local, *noa* side; and *tara whānui* "wall of honour"—the visitors' *tapu* side. This accords well with the key positions for chiefly occupants of the house—the *kopa iti* position for the local chief and the *iho nui* position for the most prominent visitor, and is consistent with the other symbolic associations of the two sides.

My thanks to Rev. Maori Marsden for extending my understanding of these aspects of meeting-house symbolism.

CHAPTER FOUR

STAGING[87]

Organisers
At a typical *hui*, about 3-500 people are fed and accommodated for a period of up to three days. Sometimes the *hui* occurs without warning, when there is a sudden death in the community, and if the dead person is nationally important, the number of visitors may run into several thousands. These people begin to descend on the *marae* in busloads a day or two after public notice of the death is given, and as a matter of course they are given a place to sleep, three hot meals a day and a feast at the end of the *hui*. The most remarkable thing about all this is the effortless quality with which a *hui* is run. There are few visible signs of organisation, no shouting of orders or elaborate delegation of duties. Live beasts are brought to the *marae* and butchered, sacks of vegetables arrive, boys go out fishing and catch eels, women collect mussels, *pipi* and other shellfish at the right tides, the *marae* lawns are mown and fires are lit in the cookshed, all with very little fuss or commotion. As the news of the *hui* spreads along the local grapevine, workers move to the *marae*, roll up their sleeves, and set about their duties with the ease of long practice.

We have already observed that most rural *marae* are run either by a local descent-group or by the community itself, and that those who run the *marae* and those who use it are mostly the same people. There is a basic rule, which is probably universal, that kinfolk should help each other in life crises, and this rule certainly applies to the staging of weddings, birthdays, unveilings and funerals on the *marae*. Other *hui* which revolve about group events such as the opening of a new meeting-house or tribal policy-making are run by the community as a whole, but in most rural districts the local network of kin and the community overlap. As a result there is a common pool of workers for all *hui* on the given *marae* (the "old faithfuls"), supplemented on occasion by kin who've moved away, and since there may be an average of about twelve *hui* a year on a *marae*,

---

87. For studies of staging in particular communities, see Metge, J. *A New Maori Migration* (1964); Hohepa, P. *A Maori Community in Northland* (1964); and Ritchie J. *The Making of a Maori* (1963).

over the years a smooth-running machinery for the staging of *hui* evolves. Different families come to specialise in particular tasks, and individuals with recognised skills act as natural pivots in their part of the work. Matiu te Hau tells the story of a *hui* he attended, where a very old man periodically hobbled over to the fire to put on some sticks and poke the embers. When asked what he was doing, a bystander replied, "He knows his job."[88] Of course all is not perfect in an imperfect world, and fights and squabbles can seriously disrupt the ready cooperation which generally prevails. Some "bossy" individuals can antagonise other workers, or a community feud might run over into *marae* business. In this case some of the workers stay away from the *marae*, and meals run late or there might not be enough food. At one *marae* I visited, several local families had taken to arriving at *hui* just in time for the final feast, and leaving shortly afterwards. They were eventually told that their presence at any stage was not welcome. Usually though, the honour of the community overrides dissension, and as a good part of the success of the *hui* rests on the local cuisine, every effort is made to provide tasty and plentiful meals.

Although the organisation of an unscheduled *hui* is spontaneous, other *hui* are planned well in advance. Weddings, twenty-firsts and unveilings are organised by the families concerned, and timed for a weekend or a public holiday, preferably in the summer. Unveilings are common over the Easter holidays, when urban migrants can return home, and in many cases football and basketball matches are organised for the same time. Other *hui* are run by the community as a whole (e.g. the opening of a new meeting-house), the tribe (e.g. tribal "seminars" or policy meetings), or national organisations such as the churches, the New Zealand Maori Council and the Maori King Movement. In all these cases there is usually an existing formal organisation which can provide planning for the *hui*.

Some extended families have a family "club", with a committee of chairman, secretary and treasurer, and a standing bank account. These clubs exist mainly to raise contingency funds for the funerals of family members, and all adult members pay a small monthly amount, perhaps fifty cents, into the burial fund. The fund may also be used for donations to the funerals of more distant relatives, but money for weddings, twenty-firsts and unveilings is separately raised. The club does not usually run the funerals of family members, because in this case all close female kin of the deceased are mourners and not expected to work, but in some families which have their own *marae*, the organisers of the *marae* and club members are the same people. In this case other local women work in the kitchen, but male members of the family help to run the *hui*. A family club sometimes sponsors a family reunion, or even organises the weddings, twenty-firsts and unveilings of its members, but these are always

---

88. McDonnell and Hilton (1971).

subsidiary functions to its main aim of ensuring family members honourable burial.

Those majority of families which have no club may improvise a committee for a particular family *hui*. Members of the committee are assigned special tasks such as ordering the food, organising bedding, running the kitchen or tidying up the *marae*, but most often the committee members turn out to be useful people rather than close kinfolk, and in effect the jobs are done by those who usually do them, not by relatives especially recruited for the occasion. These *"hui* committees", however, still contain the head of the family concerned, and provide useful liaison between the family and the standing organisation.

A community-sponsored *hui* is frequently run by the local *komiti marae*. Already mentioned as the committee which is responsible for keeping the *marae* in good order, it is activated just before a *hui* to tidy up the *marae*, and its functions readily spill over into organising the *hui* itself. The *marae* committee is appointed from local residents, not always members of original families in the area *(tāngata whenua*, "people of the land"). It has a chairman who is a respected elder, a secretary, treasurer, and sometimes a subsidiary *komiti wāhine* (women's committee). This structure is ideal for supervising the organisation and finance of a *hui* and most committee members are appointed in the first place because of their experience in this field. The chairman, often, but by no means always, acts as the *kai whakahaere* or main organiser of a *hui*, the treasurer keeps careful accounts, and the women's committee look after bedding and the kitchen.

Even when the *komiti marae* does not actively run the *hui*, they will probably be present, and at other times they have certain constant duties towards the *marae*. Families who want to use the *marae* must first make arrangements with the committee, and for weddings and twenty-firsts, a hiring fee (maybe $10) or a donation is paid towards water and electricity bills. A calendar is kept to avoid double bookings, and if a death suddenly occurs in the district all other *hui* are cancelled or shifted to other *marae* during the three days of the *tangi*. Just before the *marae* is about to be used, one of the organisers collects the keys from the caretaker, who lives nearby and is usually a committee member. The treasurer pays all power, water and maintenance bills from a *marae* account, and lets the rest of the committee know when reserves are running short. In this case they may decide to raise funds by housie evenings, sports days or dances on the *marae*, or by levying donations from local families. The *komiti wāhine* look after crockery, kitchen utensils and bedding. They air the linen before each *hui*, check the crockery and utensils and arrange for extras to be borrowed if necessary. In some communities the committee is elected, but more often people are informally chosen or volunteer, and positions can be passed around within the family. There are supposed to be regular meetings about once a month, but in practice the committee gets to work when it is needed, transacting most of its business by telephone calls and meeting only when a *hui* is planned.

For larger-scale meetings sponsored by the churches, the King Movement or the Maori Council, planning is provided from within the structure of each organisation. The Church of England, for example, runs an annual *Hui Tōpu* in the Waiapu diocese, where each Maori pastorate led by its Vicar raises funds, trains teams for competitions in action songs, *haka* and choral singing, and attends the *hui* as a group. The King Movement runs a large number of *hui* each year, including a cycle of twenty-eight *poukai* (when the Maori Queen and her councillors visit loyal *marae* in turn), and an annual Regatta and Coronation each attended by thousands of visitors. Each *marae* on the *poukai* circuit has its own main organiser and committee, and Tūrangawaewae *marae* where the other *hui* are held has a large number of committees to handle the task of accommodating thousands of visitors at a time. All these committees are subject to the Queen and her twelve-man council. Other movements such as the Ringatū and Rātana churches also hold both local and national *hui* for their adherents, and provide their own forms of organisation.

For many *hui* there is a figure who can be identified as the *kai whakahaere* or main organiser of the *hui*. This man is a respected elder, closely related to the main figures of the *hui* if it is a life crisis, and well versed in *marae* procedure. He is in charge of *marae* protocol, and may also act as overall co-ordinator for finance, ordering food, estimating numbers of guests and roughly outlining a programme for the *hui*. In general, though, he is the Master of Ceremonies, and his job is to ensure that all the rituals of welcome as well as the main ceremony run smoothly.

Before the *Hui*
When the *hui* is planned in advance, the organisers may get to work a year or more ahead of time. Large-scale gatherings such as the centenary of a *marae* or a Maori welcome to visiting Royalty are planned over a long period to avoid last-minute rush, and quite elaborate arrangements are made. Special memorial booklets are written and printed, invitations are sent out, and local concert parties rehearse for the occasion. Small family *hui* such as unveilings, weddings and twenty-firsts are planned over a period of months, and are also given careful thought.

Once the organisers get together, there are a series of informal meetings, and the time and place for the *hui* are decided. Winter is an unpopular time for gatherings, because most *marae* have no heating systems and the old people suffer from the cold. Summer and spring are favoured, because at these times farm incomes are supplemented by seasonal work, the weather is pleasant, and generous donations of potato, *kūmara*, sweetcorn and watermelon in season can be expected from local farmers. In some areas, *hui* are timed for the seasons of local delicacies, for example, in the

Whānau-ā-Apanui district, the arrival of the *moki* fish off Cape Runaway in June, or the running of the *kahawai* in the Motu River during January. Most *hui* apart from *tangi* are held in the weekends so that wage earners can attend, and public holidays such as Easter, Queen's Birthday and Labour Day are particularly favoured. Sometimes *hui* are doubled up for economy, so that a birthday and a wedding; a *poukai* and an unveiling; or several unveilings might be combined in the same occasion. As a result of all these factors, twenty-first birthdays, golden wedding anniversaries or unveilings (usually held on the first or second anniversary of death) may be shifted from their "proper" day.

The place for the *hui* is not always obvious. Weddings are traditionally held on the groom's *marae*, but increasingly European custom prevails, and the bride's *marae* is chosen. This conflict in custom can lead to disagreement and ill-feeling between families. For a twenty-first there may be some question whether the celebration should be held on the *marae* or in a local hall with catering facilities, and here the argument is likely to be an intergenerational one. Halls are sometimes favoured for a twenty-first, because there are no restrictions on liquor and the building has no traditional connotations, but elders in the family may disapprove for just these reasons. An unveiling is held as a matter of course on the *marae* nearest the cemetery where the memorial stone has been erected, and presents no particular problems. Important *hui*, however, such as welcomes to Royalty, the *Hui Tōpu* or the Maori Council's "Meet the People" can cause heated debates over venue, because they win considerable prestige for the *marae* on which they are staged. One such case was the Royal Visit in 1953.[89] Plans were made for the Queen to be welcomed at Rotorua and at Waitangi by the Maori people. The Waikato tribes, however, felt that the Queen should visit King Koroki at Ngāruawāhia as a token of friendship, a move which would amount to Royal recognition of the Maori King Movement. The New Zealand Government refused the request, saying that it was too late for the tour programme to be changed, so in retaliation the King's Council announced that they would boycott the Rotorua welcome. A delegation was sent to Parliament without effect, the newspapers took up the question, and old angers began to flare. At the last minute the Queen made a brief but very cordial visit to Tūrangawaewae, and the Kingites were appeased.

The most notorious arguments about venue invariably occur at *tangi*. It is an old sign of honour to the dead to argue about where they should be buried, and angry speeches on this topic are a feature of many funerals. Sometimes the entire *hui* is shifted to another *marae* halfway through, a *marae* that may be tens or even hundreds of miles away, and there are stories of relatives seizing the coffin from the meeting-house in the middle of the night and driving it off to the *marae* of their choice. One

---

89. Jones, Pei te Hurinui "Maori Kings" in Schwimmer ed. (1968), pp. 159-66.

account I heard, which might be apocryphal, spoke of an old kinsman who became so infuriated by the arguments over the place of burial that he backed his station wagon up to the meeting-house, had the coffin loaded in the back, and drove to a nearby cliff. There he tipped the coffin over the edge to settle the dispute once and for all. Wives may be buried with their husbands or their parents, urban migrants may be buried in town or by the home *marae,* and most individuals have several *marae* that can lay claim to sponsor their *tangi.* The arguments are usually ceremonial, though they look angry enough, but once in a while a serious split in opinion develops and real bitterness or old antagonisms are expressed. If a couple have settled away from the home *marae,* the widow and the parents of the deceased may quarrel over the place of burial. On one such occasion the parents capitulated, but threatened the widow that if she neglected the grave, her husband's relatives would come and rip up her clothes, smash her furniture and ruin her house (an old custom called *muru,* "punishment by plundering"). On another occasion the family attended the *tangi* but boycotted the burial, and as the hearse pulled away from the home *marae* the sisters and the mother wailed until they collapsed. In all these cases the conflicts express the value of the individual to his different groups of kinfolk.

Once the time and place for the *hui* are decided, invitations are sent out and the news media notified. Printed invitations (called *pānui* or *powhiri)* are circulated for unveilings, weddings and *hui* to be attended by important dignitaries, but they by no means define the guest list. All *hui* are open to the public, and anyone who has ties of kinship or friendship with its sponsors is fully entitled to attend. A "closed" *hui* would be regarded as very mean-minded. Invitations are a special mark of honour to important elders or officials, and they are sent to key people in different tribal or sub-tribal areas with the intention that they should pass the news around and recruit a party to attend the *hui.* Invitations are written in Maori, and their texts are structured something like a ceremonial speech. They begin with a warning cry *(whakaarara),* perhaps:

Kia hiwa rā!   Kia hiwa rā!   Kia hiwa rā i tēnei tuku!
Be alert!   Be watchful!   Be alert on this terrace!
Kia hiwa rā i tēra tuku! Kia hiwa rā! Kia hiwa rā!
Be alert on that terrace! Be wakeful! Be watchful!

This is an ancient chant once used by sentries patrolling the terraces of a fortified *pā.* The invitation goes on to address its audience:

E ngā Waka. E ngā hau e whā. E ngā mana
O canoes   Four winds   Great ones

E ngā iwi.   E ngā manu kōrero o runga i ngā marae
Tribes   Talking birds (orators) of the *marae*
Whakarongo! Whakarongo! Whakarongo!
Listen!   Listen!   Listen!
Ki te tangi a te manu e karanga nei "Tui, tui, tuituiā!"
to the cry of the bird calling "Unite, unite, be one!"

Tuia i runga,   tuia i raro,   tuia i roto
Unite above   unite below   unite within
Tuia i waho, tuia i te here tangata
Unite without, everyone unite in the brotherhood of men
Ka rongo te pō, ka rongo te pō
The night hears, the night hears
Tuia i te kāwai tāngata i heke mai i Hawaiki nui
Unite the descent lines from Great Hawaiki
I Hawaiki roa, i Hawaiki pā-mamao
From long Hawaiki, from Hawaiki far away
I hono ki te wairua, ki te whai ao, ki te Ao Mārama.
Joined to the spirit, to the daylight, to the world of light.

This chant calls all the tribes to unite, and reminds them of their common descent from the mythical homeland Hawaiki.

Now the guests are called to the *marae*:

Haere mai! haere mai! haere mai!
Come!   come!   come!
Haere mai ki te marae o—
Come to the *marae* of—
Tēnei te reo o ngā uri mokopuna
This is the voice of the grandchildren
Karanga maha o te hunga kua huri ki tua o te ārai
The many descendants of those who have gone beyond the veil
Mauria mai o tātou mate aituā, kia tangihia, kia mihia.
bring our dead to be wept over and greeted.

Finally the invitation lists the reasons for the *hui*, gives a detailed programme with dates and times, and an RSVP address. Because the *pōwhiri* requires a good deal of esoteric knowledge, it is written by the most expert elder on the committee, and he takes great care to ensure that it is correctly and impressively phrased. If no printed invitations are sent out, important guests are invited by telegram, letter or phone call. Particularly for a *tangi*, where invitations are quite inappropriate, toll calls are made to kin in different areas, and each person contacted undertakes to inform other relatives in his district. This kin grapevine is efficient and operates with surprising rapidity. In the home area where the *hui* is to be held, news of it spreads by word of mouth, sometimes helped along by a notice in the local newspaper or taped up in the window of a local shop. *Hui* of national importance such as welcomes to Royalty, the death of a well-known Maori or the opening of a new *marae* receive wide publicity in the press and television, and reporters, photographers and television cameras are a common sight on such occasions. Another important avenue for announcing forthcoming *hui* is the NZBC *News in Maori* on the radio each Sunday evening, when recent deaths and major *hui* are announced along with other news items.

Once the event has been planned and the invitations sent out, the organisers can begin to estimate the numbers that may attend. This largely depends on the general significance of the occasion, and if it is a life crisis, on the *mana* of the individual and his family. As one informant put it, "So-and-so is a big man, and if anything happens to his family—oh well!" The King Movement's annual Coronation regularly attracts thousands of visitors, in part because the Maori Queen is an important symbolic figure to many tribes, and partly because it is a picturesque occasion combining stately ritual with sports and cultural competitions. Funerals in general attract greater numbers than other types of life crisis, because in the case of death it is imperative that kinfolk should attend to "pay their respects". This is the last opportunity for kinsmen to pay tribute to the *mana* of the dead person, and it is regarded as an insult and most unfeeling if even quite distant kin fail to attend. The general principle that governs attendance at a *hui* is "the more the better", because a large number of visitors is a compliment to the sponsors, and a recognition of their *mana*. A "big man" should always have a big *hui*. The same principle causes visitors to prefer to arrive at a *hui* in large groups, and one often sees a small cluster of people waiting outside the gate of the *marae*, preferring to join in with a larger crowd of strangers than to "go on" by themselves. These two factors, the type of the occasion and the *mana* of the sponsors, intersect, so that while a wedding in an important family will attract more guests than the *tangi* of some humble person, a *tangi* in that same family should still have a larger attendance than the wedding. Other factors include the immediate weather conditions, and for a *tangi*, whether it falls during the week or at a weekend. Organisers of a *hui* have long experience in making these types of judgment, and they can make quite accurate predictions of the numbers to expect. An average *tangi* brings about 500 people, whereas a *tangi* in the Royal family might be attended by 5,000 or 6,000 people. A typical wedding or twenty-first attracts about 300 visitors, and so on.

According to the numbers expected, supplies are ordered, sleeping facilities arranged, and crockery and table utensils are prepared. Some farmers plant special areas of vegetables for donations to *hui*, and in any case, generous gifts of produce can be expected. Farmers affiliated to the *marae* or related to the central figure of the *hui* volunteer sacks of *kūmara* and potatoes, cabbages, pumpkins, cans of milk or cream, and on special occasions, livestock or poultry. A couple of sheep, a pig or a bullock might be sacrificed for a family *tangi* or wedding, but by the same token these gifts are returned on later occasions. Such donations show family *aroha* (love), and are part of a reciprocal system of co-operation among kinfolk. Relatives who fail in generosity are regarded with some contempt. A farmer might also lend a truck to cart things to the *marae*, or a tractor to help tidy the *marae* grounds. Loads of new hay are taken to stuff mattresses, and firewood for the earth oven and cooking fires. On one *marae* in the East Coast area a local farmer had arranged to lease eighteen acres of bush land from the *marae*, and in return undertook to supply milk, cream and firewood from the bush for every *hui*. After fifteen years of *hui*, there were only five acres of trees left on the land.[90] Housewives give bottles of preserved fruit, pickles and jam, and lend mattresses, linen, crockery and table utensils if the *marae* is running short.

Sometimes *kānga pirau* (fermented corn) is put down especially for the *hui*. Corn cobs are put in a clean bag and left in a stream of running water, to be taken up several months later and cooked as a sort of porridge. Just before the *hui*, the women go to gather watercress and *pūhā*, in the fields, or out on the reef to collect sea urchins, edible seaweed, mussels and other shellfish in plaited flax kits. Divers bring up *pāua* and crayfish, people go fishing, and all this *kai moana* (seafood) provides a prized addition to meals to be served at the *hui*. Flour, sugar and eggs are distributed by the committee, and at the last minute women bake bread, cakes and fried scones, and bring them to the *marae*.

Although most of the cost of a *hui* can be defrayed by local effort, there are some things that must be bought. Flour, sugar, salt, butter, tea, soap and sometimes bread and milk are purchased in bulk from a local shopkeeper, and these accounts are settled after the *hui*. If tinned foodstuffs such as ideal milk, fruit salad, tomato sauce etc. are bought, any tins left over can be returned to the shopkeeper afterwards or left in the *marae* store. After the *komiti wāhine* have decided on a shopping list, one of their members goes to the shop and orders the goods several weeks ahead of time, and they are delivered to the *marae* a day or two before the *hui*. These and other expenses are met in part by local money, and partly by the donations that visitors bring with them. Local funds are raised by bring-and-buys, card evenings, raffles, sports days, housie, private donations or a levy (perhaps $10) on each household concerned. Sometimes donations are also received from the local Tribal Trust Board or land incorporations

90. Wawatai (1971).

in the district, particularly at a *tangi* or the opening of a new *marae*. Weddings, twenty-firsts and unveilings are financially sponsored by the families concerned, although visitors' donations help to defray the costs. A treasurer is appointed for each *hui*, and a careful accounting of all gifts and expenditure is kept throughout. Visitors are sometimes given receipts for their donations, and such accounts enable the local people to return all cash gifts equally or with some addition at subsequent hui sponsored by their guests.

Another task to be done before the *hui* is to tidy up the *marae*, and often the opportunity is taken to make quite extensive renovations as well. A new hot water system might be installed, the buildings might be given structural repairs or a new coat of paint. Fences are checked, the *marae* cemetery is cleared and weeded, and the grass in front of the meeting-house is mowed. If large numbers of guests are expected, a marquee is erected. The buildings are aired, washed and swept, kapok mattresses are brought out and counted, and in some *marae* large ticking bags are filled with hay for temporary mattresses as well. These are laid out along the side and back walls of the meeting-house in a continuous line. *Marae* vary in the sorts of bedding available, and some even provide foam rubber mattresses for honoured guests and the old people. Women bring out the linen, wash it if necessary and give it a thorough airing. If the *marae* is short of sheets, pillowcases or teatowels, these are borrowed from member households. In the kitchen, the large black open-fire pots are scrubbed, utensils and crockery are counted and washed if they are dusty. The younger people decorate the dining-hall with large fern-fronds, tinsel and colourful crepe streamers, while the men out the back check that there is plenty of firewood and the right sorts of stones for the earth oven. The toilets are scrubbed and soap and paper provided, light bulbs are replaced, and water may be brought in a water truck if the *marae* tanks are nearly empty.

For several days before the *hui* begins, workers stay at the *marae*, sleeping overnight in the meeting-house if they've come a long way. In the beginning there might be about fifteen women and perhaps ten men, but the numbers steadily increase until there are fifty or so workers at the *marae*, working hard to make the place attractive, and thoroughly enjoying themselves in the process. Old ladies peel great mounds of potatoes singing old songs, laughing and swapping yarns. The men butcher the animals and get the fires going, children play games of tag around the *marae* and snatches of song come from the kitchen. Once in a while a triumphant *karanga* (call) is heard as an old woman pulls a batch of bread from the oven. Schoolgirls set the tables, laying down temporary tablecloths of white printer's paper from a large roll, and arranging bowls of flowers. Just a few hours before the first guests arrive, a pot of stew is put to bubble over the open fires, and benches are set out on the *marae* amid the smell of new-mown grass. At the last minute an old woman (called the *kāea*) lines her *pōhiri* party in front of the meeting house and starts to run them through the action chant of welcome:

Tōia mai-te waka!*
Haul-the canoe!
Ki te urunga-te waka!
To the resting place the canoe!
Ki te moenga-te waka!
To its bed-the canoe!
[All] *Ki te takotoranga i takoto ai te waka e!*
To its lying place to lie, the canoe!

Down the road the horn of a bus begins to blare, and in a cloud of dust and flying shingle, the first visitors arrive. The visitors, too, have gone to some effort to get to the *hui*. Quite often they have travelled hundreds of miles, taken time off work, and financed the trip from slender resources. A majority of those who travel to a large number of *hui* every year (thirty or more) are old age pensioners, and a good part of their pension goes towards bus fares and the *koha* (cash gift) to be presented at the *marae*. Some of these old people travel almost incessantly to *hui*, perhaps fifty or seventy a year, and unless they have independent resources they manage the trips only with the help of their sons and daughters. All the same it is well worth the financial sacrifice, because the old people are the star performers at any hui, and they are treated with respect for their knowledge of rituals and tradition. Because they are given a valued role to play, old age is a proud and happy time in Maori society. Apart from the interest of the *marae* ceremonials, visitors to a *hui* are attracted by the prospect of meeting friends and relatives, talking Maori, feasting on Maori foods, seeing new places and being together in a convivial, exciting atmosphere.

Once the people in a given district hear about a *hui* which concerns them, whether by direct invitation or by word of mouth, one of their number rings around to find out a convenient time for departure, then contacts the bus company to hire a bus or mini-bus. If only a small group plans to go, they will travel in private cars and meet some distance from the *marae*. A bus is hired for a group of about thirty-five to forty, and the more buses from an area that attend a *hui*, the greater the compliment to its sponsors. The hire fee varies but averages out at about $3 a person, plus $1 or more for the *koha*. Groups that travel together to many *hui* often have a favourite bus driver, and on some occasions a Maori driver in the company will volunteer to drive without wages. Before the bus

---

*Underlined text is chanted by all performers in unison.

departs, people gather at one of their homes, and a Minister or lay reader conducts a short service to give them protection on the journey. At the time of departure or several hours later due to mishaps with cars, grandchildren or sheer forgetfulness, the bus gets under way. The travelling party is carefully selected to include an adequate number of speakers, an old woman to give the *karanga*, and if possible an elder who can advise them about the etiquette on the host *marae*. It is quite impossible to enter a *marae* alone unless you are a person of very considerable *mana*, and it is preferable to go in a large group, so that unless six or seven people including several elders are interested in the trip, nobody goes. Apart from this, the composition of the party is mainly determined by the type of *hui*. For life crises, the party will probably be recruited by ties of kinship or friendship, and as long as the majority of people in the party have some links with the main figure of the *hui*, any number of their friends can come along as well. For church *hui*, common religious affiliation is the main factor; for tribal *hui*, membership of the sponsoring or affiliated tribes; and for national *hui* such as the Coronation or a Maori Council "Meet the People", it is enough to be Maori. In all cases, friends of those with a primary right to attend are always welcome, irrespective of tribal, racial or religious factors.

A bus trip to a *hui* is rarely a staid affair. Ukeleles and guitars are loaded into the luggage racks and a crate of beer goes under one of the seats, unless the *hui* is a particularly serious one. Soft drinks, popcorn and potato chips are provided, and once the guitar players get warmed up, most of the trip is occupied with singing popular European and Maori songs, sometimes with impromptu actions in the aisle. The bus stops frequently for the comfort of old people. The journey might be ten or twelve hours long, but it is hardly ever boring. If it is an important occasion, the speakers sit quietly, planning their orations and making sure they have the incantations word-perfect, and the old women run through a number of *waiata* (chants) by way of rehearsal. The journey is carefully timed so that the bus arrives at the host *marae* before dusk, and a very long trip may be broken by an overnight stay at a *marae* en route. Groups who arrive at night are jokingly called "moreporks" (a native owl), and it has already been mentioned that the night is considered a time for "ghosts and lovers", not for tardy guests. When the bus is several miles away from the *marae*, it stops by the roadside and everyone gets tidy. The men put on suit jackets and ties, and if it is a *tangi* the women change into black clothes and twine greenery from the bush into wreaths for their hair. A phone call has already been made to the *marae* from the last township, and the guests are expected. They climb back into the bus for the last leg of the journey. As they approach the *marae* the driver sounds the horn, and the local people get ready for the rituals of welcome.

Getting to the *marae* is not always so simple. At one *hui* I attended the bus took us to one side of a tidal river. The *marae*, it eventuated, was on the other side and although the local people had several small boats, they appeared to be having engine trouble. We waited for about half an hour until finally a boat chugged over from the other side and the ferry service began. The boat I boarded was loaded almost to sinking point, with an old adapted motor-mower engine at the back, a stick serving as the choke. About halfway across, water got into the petrol tank and we began to drift out to sea. Yells of encouragement came from the shore, comparing the boat to one of the canoes of the Great Fleet setting off to explore the Pacific; while our driver pulled furiously at a ripcord. Eventually the engine started again, and we were delivered safely to the *marae*. Until several years ago, we were told, this *marae* was serviced entirely by canoe. There are also some *marae* that can be reached only by horseback, or along a beach at low tide, but today, most *marae* are by the roadside, and such picturesque forms of transport are no longer required.

During the *Hui*

During the *hui* the old people are occupied with ceremonial activities on the *marae*, and younger generations take over the staging. Parking is handled by several men, who signal cars and buses to convenient places around the borders of the *marae* proper or just outside the *marae* gates. These men may be *marae* wardens, uniformed officials appointed by the local Maori Council, and apart from supervising parking they make sure that no-one brings unauthorised liquor on to the *marae*. On many *marae* there is a prominent sign forbidding all liquor, and on the odd occasion when this prohibition is flouted the wardens take care of it. Once at an East Coast *marae*, we were all inside the meeting-house watching the local people entertain their guests. At the height of a *haka*, a man came from the kitchen clutching a bloody clavicle bone he'd taken from the butcher-shed. He brandished it like a *mere*, and obviously drunk, moved along the front row of the *haka* party, chanting loudly. The local warden was a powerful and decisive woman. After watching him for some moments, she rose from her seat with an air of justice about to be executed, raised her arm, and sent him flying backwards through three rows of men. For the rest of the *haka* the man lay silent and dazed in the background, and gave no more trouble.

Once the visitors have parked their vehicles, they assemble outside the gateway of the *marae*, and in their turn they are formally welcomed. At the conclusion of the speechmaking the last orator on the visiting side puts an envelope down on the *marae*. This is the *koha* (gift), *awhina* (help) or *moni marae* (*marae* money), a cash donation collected from members of the party by the leading elder. People contribute according to ability, perhaps $2 each, and on important occasions the gift might be supplemented from the home *marae* account, or the family fund. The *koha* might be anywhere from ten to several hundred dollars, and great pride is taken in being able to present a generous gift to the hosts. This money helps pay for the *hui*, but more importantly it expresses the good nature of the visitors and the Maori *aroha* (love) they have for their hosts. Some groups prefer to give their gift quietly, and slip it to the head cook some time during the *hui*, but on the whole the public presentation is an essential part of the *koha*. In earlier times the donors sometimes marched on to the *marae* bearing a cleft stick into which a bundle of banknotes was jammed, or a branch on which the notes fluttered like leaves; and Donne once reported seeing a large brown roasted pig carried on to the *marae* with £5, £10 and £20 notes stuck all over it.[91]

On one occasion only a few years ago an old man felt that he had been slighted on his welcome to the *marae*, so he reserved his donation and later went off to the bank. As he was leaving the *hui*, at the end of his farewell speech he announced that he was about to present his *koha*. He produced a large bag and began to strew threepennies all over the *marae*. The hosts had to kneel down and laboriously pick them up, and the old man had his satisfaction.[92] At a *tangi* the gift is called *roimata* or "tears", and it may take the form of an heirloom—a greenstone *mere* (club), a *tiki* or a cloak. If it is placed with its handle, head or neck border towards the body, this means that the gift is permanent, but if it is placed towards the donors, the heirloom should be returned at the end of the *tangi*. These gifts pay tribute to the *mana* of the deceased and are received with great ceremony. A famous heirloom with historical and sentimental value might be wept over and greeted in orations as a long-lost friend. The cloak, *tiki* or *mere* is laid on the body to "keep it warm" throughout the funeral, and such treasures might be buried with the body of a very famous man.

Once a gift is laid on the *marae*, on a mat or in a carved bowl, in some areas (notably the Waikato), an old women stands to greet it with a *karanga* (call of welcome). Cash donations are collected by the treasurer of the *hui*, and he may announce the donor and the amount to the assembled gathering. In the past most donations were in the form of food, but today only the local people contribute food to the *hui*, and outside contributions are by cash or cheque.

With the presentation of the *koha* the ceremonial welcome is complete. The visitors move to shake hands with the local people, and as soon as the cooks are ready, they are called into the dining-hall. Food is the true symbol of hospitality on the *marae*, and it is a long-established custom that directly the visitors have been welcomed, they should be fed. The great importance of food throughout the *hui* makes the cooks key figures in its

91. Donne (1927), p. 57.
92. Paki (1971).

staging. When guests leave the *marae* and return home, one of the first questions they will be asked is "how was the food?", and according to their answer the prestige of that *marae* rises and falls. Some *marae* acquire a wide reputation for the food provided at their *hui*, and any gathering staged there attracts large crowds, further increasing the local *mana*. Most of the cooks (called the *kanohi wera*, "red faces"; or the *wīwī*, because they are as numerous as the blades in a clump of tussock grass *(wīwī)*, are middle-aged men and women, waiting their turn to qualify for the ceremonial activities carried out by the old people. They are all local people, or relatives of those who are sponsoring the *hui*, so they can be relied on to work hard for the honour of the *marae*. The cooks are up every morning at dawn, stoking fires, heating water, chopping meat and vegetables, and there is little rest for them while the *hui* is on. The men work outside in the *kāuta* (cookhouse), led by a head cook with long experience in earth-oven and open-fire cooking, and they are responsible for cooking the main course. In the cookhouse open fires are kept burning day and night; meat and vegetables are boiled and water is heated in great metal drums or copper steamers. The men skin and butcher the meat, and chop firewood to keep the fires going.

The earth oven is prepared by two or three experienced men with the head cook in charge. Food may be cooked in the *hāngi* each day of the *hui*, but more often these days the *hāngi* is reserved for the great feast which follows the main ceremony. The hole for the oven is dug the night before, with a drain running out of it in case it rains overnight. Early in the morning the experts dig up the oven stones which have been lightly buried after the last *hāngi* and start a fire with paper and kindling in the pit. *Mānuka* or dried brushwood is preferred for firewood because it burns without much ash, and once the fire is blazing the oven stones are stacked on top to heat. *Hāngi* stones have to be carefully selected as some types of rock will explode in the fire, and today chain harrows, firebricks, or two-foot lengths of railway line are sometimes used instead. The stones are left to heat for about an hour and a half, then they are pushed aside and the ashes are carefully shovelled out to prevent the food being tainted. The stones are covered with cabbage leaves or watercress to stop the food burning or sticking to them, and to give it extra flavour, then the food is lowered into the pit in wire-netting baskets or muslin bags, with the food that is slowest to cook at the bottom. Mutton, pork, chicken, potatoes, pumpkin and *kūmara* are the most common foods cooked in the ground. Water is sprinkled on the stones to start them steaming, then the baskets are covered with leaves or a rough-plaited flax mat, and a wet sheet to keep the food clean. Wet sacks are piled on top, then a layer of earth is shovelled on to seal in the steam. Sheets of corrugated iron or a tarpaulin may be laid on the earth for further insulation, and the *hāngi* is left to cook. The correct cooking time is about two and a half to three hours, depending on the size of the *hāngi* and the amount of food, and if the oven is dug up too soon the meal may be ruined. The head cook judges the right time to open the *hāngi* by the amount of steam coming out, and this ability is acquired only after years of experience. When he gives the word, the earth is shovelled off and the food uncovered. If the *hangi* is not properly cooked, it is a bad omen. The men carry the wire baskets into the kitchen, carve up the meat and dinner is served. Back outside, the *hāngi* stones are buried for the next time, the left-over wood is stacked and more firewood is cut to replenish the supply. The men stay around the cookshed until the early hours of the morning, joking, tending the fires, reading *Best Bets* and swapping yarns, while children play nearby, attracted by the warmth of the fires.

Inside the kitchen, women prepare the food for cooking. Broadly speaking, men cook the main course while women prepare the food and cook the dessert. Under the guidance of the female head cook, they peel vegetables, stuff chickens and cut up sponge cake for the trifles. The old women make steamed puddings and bake different types of bread— *parāoa rēwena* (leavened bread), *parāoa koroua* (old man's bread—a flat bread), or *parāoa parai* (fried bread). Sometimes a roster system has been established, but it only works approximately, and more often people do what they have always done, a task that may have been passed down through the women of their family. At Tūrangawaewae *marae*, for example, one entire kitchen and dining-hall is staffed by members of the Ngāti Koroki sub-tribe of the Waikato federation.[93] The younger women set tables, wash dishes and waitress. Meals are served at long trestle tables with forms for seating, and before each meal the tables are set by a team of women, some of whom may be trained waitresses. Plates of bread, butter, cheese, jam, sugar and salt are put on each table, with a cutlery setting and a breadplate for each guest. When the meal is ready, one or two women serve the potatoes, others serve the cabbage, the men serve the meat, and the plates are passed through serveries to lines of waitresses. Two or three waitresses look after each table, and sometimes the girls of different local families are each assigned a different table. Schoolchildren bring around the tea in big enamel pots, and carry away dirty dishes to the servery. Scraps are scraped off into a tin, and the plates are handed over to the sink area, where a team of women quickly wash and dry them and stack them up again. All the scraps are put into a 44-gallon drum outside, and eventually go to a local farmer's pigs. There are no idlers in the kitchen, and anyone who shows a tendency to hang about is soon told to work or move. Although the atmosphere is busy, the women are constantly singing, chatting and laughing as they bustle about.

Apart from the meal that is served to each group of visitors as they

---

93. Metge (1967), p. 191.

arrive, three regular meals and morning tea, afternoon tea and supper are served every day of the *hui*. For breakfast, lunch and dinner there is a basic menu of boiled meat with greens, potato, *kūmara*, bread and butter, cake and a cup of tea. Steamed pudding or seafood might be added on occasion. The "in-betweens" include a cup of tea, bread and butter, biscuits, jam and cake. At a large *hui* there are several sittings for every meal. Guests are called to eat by one of the cooks who bangs a saucepan and calls out some jocular invitation. Elders and visitors from important tribes are summoned first, then other guests, with the local people always eating last. As they enter the hall, particularly for the feast, the visitors begin to sing, and sometimes an old lady stands to *karanga* the festive-looking spread. A clergyman raps a spoon on the table, says grace, then the meal begins. Honoured guests may be placed at a special table on the stage or at the head of the hall, served by special waitresses, but they eat the same food as everybody else. Children all sit together, but otherwise the seating is informal and people sit wherever they want to.

The most important meal is the *hākari* or feast, which is served when the main ceremony is over and effectively signals the end of the *hui*. It is very poor manners to leave the *hui* before the feast, particularly on the same day, and people make scathing comments about people who leave the *marae* without bothering to join in this last festivity. The menu is elaborate and there is always plenty of food. The hosts are most happy when a guest leans back, lets out his belt a notch and says *"Ko te taua tā te kai"* ("The battle has gone to the food"). The first course is mutton, beef, chicken and pork from the *hāngi; kūmara,* pumpkin, potatoes and greens. The second course includes trifle, custard, cream, steam pudding, fruit and jelly. Plates of seafood, soft drinks, cakes, biscuits, fresh fruit and sweets are stacked on the table, and sometimes there are pungent delicacies such as dried shark, eel, and fermented corn as well. All this food is attacked manfully, because if it is the duty of the host to provide the feast, it is certainly the duty of the guests to eat it. As the waitresses carry around steaming plates of food, some of the more exuberant of them, aided perhaps by a glass of sherry intended for the trifle, start to sing. These songs are old ones, taken from the days when a feast was served outside by waitresses who brought the food in plaited baskets, singing as they came. The custom was called *"tuku kai"*, and was vividly described by James Cowan in 1910:[94]

"At a *tuku kai* I witnessed not long ago, on the occasion of a large congress of the tribes, there first advanced a long line of merry girls and women, each carrying a plaited basket or *kono*, of green flax, containing a steaming 'first-course' of potatoes and pork, hot from the *hāngi*. As they came they chanted a lively song keeping time with a skipping dance . . .

---

94. Cowan (1910), p. 157.

swaggering and swinging their plump bodies from side to side. Then they retired in good order for another course. Next a number of young men advanced in two long lines, yelling a *haka* song as they did so, each bearing a loaf of bread or a handful of biscuits, and others carrying buckets of tea, all of which were laid out on the grass in front of the visitors . . . Then a squad of Nga Puhi came forward, carrying more bread, and pannikins for the tea . . . 'Here we come,' chanted their leader, 'bringing our gift—the fifteen pannikins of Nga Puhi!' . . . Then there marched up, bringing more *kai*, headed by a brass band of Maori youths playing a quick-step, a party of Ngati-Apa and Ngati Raukawa people. Ngati Apa were headed by an enormously stout woman, whose fat body quivered and shook as she danced along the line, grimacing. The Ngati Kahungunu people in their turn advanced, singing as they stamped, . . . and swishing their flax waist mats as they swung up to the dining-room—the grassy-green—and laid their offerings on the ground."

After the feasting has continued for thirty minutes or more, men from the visiting parties stand and ceremoniously thank their hosts, and chatter begins as the urgency of eating subsides. Another way of thanking the cooks is for the visitors to muster a party, and to perform action songs as a token of gratitude. By this time there is warm friendship between hosts and visitors, and when the guests at last reluctantly stand to take their leave, the local people pile any food left over into boxes and put it in the bus for them to eat on the way home.

Throughout the *hui* visitors are not only fed but also given a place to sleep. "Stay here and let the fleas bite your bottom" is a joking admonition to visitors who show a tendency to hurry home in the evenings. With cars and buses providing easy transport, many people travel to the *hui* and return home, the same day, but visitors who have come a long way may sleep overnight in the meeting-house. Beds are made up on mattresses on flax mats laid round the walls, and visitors provide their own blankets. As soon as a group arrive on the *marae*, they are welcomed, given a meal, and then shown to the meeting-house. Here a local woman shows them where they are to sleep, and they unload their bags and arrange themselves into groups of family or friends before returning to rejoin the activities of the *hui*. Guests are traditionally placed along the right hand wall as you enter the meeting-house, with their chief in the place of honour under the front window, and their hosts along the opposite wall. Apart from the division into visiting parties and hosts, there is no formal segregation by age or sex in the sleeping arrangements, but parents with small children sometimes stay with relatives rather than risk disturbing the meeting-house at night. When there are a large number of guests, most of the local people sleep at home, and private billets, a nearby *marae* or a marquee may be pressed into service to accommodate the overflow. Inside the meeting-house there are a number of rules to follow. Clothes, particularly women's clothes, should not be hung up on the walls, because clothes are "common" and it is wrong for them to be suspended above the heads of chiefs. Women should never step over the legs of a man, no matter how crowded the conditions, because women are "common" *(noa)* and men are sacred. Food cannot be brought inside the meeting-house, because food is common and the house is sacred. All these rules derive from ancient *tapu* laws, and are quite often violated, partly because the laws are not always taken seriously today, and sometimes out of ignorance. The rule about food is widely known, but the others are known only in the more conservative areas.

In earlier times distinguished visitors were provided with the extra comfort of a woman to sleep beside them. It seems that once when Bishop William Williams was visiting Taupo, the chief thought to do him this honour and sent a local maiden to his hut. Shortly afterwards the girl returned in tears, because the Bishop had sent her away. The chiefs pondered over this behaviour and discussed it at some length. Te Heuheu came up with an explanation: "The Bishop is a great man. He comes from a great country, the country of our Queen, and we have treated him as a commoner. We have sent him one handmaiden whereas we should have sent him ten. Let ten be sent." So they summoned the ten loveliest girls in the village, had the women comb their hair and put jade ornaments round their necks and feather cloaks over their shoulders, then sent them to the Bishop's hut. The Bishop was amazed and angry, and ordered them to leave at once. Weeping with humiliation, the girls returned. The chiefs in solemn conclave decided that the Bishop must be mad, and still perplexed, they filed off to bed.[95]

Activities in the meeting-house begin after the evening meal. About 7 pm everyone assembles for evening prayers, led by a local lay reader or a clergyman attending the *hui*. These services are interdenominational, and it is not uncommon to find an Anglican minister, a Roman Catholic priest and a Ringatū *tohunga* (priest) each taking part. The congregation sit quietly round the meeting-house on mattresses and mats, and rise to sing the hymns. Prayers are recited in Maori, and some parts of the service are chanted together in harmony.

The minister or an old woman in the congregation starts the hymns, and most of them are known by heart. The unaccompanied music of a service in the meeting-house is very beautiful. The best singers invent their own harmonies, and the others keep to basic chords that give a rich and simple total effect. The service also includes a sermon in Maori, where the minister doubles as orator and preacher, combining the patterns of *whaikōrero* (oratory) with a religious message. The combination of tradition and theology is on occasion ingenious, and I have seen a minister

95. Donne (1927).

recite a string of Biblical genealogies in traditional Maori style, brandishing a walking-stick and using all the tricks of the orator to dramatise his sermon. Most Maori ministers are linguistically versatile, and can freely switch between the styles as well as the languages of Maori and English. Parts of the service are given in English if there are a number of young people present. After the evening service people sit around and chat, and start changing for the night. Women use a complicated ritual with a blanket for changing in the meeting-house, but those without the necessary skill take dressing-gown and toilet bag to the facilities outside, and change there. Separate facilities are provided for men and women, with hand-basins, toilets and cold showers, and although there is little privacy, no-one takes much notice. People sometimes sleep in their clothes, but most often they bathe and change, then return to the meeting-house for the evening's activities.

Before long the evening speeches begin. These are quite different from the formal and strictly ordered speeches given during a ceremonial welcome on the *marae*. People stand when they want to, and discuss any topic which is on their mind. In some areas speeches circulate round the house, starting with the leading local elder by the door, and ending with the guest of honour in his place by the front window; but today this formality is rare. On other occasions speakers stand at random to discuss burning issues of the day, re-tell traditions, and sometimes just to be amusing. Unlike the speeches of welcome, bound by ritual patterns, the evening speeches are loosely structured and discursive. In this relaxed atmosphere younger men and even women stand to speak, although they would be censured if they tried to do so on the *marae*. In this context the best speaker is the most entertaining, and elders who display formidable learning on the *marae* stand in the meeting-house at night to show a lively turn of wit. These speeches continue into the early hours of the morning, interspersed with action songs and *waiata* (chants), and at a *hui* nobody gets much sleep. As soon as heads begin to nod someone else stands up to speak or sing, and everyone wakes up again. As the night goes on the action gets livelier and people take to "passing round the walking-stick", a game where each performer nominates his successor by handing over a carved staff. People are unselfconscious about taking their turn, and sing or clown with gay abandon.

Sleeping arrangements at the *hui* are informal—"everybody sleeps together like one big family", and couples who show more than familiar affection do so at their own risk. An elder who notices them is likely to leave his oratory for a devastating commentary on their cuddling. If the couple are unmarried they may find a wedding day being arranged on the spot. In Northland these arrangements are called a *tomo*. Pat Hohepa has described one occasion when this happened: "Motu [a local elder] mentioned that a certain unmarried couple had slept together openly during the *hui* and it was his desire that this reason for a *tomo* be investigated . . . At this, the crowd looked over to where the couple were sitting; the young woman blushed and dropped her eyes while the young man stoically observed his stockinged feet. Pere, father of the girl, . . . stood up, his face indicating his grief. After a long silence he spoke, his words interspersed by lengthy pauses. 'My daughter gave birth to a child a year ago . . . This same person was the father . . . my wife had never met him for he did not want to marry my daughter . . . just when my wife had arranged to meet him . . . she died.' At this point, Pere wept. He then looked up again and said, 'It is for you, my people, to decide this case.'

"There followed an uncomfortable silence when Pere sat with his head in his hands, and in that silence adverse comments regarding the young man were plainly audible. After this silence had persisted for some time, Waitaki, a white-haired elder, stood up and said 'My thoughts on this matter are, it is little use our proceeding with a *tomo* if this couple are not over twenty-one. I suggest that they be asked whether they are over this age of consent.' When he sat, the murmur of the crowd indicated that this was a good plan.

"Motu, at this point, stood up again, and walked over to where the couple were sitting and asked them if they were both twenty-one, the girl answering in the affirmative. He then asked them to stand up, and turning to the girl first he said 'Do you agree that this man be your husband?' The girl said, '*Ae!* (Yes!)' At this point the crowd clapped and cheered. When there was silence, Motu turned and asked the young man the same question, but although that person was unmistakably Maori, he did not seem to understand the question. The girl was asked to explain and translate this before Motu once more asked the same question in Maori. There was a noticeable tension in the air, a silence shattered by a tumult when the young man said '*Ae!*' quite loudly. After the tension and tumult, Motu introduced a change of atmosphere by saying light-heartedly to the crowd, 'The only thing that remains is to decide the wedding day.' Laughter greeted this suggestion and this continued when Motu coughed loudly several times, held his throat as if thirsty, took a hat off the nearest hat-wearer, placed ten shillings into it, then sat down after leaving the hat on the floor. This obvious hint resulted in many persons placing contributions into the hat while the speeches continued."[96]

It may be almost dawn when the last orator finally drops off to sleep, and the chorus of snores about the meeting-house is at last unpunctuated by speech-making. If it is a *tangi* and the night before burial, the speakers stay awake to keep the dead person company through his last night on earth. Although the evening ends late in a meeting-house, the morning begins early, and the old people begin to stir again about 6 am. A service

---

96. Hohepa (1964), p. 83.

is held in the half-light of morning, with some people still asleep and others rising sleepily for the hymns, their blankets wrapped about them. Gradually everyone wakes, washes and dresses, mattresses are rolled back to the walls, clothes are packed tidily away, and it is time for breakfast.

Guests at a *hui* are not only fed and accommodated, but also entertained, and at any *hui*, stately rituals and high spirits are never far apart. An old woman who but an hour ago was wailing on the *marae* may be seen performing a comic *hula*, waggling her hips at one of the elders. In between the chanting and oratory of different ceremonial welcomes, people sit around singing or playing cards. At a funeral on the night after burial, a beer party is often held to sing, dance and drink away the death, while at a wedding the guests may be welcomed with weeping and calling on the dead. This mixture of grief and happiness seems strange to outsiders, but not on the *marae*. Wailing is an integral part of the rituals of encounter because wherever groups meet they remember those who have died since they were last together. On the other hand, conviviality and clowning are also a natural part of the meetings of friends and kinfolk. On the *marae* life is all of a piece, and there is no attempt to enforce one type of emotion or another.

One form of entertainment common to most *hui* is the visit to a local pub. In the afternoon and evening, particularly after dinner, people begin to drift away from the *marae* to spend a couple of hours at a nearby pub. While the elders carry on speech-making in the meeting-house, the rest drink beer at the pub, sing, and discuss the *hui*. Particularly they sing, some of the songs in Maori and others old favourites of the war years or vintage Hit Parade productions. Jugs of beer are brought to the table, the guitar player warms up, and soon everyone is standing in lines performing action songs, or sitting around and singing. On occasions virtually the whole of the hui shifts to the pub, and these convivial moments have become an accepted part of the proceedings (although some of the old people still disapprove), and an added attraction to the *hui*.

Action songs are also performed as entertainment on the *marae*, and as a modern alternative to the ancient *waiata* (chants). It is interesting that while people greet a *waiata* with murmurs of approval in Maori (*"Tēnā koutou!"*, "greetings"; *"Kia Ora!"* or its English equivalent, "Hear! Hear!"), they greet action songs with applause. Applause is only given on the *marae* for non-traditional performances, say a young Maori or a European giving a *whaikōrero* (speech), and it is unconsciously used as a European form of approbation appropriate to European-influenced activities. The action song is a recent innovation; the first ones were composed early this century by men such as Sir Apirana Ngata and Paraire Tomoana. They took popular European tunes, composed words in Maori and added actions, each with its own appropriate meaning. The songs are performed by highly-trained parties of men and women, who sing in harmony and perform the actions in unison. Action songs are particularly popular with the young people, and hundreds of action song clubs have been set up in schools, universities, training colleges and churches. Many of the *hui*, for example the *Hui Tōpu* of the Anglican church, or the King Movement's annual Coronation, cater to this interest, and run culture competitions as part of their activities. Apart from action songs, different types of war dances, stick games and *poi* dances are performed, and these competitions attract large numbers of people to the *hui*. If an important dignitary is to be welcomed to the *marae*, a concert party is often invited to perform the *pōwhiri* (action chant of welcome) and to entertain the visitors after the official welcome. Another occasion when action songs are used is at the end of an oration. If the group don't know any *waiata* (chants), they sometimes give an action song instead. Finally, and this has already been mentioned, action songs can be performed after a meal to thank the cooks for all their work.

Another far more informal type of dance is the *Kopikopi*, a local form of *hula* performed mainly by old women of the Waikato tribes. The Waikato area is the home of the Maori Queen, and when she visits her loyal *marae* she is usually accompanied by the King Movement's brass band. After the main meal of the *hui* the band assembles on the *marae* and starts up a lively quickstep. One by one the old ladies move on to the *marae* and begin to *kopikopi*. They gyrate their hips, roll their eyes and flirt comically with the elders, always to the great delight of the crowd.

A social is also included in the more festive types of *hui*, particularly weddings and twenty-firsts. After dinner the dining-hall is swept and cleared, then some local boys bring in drums, amplifiers and electric guitars, and start setting up a sound system. Once the microphones are working and the guitars tuned, the band strikes up and people begin to drift into the hall. There might be a small charge at the door (say 20 cents) to pay for the band, but often they play for nothing. Everyone comes along, from the smallest children to the elders, and the band plays waltzes and foxtrots for the older generation and electric rock for the younger. Soft drinks, ice blocks and cigarettes are on sale at the shop outside, while inside little children twist, their elders whirl in graceful waltzes, and the young people meet and flirt. Sometimes there is a talent quest to climax the evening. The MC jokes and calls people up to the microphone, where they compete for small cash prizes to generous rounds of applause. After more dancing the band strikes up the last waltz, and the dance is over. People move outside, smoking, chattering and laughing, and stand around a while before going back to the meeting-house to sleep.

After the *Hui*

The next morning after breakfast farewell speeches are exchanged, any last gifts are presented, and visitors shake hands and press noses along the long line of their hosts. By now, guests and local people are on the best of terms, and the farewells are regretful. As the visitors climb into the bus the local people press boxes of food on them for the journey. Relatives hug each other for the last time, and exchange messages for other relatives or friends. Then with vigorous waving on both sides, the bus roars off down the road, sounding its horn. When the last guests have gone the local people start cleaning up, and the *hui* is effectively over. Cleaning up takes the rest of the day, and probably most of the next day as well. All the dishes and cutlery are counted and stacked away. Sheets and pillowcases have to be washed, ironed and stored; mattresses are stacked up in the meeting-house, and all the buildings are swept and mopped. Any rubbish on the *marae* is raked up and burnt. Borrowed benches, mattresses, linen, plates and cutlery are returned to their rightful owners. All the fires are doused and raked over, cooking pots are scrubbed, and any left-over food is collected to be auctioned among the workers, or given to people who contributed generously in the first place. After the cleaning up is finished, the workers sit around discussing the *hui*, and deciding whether it was a success. If there is any beer left over they have a quiet drink, then return home for a good bath and a sleep. During the cleaning up the committee has set a date for the final meeting, and this may take place the next weekend. The committee gathers on the *marae* or in one of their homes, and after an initial exchange of *mihi* (welcoming speeches), the treasurer reads a statement of all donations and bills received. Often the generosity of the guests leaves a credit balance; for example at one *hui* I attended the bills amounted to $350 and the donations to $445. Any extra money is paid into the *marae* or family account, depending on who is running the *hui*, or to the bereaved family after a *tangi*. A detailed list of donations is kept so that each can be handsomely repaid when the time comes. If the *hui* runs at a loss the deficit will be met by those who attend the meeting, or out of the *marae* account. After the financial report the treasurer is empowered to pay all accounts, then everyone sits around and discusses the *hui* all over again. Incidents are recalled, speeches remembered, and any local idlers come in for heavy criticism. This meeting is the last direct activity rising out of the *hui*, although its effects may reverberate in local politics and gossip for a long time yet to come.

In these last two chapters we have set the scene and described what goes on backstage at a *hui*. In the next chapters the actual ritual performances are discussed, for it is these that define the *hui* as a special class of occasion.

CHAPTER FIVE

THE RITUALS OF ENCOUNTER

Introduction
The ceremonial part of a *hui* begins when guests start arriving at the *marae*. Each party of visitors *(ope* or *tira)* is separately welcomed with a formal ritual which includes calling, chanting, wailing and oratory, and it is this that we may call the ritual of encounter. On the *marae* it may be called the *mihi*, or simply, the 'welcome'. In earlier times when warfare was endemic and strangers were probably enemies, these rituals were used as a finely-balanced mechanism to manage encounters in peace. Even then they were not always successful, because between traditional rivals tempers ran high, and an exchange of insults or some unwitting offence could spark off hostilities on the spot. Sometimes unscrupulous chiefs would welcome visitors to their *marae*, and lull their suspicions by following the ritual through, then with a signal to their warriors slaughter them all. One such plot gave rise to a chant which is today used as prelude to a speech. An East Coast chieftain called Apanui had been invited to a gathering at Taupo, and on the way he stopped in Rotorua at the *marae* of an acquaintance, Huri Tū Moana. Like other chieftains of his time, Apanui had a pet parrot which he had taught to talk, and the bird flew on ahead of the party to Huri Tū Moana's *marae*. Here it noticed that the earth ovens were ready, but no meat had been provided; and the local men were all sitting round sharpening their weapons. It was clear that they were planning to kill their guests at some point in the welcome, and consign them to the *hāngi*. As Apanui's party approached the *marae* the bird flew to the ridgepole of the meeting-house and warned them with this chant:

Uia te manuhiri me ko wai?
Ask the visitor who he is?
Te Kuti, Te Wera, Te Hauā
He is descended from Te Kuti, Te Wera, Te Hauā
Ko Apanui
His name is Apanui
Moi, moi, moi, haere mai!
Moi, moi moi [a call], welcome!

Kāore he kai o te kāinga nei
There is no food in this village
Tou apiapi, tou apiapi
The *marae* is crowded
Kēhū kēhū
The people are getting ready
Haere mai te kokikokū
Welcome to you
Ko Huri Tū Moana
Huri Tū Moana
Te ō te ō.
shall be the food.

Forewarned, Apanui entered the *marae* and before the local people could attack, his warriors fell on them and killed them all. Instead of the visitors, the hosts provided the feast, and after dinner Apanui and his men went on their way satisfied.[97]

The long description by Maning of an early *hui* given in Chapter 2 made it clear that right throughout the rituals of encounter no-one could be certain whether the outcome would be peace or war. The sham battles and war dances described in early accounts were meant to be intimidating, warning the other side not to try any tricks, and if they detected any weakness in their opponents they were likely to take advantage of it. *Utu* accounts were so complicated that one never knew whether the other side was storing up some ancient insult for revenge.

Today there is no fear of warfare, but suspicion and hot pride can still be powerful underlying factors in rival group encounters on the *marae*, and the rituals are often played out in a keenly competitive spirit. Actors on both sides exert themselves to give an impressive performance, with the fundamental principle that the more distant and powerful the other party, the more perfect your own part in the ritual must be. Although there are no longer likely to be physical attacks on visitors to a strange *marae*, there may still be baleful spiritual influences about, and part of the ritual is aimed at warding them off. In the old days distant tribes were thought of as sorcerers and witches, and this attitude has not entirely vanished. At one *hui* I attended the visitors were from a powerful tribe of another district. After they had gone a local woman found a coin on the *marae*, and before she went off to spend it she spat on it in case it was theirs and might harm her. People often say they are scared of going to a strange *marae*, and this is something more than shyness. Visitors prefer to visit distant *marae* in large groups, and enter in the daytime, when local "ghosts" are less likely

97. Eruera Stirling (personal communication) (1971).

to be about. After the welcome the old people look around for water, so they can lift the local *tapu* before they eat. One must emphasise, however, that this sort of suspicion applies only to the meetings of strangers, and kinfolk and friends are quite free of it. In most encounters the people know each other well, and the atmosphere is relaxed and easy. The greetings on these occasions are more expressive of *aroha* (love, warmth) than anything else. It is only when groups with traditional rivalries meet on the *marae* that the ceremony is performed in full elaboration, and the atmosphere is tense.

At this point it is perhaps appropriate to set the scene by describing one fairly ceremonious ritual of encounter. The visitors in this case are about to enter a strange *marae*. They stand around near the visitor's gateway chatting or tidying up, then move into position—the old women in front, in black dresses, black scarves, and wearing greenstone ornaments; younger women next, then the men, with the more notable elders at their head. A warden comes out and gives them the signal to enter, and the ritual begins. The chief elder of the visiting party calls out a protective incantation *(waerea)* from the gateway of the *marae*, to shield his people from any hostile influences within, and an elderly local woman standing in the porch of the carved meeting-house begins a high wailing call of welcome *(karanga)*: "Enter and bring your dead, we shall weep for them together." The local people rise, the caller for the visitors replies, and the two old ladies call and answer while all the women present set up a chorus of keening, sobbing and wailing for the dead. A party of women standing in front of the meeting-house begin the action chant of welcome *(pōwhiri)*, metaphorically addressing the visiting group as a prized canoe which is being hauled on to the *marae*. The visitors move slowly towards the meeting-house, halting at least twice to drop their tears on to the grass of the courtyard in honour of the dead. The old ladies continue to wail, and wave sprigs of greenery in gestures of welcome. The visitors stop at some distance from the meeting-house, and all displays of grief are redoubled —wailing reaches a crescendo, and handkerchiefs are produced in quantity *(tangi)*. This may last for ten to fifteen minutes. The old ladies of the host group are seated in the front porch of the meeting-house; their orators sit silently on a bench to the right of the house; and all other locals are either standing around watching or busy in the background cooking, washing dishes and minding children.

As the weeping subsides the visiting men leave their women and sit on the bench for visiting orators, opposite the local speakers; and the women move to join the local ladies on the porch, pressing noses with each in turn, or go to benches set out behind their menfolk.

Now the oratory *(whaikōrero)* begins. A local elder stands with a shout *(whakaarara)*: "*Tihei - mauri ora!*" ("I sneeze, it is life!"). He walks on to the *marae* and faces the visitors. He is bare-headed, wears a suit and tie, and carries a carved walking-stick. He stands there and launches into a *tauparapara* or traditional chant, accompanied by vigorous actions and defiant brandishings of his stick. This display gives the orator's credentials and establishes his skill. Then he starts his oration. He strides along in front of the visitors, stops, delivers a few sentences, then turns on his heel and strides back again. His welcome to the dead, to the living, the recitation of genealogy and delivery of humorous asides are all given in these short bursts of speech. As his speech draws to a close, the orator starts up an ancient song *(waiata)*, and is joined and supported by members of his group. The song finishes, and he rounds off his performance with a few last words. In some tribes all the local orators speak in turn until their side is finished, then all the visitors—a style known as *pāeke*. In other areas orators of the two sides alternate *(utuutu)*. Ritual experts make it their business to be aware of such regional differences, which can be humiliating traps for the unwary.

One of the host speakers now calls the visitors over to shake hands. The local people line up in front of the meeting-house, and the visitors move along the line, pressing noses and shaking hands with each in turn *(hongi)*. Now the *mihi* for this group is complete. They have been given honorary local status by the ceremony, and are no longer threatened by *tapu* qualities on this *marae*. They take their bags to the meeting-house, then move to the dining-hall for a meal.

On this occasion no challenge *(wero)* was given, because there was no celebrity among the visitors, but if it had been performed, it would have followed the protective incantation *(waerea)*. Adjacent activities in the ritual of encounter may overlap, so that for example, at one point in the ritual the call *(karanga)*, wailing *(tangi)* and the action chant of welcome *(pōwhiri)* combine in one great medley of sound; but the order in which each ritual activity begins is clear, and this gives the ritual of encounter its structure. The *waerea* (protective incantation) is started first, outside the gates of the *marae*, then the *wero* (challenge) is given at the gateway, followed by the *karanga* (call) as the group begins to enter the *marae*. As the visitors advance, the *pōwhiri* (action chant of welcome) is performed, then they stop and stand to wail *(tangi)* for the dead. The visitors are seated and speech-making *(whaikōrero)* begins, then both parties shake hands and press noses *(hongi)*; and the ritual is over: i.e. *Waerea+wero karanga+pōwhiri+tangi+whaikōrero+hongi*.

The structure of the ritual of encounter adapts to factors such as the relative *mana* and distance of hosts and visitors, and although at a single *hui* the ritual is repeated perhaps twenty times or more as different groups arrive, each performance is distinctive. The principle that governs this variation is that the more strange and powerful the other group, the more ritual is given. The *waerea* or protective incantation, for example, is only used on entry to a strange *marae*, and it would be something of an insult if it were used on any other occasion. The *wero* or challenge is performed only for celebrities, perhaps the Governor-General, the Minister of Maori Affairs, the captain of a visiting rugby team or some high official of church or state, and the more distinguished the visitor the more chance there is that there will be two or even three challenges. The *pōwhiri* or welcome chant is given for important groups, and will probably be left out altogether if friends or kinfolk enter the *marae*. The number of speeches increases with the *mana* of the visitors. Two local speakers can provide a minimal welcome, but if a group of traditional rivals enter the *marae*, an oratory contest is likely to develop; and as many as twelve speakers might stand for either side before one group finally run out of men. The ritual is simplified for friends and kinfolk, not as a slight on their *mana*, but quite literally expressing the attitude "let's not stand on ceremony".

The rituals of encounter in some form or other are used whenever Maori groups formally assemble, and it would be an ominous sign of they were omitted. Cowan tells of a time when a Government survey team was sent into Tūhoe country to route an unwanted road. They came to the *marae* to parley with the local chiefs. No call of welcome was given, and the chiefs sat around the *marae* in grim and scornful silence. Only when the visitors began to speak, the chiefs sprang up, and, one by one they cursed the Government and all its works.[98] On normal occasions the appropriate ritual is followed through in all its parts. The usual context is the *marae*, but even in private homes, in public halls, at dances or committee meetings where Maori people gather, the ritual is used to open up the proceedings. It is flexible in timing, and can adapt to almost any situation. Once when Sir Apirana Ngata was making a railway journey from one part of his constituency to another, the train made a whistle stop at a particular station. A crowd was there to greet him, so Ngata jumped to the station platform, was called, wept over, greeted in oratory and replied, then pressed noses with his hosts and got back on the train just as it started to move, all in the space of about five minutes. An even more remarkable application of the ritual was made in Ruātoki, in 1901. In that year the Government presented a herd of pedigree goats to Sir James Carroll, to be reared in the Urewera country. A Chief was sent to collect them, and they were brought by steamer to Whakatāne then herded to Ruātoki. They arrived on the day that a high-born woman died, and a formal letter was at once dispatched, inviting them to the *tangi*. Tupara, the chief in charge of the goats, dressed the head goat in a feather cloak, stuck a *huia* feather between his horns, then sent a messenger to the *marae* to warn them that the travellers were on their way. As the herd approached the *marae*, the women set up a cry of welcome, and the

98. Cowan (1934), p. 73.

pōwhiri action chant was performed. The goats were led into the meeting-house, where the floor had been covered with fine quality mats, and the speechmaking began. First an old chief called Rakuraku arose and said, "Illustrious strangers, I greet you who have been sent hither, a treasure for the Tūhoe tribe. Welcome!" Then Te Whiu addressed them, and promised to give them all his common she-goats for their wives. Finally a tattooed warrior called Te Kauru stood, and pacing to and fro in front of the goats, proclaimed: "Welcome Tupara. Bring to the house of our ancestors the pets of our relative Mr Carroll. Let all these goats be a joy and a delight for the women and for the old men. But I am wondering in my heart why we Tūhoe people should be so greatly favoured even above all the Europeans. What have we done to deserve such a singular mark of affection! Long life to you all!" Now that the host speeches were over, Tupara stood on behalf of the goats and replied, "I shall act as an interpreter for the Billy Goat and tell you what he says:

"O Tūhoe, salutations to you, the living representatives of your elders who are gone! I thank you for the warmth of your greeting. We have come from the distant islands to see you Maori people, of whom I have heard so much, and now I am rejoiced to have met you and to have seen with my own eyes the tattooed faces of your elders, who look like graven images. [Tremendous applause.] I have been sent by Timi Kara for you people to tend and care for, and you must be very kind to me and my wives. For if you treat me cruelly, my descendants will go forth to other tribes and an evil reputation will fall upon Tūhoe. Kia-ora!"[99] And this, apparently, is a true story.

Actors

In other, less remarkable situations, the main actors are all elderly people with the exception of the challenger, played by a young man. There is a great emphasis on the past, on the ancestors, and on the world of the dead in the rituals, and in this context the old people are most at home. The old people, too, are more *tapu* than the young. They have had time to acquire esoteric knowledge and to become expert in the rituals, and with old age they draw nearer to the shadowy world of legend, the long night of the underworld or *Pō*. The elders attend a great many *hui*, listen to hundreds or even thousands of speeches, and in the process they absorb chants, proverbs, genealogies and traditional stories. If an old woman hears a call or a *waiata* that particularly appeals to her, she goes to someone who knows it to get the words, then practises it in the corner of the meeting-house, or later at home. An old man listens to other speakers, checks their genealogies, adds to his own, and stores up fine turns of phrase for future use. A number of old people I know carry a small note-

99. Cowan (1934), pp. 74-80.

book around with them to *hui*, filled with random jottings of this sort. Often at a *hui* in a quiet moment the elders sit around telling stories, explaining chants and practising them together, and the *hui* itself is by far the best school for its own rituals. Away from the *marae* the old people refresh their knowledge by looking over family *"whakapapa"* books, written by a father or a grandfather and filled with chants, miscellaneous bits of information and family history as well as genealogies; and some of the more erudite elders delve into scholarly studies of their own tribal history, e.g. *Tuwharetoa*, by John Grace, *Te Arawa* by Don Stafford or *Tuhoe, Children of the Mist* by Elsdon Best. The old people of some districts regularly gather at one of their homes or at the *marae*, to keep alive their esoteric knowledge. At Ngāruawāhia, for example, there is a weekly *waiata* class for local elders at the *marae;* and up till quite recently the elders of the Aupōuri tribe of Northland used to gather from time to time at one of their homes in closed session, to discuss local history and genealogy. On the way to a *hui*, in the bus or car, the old people of a party mentally rehearse the forms that they will follow, carefully choosing incantations or *waiata* suitable to the occasion.

The esoteric knowledge associated with *marae* rituals is a prized possession, first brought down from heaven by the god Tāne in the *kete tuauri*, one of three "kits of knowledge", and it has been *tapu* ever since. The elders are revered as keepers of these traditional treasures, and every time one of the old experts dies, he is mourned as irreplaceable. On every *marae* they lament, "our elders are gone, and we, the younger generation, are not fit to greet you"; and they fear that as the orators and singers pass away the *marae* rituals will also die. The human cycle is speeded up on the *marae*, for a man's life span as an elder is only twenty to thirty years (say from fifty to eighty years old); and by the time he has become an expert it is not long before he must inevitably die. For this reason it seems that the rituals of the *marae* are perpetually on the edge of extinction, because no sooner does an orator arise than he is felled by death. All the same the rituals have survived with little change for 200 years since earliest contact, and they continue to be practised on *marae* all over New Zealand. In the words of the proverb, *"Ka pū te ruha, ka hao te rangatahi"* ("When the old net is drawn in, the new net goes fishing"), and the rituals go on.

Specific chants and *waiata* may be lost. Some of the elders are reluctant to pass on their knowledge to the younger generation, because it is the rarest chants that are the most prized, and if they pass into common currency, much of their *mana* is lost. An old man might say a favourite *tauparapara* (chant), "It is my blanket, and if I give it away, how can I keep warm?" For this reason tape recorders are sometimes regarded with suspicion, and there is a particular fear that the knowledge might be commercialised.

Others of the old people prefer to "give out" what they know, to save it from extinction. They write it into *whakapapa* books, share it with younger kinsmen who want to learn, and tape chants and songs for university archives, or for radio broadcast. There are now weekly programmes in Maori on the radio, where elders of different areas discuss local traditions, explain their chants and *marae* etiquette; and university archives have substantial collections of field and interview tapes of Maori verbal art. *Whakapapa* books are a family possession, kept hidden away in a suitcase or on top of a wardrobe, and brought out only to refresh the owner's memory or to teach a kinsman. Ironically, the younger generation do not usually become interested in tradition until they too, are approaching *kaumātua* status, and by then it is often too late. The father or uncle has died, and most often the *whakapapa* book is buried with him. These books, because they are *tapu*, have to be carefully handled, and should never be taken into a kitchen *(noa)*, or anywhere near food.

The most natural way for young people to learn *marae* rituals is to be there when they are practised, and when the right time comes, to take an active part. At rural *hui* there are always children and young adults about, and those who are interested can sit, watch and listen. A young man may give his maiden speech at a family *tangi*, when he speaks for his brothers and sisters, or on a trip to a nearby *marae*. One man told me about the first speech he ever made: "We were visiting Whakatōhea, old Ngākohu Pera's *marae*. When we got there, all their young chaps stood up to *whaikōrero*. I thought I was all right, because we had plenty of old fellows to speak for our side, but when our turn came round, the old blokes made me stand. They told me, 'You go first and we'll follow up and cover any mistakes.' Those old boots! So I stood. I didn't have a *pātere*, no *wai*, nothing. I didn't know anything. But anyway, I made my maiden speech and passed with flying colours, although I didn't think much of it. And it's stood me in good stead ever since, you know."

Young men who've grown up on the *marae* have plenty of material to draw on for the body of their speech, but the chants have to be specially learned. Aspiring young orators practise at home in the cowshed, or get together for special sessions. One man who is now a notable speaker said that when he was learning, he and a mate got drunk one night and decided to practise. They got a crate of beer and wrapped it up in a blanket, and proceeded to deliver a series of inspired funeral orations at this makeshift "corpse". The old people in general don't approve of speeches being practised out loud away from the *marae*, especially funeral orations, because the references to the dead which are part of any speech are bad luck in any other context. *Waiata* are learned by standing up to join the elders when they sing, and gradually learning the words. Sometimes today they are learned from tape recordings taken at the *marae*, or from Sir Apirana Ngata's book *Nga Moteatea*, which gives the words of almost 100 songs. Some of the old people carry round a copy of *Nga Moteatea*, but it should never be used at a *marae*, and the one time I saw an old lady singing from it she was told to put it away. At Tūrangawaewae *marae* in Ngāruawāhia, a weekly *waiata* class is held for the elders and some of the young people to practise old songs and learn new ones. Also recently, a *waiata* school was held at the University of Auckland, and Maori people assembled there to learn from a Tūhoe and an East Coast elder in weekly sessions sponsored by the Maori Women's Welfare League and the Archives of Maori and Pacific Music. The *tauparapara* or the chants which precede a speech are usually learned from an elder relative, written down and then memorised.

Another way of training the young people is to hold a *Whare Wānanga*, or school of learning. This institution dates from pre-contact times, when the high-born young men of the tribe gathered in a *tapu* house or out in the bush at night, to learn the local genealogies and traditions. They sat in complete darkness and memorised texts and genealogies by chanting them out loud. The teachers were *tohunga*, elders expert in their field, and some of their schools came to be famous, for example Te Rāwheoro on the East Coast, or Te Mātorohanga's school in the Wairarapa. The entire proceedings were surrounded by strictest *tapu*. The *Whare Wānanga* of today is rather different. Recent schools sponsored by the Ngāti Porou and the Tūhoe people have been held at weekends or in public holidays, so that the young people can leave their jobs in the city and return home to sit at the feet of their elders for a time. They gather at a *marae*, and the elders stand in turn to lecture their younger kinfolk, while tape-recorders or scribes record the proceedings. These gatherings are open to both men and women. The Tūhoe schools have been closed to outsiders, since they prefer to keep their traditions within the tribe, but other *Whare Wānanga* are open to university students, lecturers, and people from many other tribes as well as local people. At these *Whare Wānanga*, also called "seminars", genealogy, local legend and *marae* etiquette are discussed and explained to the younger generation.

A more individual training is in the form of an "apprenticeship" to an elder kinsman. If an older man wishes to pass on his knowledge before he dies, he looks among his younger relatives and picks out one who seems both interested and capable, and begins to teach him. Usually today, this is quite an informal arrangement, but in earlier times the young man was "*tohi*'d", or specially dedicated so that he would put the knowledge to good use. Here we might examine the life history of a well-known elder, Eruera Stirling, to see how he was taught. He was born at the end of last century, at Raukokore on the East Coast. His mother, Mihi-Kotukutuku, was a high-born Whānau-ā-Apanui woman, and his father, Duncan Stirling, was a part-Maori from the South Island. There were signs at his birth that he should be *tohi*'d for sacred learning. His mother had a long and difficult labour. At first she lay inside her house, but the child could not be delivered, and an old prophetess called Hiria-te-Rangihaeata had to be called in. She recommended that Mihi should be taken to an old *raupo* hut in the bush, and when this failed she decided that the child would have to be born outside. His mother was carried across a creek, and laid on mats under a grove of *karaka* trees. Hiria sent some women to Kirieke beach to report on the state of the tides. When they came back they told her that the tide had just begun to ebb, and the old woman predicted that when Matariki constellation (Pleiades) stood over Tikirau hill that morning, a boy would be born. It happened as she foretold, and she claimed the boy as a foster child. When he was weaned Hiria and her husband, Pera te Kaongahau, took him to their home, and he lived with them for about seven years. When he was eight years old Pera took him to a local *wai tapu* (sacred pool) for the *tohi* ceremony. First they both undressed, then Pera told him that he must dive three times into the pool, bringing up a pebble from the bottom on his third dive. Eruera followed these instructions, and each time he dived the old man chanted a *karakia* (prayer) which was to fix firmly in the boy's mind everything he was taught. On the third dive he found a pebble, and brought it up in his mouth. Once he was out of the water, Pera told him to throw the stone back into the pool, and so the *tohi* ceremony was completed. After that each night the old man taught him, reciting chants and genealogies in the dark and observing strict *tapu* rules. By the time he was about ten Eruera had memorised a number of chants and genealogies. From school he won a scholarship to Te Aute Maori College, where he studied the Maori language and learnt more about Maori traditions. After he left Te Aute he began to travel round the country with Sir Apirana Ngata, attending *hui* in many different tribal districts, and here he learnt of tribal differences in *marae* procedure and consolidated what he had been taught as a child. Now after more than forty years of activity on the *marae*, Eruera Stirling has a wide command of genealogy and chants, and is generally acknowledged as an expert in all fields of *marae* ritual.

The *Whare Wānanga*, the *tohi* and just sitting around listening are all ways that *marae* rituals have been traditionally passed on, but today they are not always adequate. Although at rural *hui* the young people are there at the *marae*, they are busy working or playing, and don't take much notice of the old people's ceremonial activities. It is difficult for young Maoris reared mostly in a European world to take "that old stuff" seriously, and many of them are bored by it. It is not until they are twenty or so that *Maoritanga* becomes important to them, and they realise what they have missed. By then many of them are living in the cities and no longer in close contact with a *marae*. Despite the difficulties, there are a surprising number of people who make determined efforts to recapture the knowledge they ignored as children. This is partly because the *marae* is still the major political arena, and young leaders who want to influence their people have to master the ritual forms; but even more than this, the *marae* and its rituals have become caught up in a search for identity. Particularly in the cities, where young Maori people are raised in an environment that is not very different from that of their European neighbours, the *marae* has come to have a new sort of importance.

Most young Maoris born in the city cannot speak Maori, have never been to a *marae* and know nothing of its rituals, but their faces are Maori and that marks them. Their position is bitter, because they are Maori with none of the compensations. As children in urban schools they are teased and sometimes taunted for being Maori; as adults they may be refused accommodation or jobs on the same grounds, but as Maoris they live in a cultural vacuum. Even their own people criticise them. "Look at this young boy," says an old man on a *marae*, "black as the ace of spades and can't speak a word of Maori!" Some of them join gangs, such as the "Stormtroopers", "Nigs", or the "Mongrel Mob", and find identity there, while others look to the *marae*. In recent gatherings of Maori secondary school students, one of the main points raised was that they wanted to learn Maori and *marae* etiquette. The *marae* is a Maori place, where Maori arts are practised and Maoris gather. Its rituals recall a legendary time of great navigators and warriors, and genealogy bridges that time to the present. On the *marae*, people are aligned into tribes and identified by *whakapapa*, and being Maori is a matter of pride. Although many young urban Maoris look to the *marae*, it is not easy for them to take their place there. If they can't speak Maori, they can't understand what is being said, and if they don't know the rituals, it is easy to do the wrong thing. For those who are keen enough to learn, however, there are a number of possibilities. Some urban families hold private language classes for their children, taking off one evening a week to talk and study Maori. Increasing numbers of urban schools offer Maori as a subject, and at Hillary College in Auckland special lessons in *marae* ritual were given for a time. At the Maori boarding schools, like Queen Victoria School for girls, or St Stephen's School for boys, Maori is a major part of the curriculum, and oratory is fostered in school competitions. The schools' culture groups visit *marae* frequently, and these schools are probably the best channel for transmitting *Maoritanga* in the cities at present. At Victoria University in Wellington and the University of Auckland, full courses in Maori language and culture are offered, with special classes in the art of oratory. For working adults there are night classes offered by University Extension or at local schools, in Maori and *marae* etiquette. Most recently, a University affiliated group called "Te Reo Maori" has conducted its own courses in oral skills and oratory. Outside the educational system are the culture clubs, run by young people in churches, schools, training colleges, and universities. These culture clubs concentrate on the performing arts; action songs, *haka* and *poi;* but they are beginning to teach *karanga* (calls), *waiata* (songs), chants, and the rudiments of oratory to their members. The *wero* or challenge is usually taught through these clubs. Ngāti Pōneke Club in Wellington has gone a step further and offers a Saturday morning class in Maori for members' children. The Maori Woman's Welfare League held a competition in *waiata* at one annual conference, and through all these non-traditional channels *marae* skills are being passed on.

All the same, these organisations reach only a small minority of urban Maoris, and it is difficult to predict what is going to happen to the *hui* and its rituals in the city. Those who are at present carrying on the rituals are the parental generation, raised in country areas close to a *marae*, but with the rising generations, born in the towns away from the *marae*, the forms of the *hui* may radically change. Even in some country areas this has happened, for example in a few Northland communities, where the prolonged influence of the missions followed by the influence of the Rātana church have almost obliterated traditional ritual forms. At one community I visited *waiata* were replaced by hymns, and chants were replaced by Christian prayers. Changes even more fundamental than this may come to urban *marae* rituals in years to come.

Although the main actors in the rituals of encounter are mostly elderly specialists, these are some exceptions. A man is usually about fifty or fifty-five when he graduates to *kaumātua* (elder) status and becomes a regular speaker for his group; but this age requirement is lifted for men who occupy important positions in the community. Maori ministers, welfare officers, university and training college lecturers, doctors and lawyers are regarded as exceptional cases and are permitted to speak on the *marae* at a much earlier age. This is also true for men with particularly forceful personalities. In all these cases *mana* overrides age, and qualifies them to act as honorary *kaumātua*.

If the actors at a *hui* are first divided by age, so that old people dominate the ceremonial area while the younger generation act as workers, another great division is that of sex. We have already seen that among the workers the women work mainly in the kitchen, preparing food and cooking the pudding, while the men work outside in the *kāuta*, cooking the main course. In the ceremonial area too, the actors are strictly divided by sex. Women give the call of welcome *(karanga)*, wail *(tangi)*, and sing the ancient songs *(waiata)*. After a man completes his speech the women stand to sing with him, and this song is said to be the *kinaki* or "relish" for the oratory. Women also dominate the action chant of welcome *(pōwhiri)*, although men join in. Solo opportunities for women are mostly restricted to the *karanga* or call of welcome; old ladies with clear strong voices and a knack for choosing the right words (sometimes referred to as "bugles"), are widely admired. In general, however, women play a supporting role in *marae* rituals.

Oratory is the central activity of the ritual, and in most tribes it is limited to men. On the East Coast and it is said, in Northland, this role is waived for high-born women, but if such a women should stand to speak on a *marae* outside her own tribal area there would be violent protests from the local elders, and it is said that in the old days she would have been killed. "Only the cock was made to crow," say the men, "If the hen tries, wring her neck." A male orator should also be of high descent, although this qualification is subordinated to age; and sons of a living father and younger brothers are not permitted to speak, particularly in the Tūhoe and Te Arawa areas. Apart from oratory, men also give the *poroporoaki*, a farewell call as they enter a bereaved *marae*; join in action chants of welcome *(pōwhiri)* and songs *(waiata)*; and they retain overall control of the ceremonial proceedings. When a group seats itself at the *marae*, men sit at the front benches and women sit at the back. The sexual division relates to the principle that men are *tapu*, and therefore qualified to perform *tapu* activities such as oratory, and women are *noa*. Only if a woman's birth is so high that her *mana* overrides her *noa* status can she stand to speak, and then only in some tribes.

This does not mean, however, that women are lacking in influence on the *marae* or elsewhere. It is notable that whenever a man oversteps the bounds of *marae* protocol, it is nearly always the women who carry out corrective action. If he speaks too long and fails to hold the attention of his audience, the old women become restless, whisper to each other, then make quite audible comments of *"Hōhā!"* (boring) or *"Kia poto te kakau o tō paipa!"* (shorten the stem of your pipe!) If these tactics fail, an elderly female relative of the speaker may stand and announce *"Anei tō wai!"* (here is your song), then starts to sing, effectively cutting him off. Drunks get similar treatment. If a speaker becomes insulting or cuts across major rules of *marae* procedure, the older women apply the ultimate sanction of the *whakapohane*. They stand, turn their backs on him, then bend over and raise their skirts in pointed derisory comment. Also on many *marae* the greater part of *hui* organisation falls to the women.

Apart from the age and sex dichtomies, the other great division among actors is between locals and visitors. *Marae* rituals are structured as a balanced exchange between locals *(tāngata whenua)* and visitors *(manuhiri)*. This is particularly clear in oratory, where local and visiting orators either speak alternately or in separate blocs, depending on the tribal area; and in the *karanga*, where local and visiting callers call and answer. The two groups stay spatially separate and opposite throughout the ritual, facing each other across the *marae*, and it is only when the ritual is over that they merge in the *hongi* line. Locals perform the *wero* (challenge) and the *pōwhiri* (action chant of welcome); and visitors give the *waerea* (protective incantations). Both groups play a part in the *karanga* (call), wailing for the dead *(tangi)*, oratory and pressing noses *(hongi)*. Taking the elements of the ritual of encounter in turn, then, we can describe the actors for each stage as follows:

waerea	[visitor, male, elder]
wero	[local, male, young]
pōwhiri	[local]
karanga	[female, elder] local and visitor alternate.
tangi	[female]
whaikōrero	[male, elder] local and visitor alternate *(tū mai tū atu)* or all local then all visitor *(pāeke)*
hongi	all actors

One can observe that the ritual begins with maximum separation between locals and visitors, then moves to a stage where their activities alternate. It is not until the very end of the ritual, when the visitors move over to the line of local people and press noses, kiss or shake hands with each in turn that all the actors are involved at once, and the groups truly "meet".

Language

Maori is the ceremonial language of the *marae*. Maori as an everyday language is retreating, and it has been previously estimated that perhaps 10% at most of the Maori population now speak Maori fluently. Many of the non-fluent population have a partial command of the language, or a passive understanding of it, but this sort of command is not adequate for the verbal skills required on the *marae*. Maori persists as an everyday language in isolated rural communities in Northland, the Urewera and East Coast districts, where most of the inhabitants are Maori, but even here it is used mainly among the older generations. Communication across generational lines is in English, or in a common but more complex situation, the elders address children in Maori, and are answered in English. Only in a limited number of families is Maori routinely used by all members. In urban situations Maori is rarely used in everyday life, mostly by older people raised originally in one of the Maori-speaking country districts. As the balance of Maori population shifts from the country to the towns, this trend might be expected to accelerate, especially in the city-born generations. An everyday language can effectively survive only in contexts where most of the population speak it, and most of the social transactions of its speakers are carried out with other speakers. This situation is true of English, but certainly not of Maori in New Zealand cities. It was estimated in 1913 that 90% of Maori children could speak Maori; by 1950 the estimate dropped to 26% with about 60% passive "understanders", and that was before the post-war urban migrations really began to take effect. Most Maori people believe their language is dying, and blame both parents who do not teach it to their children, and the school system, where Maori was outlawed for almost 100 years. There is a recent accelerating trend in secondary schools for Maori to be offered as a subject—in 1970, thirty schools were teaching Maori to 2,400 students; and in 1973 the figure rose to 1,976 schools teaching 6,850 students—but since language instruction does not begin until the students are thirteen or more, it is difficult for them to gain complete fluency. Other groups such as culture clubs, night schools and family classes also teach Maori to a limited number of learners; but once people become interested it is usually too late for them to fully master the language. The average age that people discover interest in *Maoritanga* is in their twenties and thirties, and by then it is notoriously difficult to acquire a second language.

Given this situation, it is perhaps surprising that Maori is still regarded as the only proper language to use on the *marae ātea*. Feeling is quite strong about this, and although English is sometimes used in a speech for emphasis or for comic effect, it is interspersed with fluent Maori. English is often heard in the background among the cooks, workers, and spectators, but rarely on the speaking ground itself. It would be quite impossible to give any of the old chants or songs in anything but Maori, since the text has to be delivered word-perfect, and any mistakes or deviations from the original are regarded as ill omens. Although Maori is to all intents and purposes becoming a ceremonial language in New Zealand, within its context it rules supreme. Those who can't speak Maori, even elders, rarely stand to express themselves on the *marae* unless they have to, and in that situation they apologise for speaking English and try to preface their speech with a few sentences in Maori. At one *hui* I attended, the Minister of Maori and Island Affairs was the honoured guest. Two old men, both Maori speakers, thought to make things easier for him, and delivered their orations in English. They were cried down and criticised, and soon after left the *marae*. Their use of English was regarded as an insult to the Minister at worst, and a foolish mistake at best. "He'll think we've all gone *pākeha*," people said with considerable disgust. English is sometimes used as a concession to young people or Europeans, but people would rather provide an interpreter and continue to conduct the proceedings in Maori. This gives them an opportunity to play bilingual games; as one man put it: "We say what we mean in Maori, and something else in English." A perfect example of this stratagem is given in J. B. Condliffe's biography of Sir Peter Buck (Te Rangihiroa). In 1908, a group of United States naval officers were being welcomed to Ohinemutu, and Buck was the interpreter. An old man from Rotorua, *taiaha* in hand, gave an impassioned speech, working himself into a frenzy. Sentence by sentence, Te Rangihiroa interpreted him. "Greetings, greetings to you our kith and kin, who like our ancestors of old have crossed the great sea of Kiwa." [Bishop] Bennet (who was sitting on the sidelines) began to chuckle as words poured from the speaker and Dr Buck maintained the even tenor of his interpretation. "You have come to this land in your canoes—just as did your ancestors from the English motherland in the Mayflower to found a new nation—so did our ancestors sail the tempestuous seas to found another land." Asking why he was laughing, the future Bishop explained, "Peter is making it all up as he goes along. The old man is working himself into a passion because of the neglect of the drains at Whakarewarewa!"[100]

Maori is prized as one of the treasures *(taonga)* of the people, and chants, proverbs, genealogies and fine phrases are all valued as gifts from the ancestors. People become connoisseurs of oratory, and take a real delight in spirited performances. "After eating, we love to talk" says an informant, and this means talking in Maori. English is a tool for communication, but Maori is regarded as an art-form. This love of language is one of the reasons why Maori continues to be spoken on the *marae*. The other reason is that the *marae* is tapu, and so are the old chants and songs. In ceremonial situations traditional language forms are most appropriate, and *marae* language is full of archaisms. The linguistic conservatism of ritual situations is well-known, for example in the Church of Rome, where Latin continued to be well used after it was a "dead" language, and something of the same principle applies to the *marae*. There is safety and sanctity in the old ways of speaking, and people defend them strongly, so that although Maori may fade altogether as an everyday language, one might expect it to remain the ceremonial language of the *marae* for a long time to come. In this case special experts in the language would have to be trained, and there are signs already in the cities that this is happening. Young people who are drawn to the *marae* and the culture it represents learn Maori as a first step. The way they learn it, out of books, in class or from tapes, is very different from the natural learning process for language and requires a special dedication. Aspiring young orators, instead of learning to speak the language fluently, memorise special set speeches, rather like a priest memorising the Order of Service in Latin; and there are a surprising number of people who, in adulthood, set about learning Maori from scratch. This is because the *marae* is coming to have a special significance. In the country it was a matter-of-fact sort of place where people conducted their gatherings. In the city, to those of the younger generation who do not know it well, the *marae* is becoming a sort of shrine, a holy place of *Maoritanga*. Because they want so much to play a part there, many of the young people make extraordinary efforts to learn the language of its rituals. For those who do not learn Maori but are still interested enough to attend a *hui* from time to time, the activities

---

100. Condliffe, (1971), pp. 77-78

on the *marae* acquire a new mystery simply because they do not understand what is being said. Most often they are impressed, although some young informants say they get bored at the *marae* because they cannot understand, and others feel that its rituals are ridiculous and out-of-date. As long as significant numbers of young people are attracted enough to the *marae* to learn Maori, however, it is likely that the rituals of encounter will continue to be practised.

Ritual Units
In this section, each of the elements of the welcome or *mihi* will be discussed in turn. To set the scene, let us imagine that it is midday on a hot and sunny Saturday. The *marae* is already packed with people, sitting on rows of benches in the heat and watching while one group of visitors after another are formally welcomed. Up on the porch of the meetinghouse the old ladies of the district chat among themselves, while down below sit the local orators, overheated in suit and tie. The *marae* is in open country, surrounded by paddocks with grazing sheep. The visitors that concern us are standing outside the *marae*, keeping a close eye on the activities within. They expect to be welcomed next. As the sixth speaker on the *marae* sits down, they move, but it is a false alarm and another speaker gets to his feet. After two more speeches the welcome is over, and a local man comes to tell them that their turn has come. They assemble in a close party and move towards the gateway of the *marae*. The welcome is about to begin.

Waerea (protective incantation)
The *waerea* is used when a group is about to enter a strange *marae*, and is delivered by their chief elder in a long, continuous chant. The purpose of the incantation is to "*waere*" or clear their path of any supernatural obstacles set there by local sorcerers, and it dates from the time when people believed that strange communities were hot-beds of black magic (*mākutu*). A belief in black magic still lingers, and elders of the Waikato and Taranaki tribes still use these incantations on entry to a strange *marae*. The *waerea* is begun outside the gateway of the *marae*, and the elder keeps chanting it as his group advance, gathering protection about them as they approach their hosts. The incantations are full of archaisms and obscure references which make them difficult to translate, but add to their mystery and *mana*. One *waerea* was quoted by Maharaia Winiata as follows:

Ko tihi - E Mauri ora!
Uea - waerea te one tapu
Kahura ra tangata-a-uta

Me turaki atu ki tangata-a-tai
Ka hurara tangata-a-tai
Me turaki atu ki tangata-a-uta
Pera hoki ra
Te Korepe nui, Te Korepe roa
Te Waahi awa, te toetoe awa
Whakamoea tama i te ara
Whakamou tama i te ara.

Ko Tu, ko Rongo
Kau raka Tama e uhia
Tukua atu Tama kia i waho i te tawhanga-whanga
He putanga Ariki, no Rongo
Mai ea, mai ea, mai te tupua
Mai ea, mai ea, mai te tawhito
I hara mai koe ia whaka Hotunuku
Ia whaka Hoturangi
Ko te manawa, ki taku Manawa
E taane ka irihia
Whaano, whaano, hare mai te toki
Haumi e, hui e, taiki e!"[101]

This text is just the first part of the incantation, and different elders have different ways of finishing it off.

The *waerea* is only rarely used today, most often by Waikato elders, who as the Queen's representatives travel widely throughout New Zealand. In most cases, however, people are entering *marae* that are already familiar to them, and no *waerea* is required, and in most tribes there are no longer elders who know a *waerea* to use even when it would be appropriate. In this situation the *waerea* may be replaced by Christian prayers, for example the prayer that begins "Fence us off from all evil", but these are recited before the party leave on their trip or outside the *marae*, and not as part of the ritual of entry.

Wero or Taki (northern term)—(ritual challenge)
The modern *wero* is the abbreviated descendent of a whole series of warlike evolutions that were once performed whenever strangers met. In peace and war strangers were greeted with the same ritual forms, because an unknown group might always be planning treachery, and a display of strength could dissuade them. Early observers of these encounters remarked that it was almost impossible to distinguish peaceful overtures from warlike ones, and just to be sure, groups who are meeting for the first time went armed and in full strength. The encounter began with a

---
101. Winiata (1967), p. 21.

firing-off of muskets on both sides, then the local warriors, stripped naked and armed, started up a wardance. The visitors followed with a *haka* of their own, and knelt down facing their hosts. A challenger came running out towards them, taunting them, leaping and making faces; he hurled a dart *(kōkiri)* into their midst and raced back to his own people with one of the visiting warriors hard on his heels. On some occasions there might be three challenges together, or one after the other. The last challenger was chased by the visitors in a body, and as they approached the local people the sham fight began, "a pell-mell sort of encounter in which numerous hard blows were given and received".[102] If the challenger was caught, he was especially roughly handled. The sham fight was a dangerous part of the ritual, because fighting could easily break out in earnest, but if it ended peacefully both sides joined in the *haka*, then pressed noses and wailed for the dead. After this the speechmaking began, followed by a feast, and the encounter had been successfully initiated. One such encounter was witnessed by Nicholas in 1814:

"The moment we were perceived, one of their women made a signal to us, by holding up a red mat and waving it in the air, while she repeatedly cried at the same time . . . '*haromai, haromai, haromai*' (come hither). Duaterra and Shungi, standing up with an air of unreserved confidence, fired off their loaded pistols . . . and instantly a report from six or seven muskets was heard to reverberate in our ears; and spears and firearms coming together in deafening collision, the noise very soon became insupportable. It would be hard to say which was more tormented during this conciliatory exhibition, the ear or the eye; for the war-dance now commencing was attended with such frightful gesticulations and such . . . convulsive distortions, that to see was no less painful than to hear. Yells, shrieks and roars, answered in responsive discord to all the clashing fury of their weapons . . . The warriors . . . stood up brandishing their paddles and making furious gesticulations, and we soon discovered that this was the signal for the sham fight to begin . . . One of Duaterra's warriors, running up and down along the beach with a long club made of whalebone in his hand, shook it at our party in token of defiance, and appeared daring them to leave their canoes. This menacing hero was suffered for sometime to pass unnoticed, the fury of our warriors not being yet worked up to the proper pitch; however, it was not long before this crisis arrived, and leaping on shore, they pursued the insulting challenger, who took to his heels the moment they had landed . . . The general attack was now to commence . . . The widest vociferations of the savage clamour were heard from both sides, and Duaterra's party being bravely repulsed for the moment . . . pursued by their adversaries, who, with their lances and spears, seemed to threaten their total destruction . . . After much terrible fighting, though never dangerous, both

---

102. Earle (1909), p. 101.

sides resolved to put an end to their hostilities in the same good humour with which they had commenced, and joined together in the dance and war-song."[103]

War dances are still being actively composed in New Zealand, but today they are mainly performed on the *marae* as entertainment. It is now extremely rare for visitors to perform a *haka* on entry to a strange *marae*. One occasion reported by Pine Taiapa was at the funeral of Sir Apirana Ngata, the great East Coast leader. When Tūhoe came to the *tangi* they were headed by two men carrying Ngata's portrait, and behind them in his honour marched a group of warriors bearing spears. As they approached the *marae* Tūhoe broke into a war dance. Ngāti Porou were not slow to reply. Ahipene Mutu, a huge, muscular man, called out, "*Kua takahia tātou, Ngāti Porou*" (We are trampled on, Ngāti Porou!") and began the famous war dance "Uhia!" All the local warriors leapt to their feet, and the roar of their voices met and drowned the Tūhoe out.

Locals now perform the war dance in honour of a distinguished visitor. After he is seated on the *marae* action songs and *haka* are performed for his entertainment, but this is regarded as diversion, not really as part of the ritual. *Haka* are taught in culture clubs, and are performed by men, lined in rows, bare-chested and wearing *piupiu* (flax kilts). They are chants of defiance, and as the warriors roar out the words they stamp their feet, roll their eyes, poke out their tongues and give the strong, aggressive actions in unison. One such war dance was composed on the East Coast after V-J Day in World War II:

Leader:
Kia kūtia! [all] *Au! au! Whiti! whiti! e!*[104]
Close your ranks—*au! au!* cross over! *e!*
Ka pāhi Itari! ka poharu Tiamani! Ka miere Tiapani!
Italy is finished! Germany is sunk! Japan is lost!

All:
Ko tō arero tēnā
Wasn't that your tongue (Hitler's)
E whatero i mua rā
You stuck out before
I ō rangi koroke whakapohautia
In the days of your rule
Kei te poharutanga, pou! pā!
Now you are finished! pa!

103. Nicholas (1817), Vol. I, pp. 127-9, 196-7.
104. In all chant texts, those words underlined are recited in unison by the chorus. Words not underlined are performed solo by the leader.

Leader:
Ka tohe au, ka tohe au
I will persist,

All:
Ka tohe au ki a Hitara
I shall keep after Hitler
Ki taku karaka i whakaura i te waru
My karaka berry boiled in the eighth month
E tū nei kāti Kāwana
Here stands the obstacle of the Allies
Kia kutia! au! au! kia wherahia! au! au!
Close your ranks au! au! open them! au! au!
E! kia rere atu te kōhuru
Let this murderer run
ki tawhiti titiro mai ai, ae! ae! aa!
And look at me from afar, Yes! Yes! aa!

When General Freyberg visited Gisborne after the war, a Ngāti Porou orator, referring to this war dance, asked him to produce Hitler's tongue as a trophy and a proof that the war was won.[105]

The war dance, then, is no longer a usual part of the rituals of encounter. The sham fight, too, has completely vanished from the ritual, nor is it ever performed in any other context. The *wero* or challenge is the only part which survives as a regular part of the *marae* ritual today. It is performed when an important visitor is about to enter the *marae*, and is a symbolic way of acknowledging his *mana*, at the same time expressing the strength of the local people. The *wero* begins before the visitor steps foot on the *marae*. As he stands at the gateway a young warrior (the *kai-wero*, or "challenger") in *piupiu* (flax kilt) and embroidered *tāniko* bandolier runs out, brandishing a *taiaha*, leaping, grunting and grimacing. He moves lightly, lifting his heels high to show agility, and threatening the visitor with his weapon. Close to the visitor, the warrior whirls his *taiaha* in an intricate drill, watching his face to see if he is intimidated. Slowly the challenger kneels, and taking a carved baton or stick *(rākau* or *mānuka)* from his waistband, he places it at the visitor's feet. In Taranaki, the district of Te Whiti the prophet, the challenger puts down a white feather, Te Whiti's symbol of "peace on earth, goodwill towards men". Then he stands and resumes his weapon drill, while the visitor impassively bends to pick up the baton, in token of peace. The baton should be laid pointing towards the visitors,* because if it is laid across his pathway it is a

---
105. Ngata (1943), p. 4.
* My thanks to Sir James Henare for this corrected version.

direct challenge to war. Women, even the Queen, should not pick up the baton; and traditionally the visitor himself should not touch it, but have one of his companions pick it up. The procedure of the *wero* varies according to the *mana* of the guest, and a particularly distinguished visitor may be challenged two or three times. In this case, the first challenge is called the *"rākau whakaara"*, or "warning baton". After it has been taken the challenger turns and runs back to his own people, and the second challenger emerges. He leaps about and whirls his weapon, eventually approaching close enough to lay the second baton, or *rākau takoto* (baton laid down). It is this baton which truly determines whether the party have come in war or peace, and it is sometimes called the *rākau taua* (baton for a war party). If this baton is peacefully collected, the challenger retires, and a third and final challenger approaches. Rapidly stamping his feet "so that dust flies on the *marae*", he performs the weapon drill, grunting and poking out his tongue. Then the warrior kneels, and lays down the final baton or *rākau whakawaha* (baton that clears the way), carefully watching his man. When the third baton is taken, the challenger whirls round, raising the *taiaha* high above his head with its blade facing into the *marae*, and leads the visitors in. There are tribal variations in detail, and in the names of the different batons, but broadly speaking this pattern holds.

In earlier times each challenger was chased by a visiting warrior, and if he was caught the local people were disgraced. The challenge is rarely taken up today, but in recent years when the former Governor-General Sir Bernard Fergusson visited Ahipara in Northland for the first time, the old custom was revived. When Sir Bernard arrived at the *marae* with the official party, he had a young man at his side, stripped for action. The challenger came down the *marae*, all threat and gesticulation, his weapon whirling close to the Governor's face. He knelt down, placed his baton, then started to run back to the meeting-house. About halfway he was felled by a flying tackle from behind—the Governor-General had followed the old custom, and met the challenge with a warrior of his own. The laughter and applause was tremendous, and the Governor's stocks in *mana* went sky-high.

The challenge is performed only to celebrities on their first visit to a *marae*, while they are still *waewaetapu* (sacred feet). It is the only element in the ritual which singles out an individual visitor for particular welcome, although visitors may be welcomed by name in the speechmaking. People who qualify for a *wero* hold some high office—MPs, Bishops, Cabinet Minister, the Prime Minister, Governor-General or Royalty; and well-known elders, despite their great *mana* in Maori circles, are not generally challenged. It seems that the *wero* acknowledges the power of the institution symbolised, rather than the man, and acts as a defence of the local *marae* from such high-powered invaders. Because the challenger represents the military strength of the tribe the part is played by a young man rather than an elder.

According to Eruera Stirling, the *wero* should never be used at a *tangi*, either as a challenge to visitors or to the dead. Although some experts claim that this is appropriate, Stirling says that the few times he has witnessed the *wero* in this context, it was an improvisation not based on traditional precedent. "The man is already dead, so why do that to him?"

Today the *wero* is not entirely serious and people are amused rather than intimidated by the warrior's antics. Challengers are mostly trained in culture clubs, which specialise in entertainment, and the *wero* becomes pageantry, not threat. There are a few traditional experts, for example Peter Awatere, who have been trained in accurate weapon drills, and understand the background of the *wero*, but these men are exceptional.

Karanga (call)

As soon as the visitors begin to enter the *marae* an old woman standing in the porch of the meeting-house or out on the *marae* starts up the call of welcome. She usually stands to the right side of the meeting-house (facing out), dressed in black, and she beckons to the visitors with slow, graceful sweeps of the greenery she holds in her hand. Sometimes there are three or four callers on the *marae*, and as the visitors advance the old women retreat, calling and waving their greenery. Because they lead the visitors into the *marae*, they are called the *pae arahi* (leaders over the threshhold). In front of the visitors walk their callers, also dressed in black, and all these old women call and answer as the party slowly advances. The *karanga* is a long, high call which sends greetings, invokes the dead, and brings an emotional atmosphere to the *marae*. The best callers have ethereal but carrying voices, in the words of an informant "like a bird, high, light and airy". Their calls are long and effortless, floating away to a sigh. The old women, sixty years old or more, usually give the *karanga*, and the best of them are known as "bugles" for the clarion quality of their calls. They invoke the dead in language borrowed from mythology, and suit the words to the occasion. Expert callers use ancestral names from genealogy, and the names of local rivers and mountains. As their voices call and answer, calling on the dead, the people on the *marae* are taken to the brink of tears—"Those old dears, they make you cry..."

Properly speaking, local callers should give the first *karanga*, but this does not always happen, and a *karanga* from outside the *marae* may be the first warning the local people have that a party is about to enter. As one call begins to fall and fade, another should begin, so that *karanga* alternate back and forth between the groups, but more often the *karanga* mix and clash. One old woman told me: "It's supposed to be that when one finish the other call, but you get one in the middle of the call, one finishing, and one starting up, all together"; and this is a fair description of what actually happens. Some visiting parties have no caller at all, and in this case the local people might send an old woman to bring them in, or else the local calls go unanswered. If the visitors are an important group, the local people in some areas stand at this time as a token of respect. The callers are women, but on some occasions an elder will stand and call out at the same time, *"Haere mai,*—(Tribal name), *haere mai"* (welcome, welcome).

According to some experts the local calls are named *maioha* (welcome), and visiting calls are *tīwaha*, but this distinction is not widely used. A few callers are especially dedicated *("tohi")* for the *karanga*, but most of them learn by observation and from elderly female relatives. Some culture clubs also teach girls to *karanga*. Young women do not call if there are older women present, and they are usually well into their fifties by the time they start to *karanga* regularly. One old lady expressed this rule by saying "Usually the young ones don't call. It's for the older ones to come to the front and call, otherwise it makes the visitors look small. If there's no old ones, though, then the young ones must step forward."[106]

Each *marae* has its recognised callers, and visiting parties try to bring at least one caller with them. People have to be chosen to call, and self-appointed experts are not particularly welcomed. On one occasion when the Maori Queen was visiting an East Coast *marae*, a young local woman moved forward and began to call. The elders were annoyed at her presumption, and sent someone out to fetch her back. An elderly Tūhoe woman who knew the true art of the *karanga*, was invited instead to welcome the *manuhiri tuārangi* (distinguished guest); and the young pretender received a stern lecture for her impudence.

The words of the *karanga* have a great deal in common with the language of Maori oratory, and people say in fact that *karanga* is the women's equivalent of speechmaking. The calls, of course, are much briefer than a speech, but they draw on a common range of mythological and poetic phrases, and follow roughly the same topics.

Local callers welcome their visitors and summon the dead:

Haere mai rā i te reo o te rā, haere mai rā!
Come in the voice of the day welcome!
Haere mai rā e kui mā, e koro mā i te pō
Come old women, old men from the underworld
E tama mā, i te karanga o tō tātou tipuna whare e tū mai nei
Come, children, to the call of our ancestral house, standing here
Huhuingia mai rā o tātou mate kia tangihia i te rā nei
Gather our dead to be wept over today
Haere mai rā!
Welcome!

106. Elsie Turnbull, interview 1971.

Visitors address the ancestral house, and farewell the dead:

Karanga rā te tupuna whare ki te kāhui pani
Call, ancestral house, to those who mourn
Ki ngā iwi e, karanga rā!
Call to the tribes!
Haere rā ngā mate o te tau, o te marama,
Farewell the dead of the year, of the month,
O tēnei rā e! Haere atu rā!
Of today—farewell!

The old women call back and forth, elaborating variations on these basic themes, and continuing to invoke the dead:

Local:
Hoki wairua mai rā e koro mā!
Return in spirit, elders!
Ki te karanga ki te pōwhiri i tā koutou kāhui pani
To the call and welcome of those who mourn you
Tēnei te pare kawakawa i a rātou
They wear the wreath of kawakawa leaves
Ka tū ki a koutou, karanga . . .!
For you—call!

Visitor:
Haere atu rā ngā mate o te tau, o te marama, o te wiki
Farewell the dead of the year, of the month, of the week
Kua huri atu ki tua o te ārai e!
Who have gone beyond the veil!
Haere atu rā!
Farewell!

If there is a distinguished visitor in the party arriving on the *marae*, the local callers give a special *karanga:*

E te manuhiri tuārangi
Visitor from afar
Nā taku pōtiki koe i tiki atu i tahu atu o te rangi,
Brought here by my beloved from the horizon of the sky,
I kukume mai! Haere mai! Haere mai!
Dragged here! Welcome! Welcome!
Haere mai! Haere mai!
Welcome! Welcome!

This *karanga* is said to have been first used in times of legend, when a young girl was captured by a monster called Te Ngārara-hua-rau, and taken to be his wife. She managed to smuggle a message to her kinfolk, warning them that she planned to bring the monster to visit their village. They should welcome him ceremoniously, but that night when he went to sleep, she would slip out and his house should be put to the torch. She persuaded the monster to make the journey, and as they approached the village, her relatives greeted him with this call. That night he was killed, but later the girl bore a child, half-human and half-monster, in retribution for her treachery.[107]

At a funeral, the calls summon the person who has died:

Local:
Hoki wairua mai rā e koro e!
Return in spirit, old man!
Huihuia mai rā o tātou mate tarurunui
Gather our great crowd of dead
Ka wehe ki te pō nui e, haere mai rā!"
Who have gone to the underworld, welcome!

Visitor:
Noho mai rā e koro i runga o tō tipuna whare,
Rest there, old man, upon your ancestral house,
Takoto mai . . . i!
Lie there!

On each occasion and with every new party of visitors, the words of the call are different, improvised by the old women to meet each situation as it arises, but they have common stylistic features and are drawn from a limited repertoire of phrases.

One of the most interesting aspects of the *karanga* is the summons it issues to the dead. By the time the callers have finished the dead are almost tangibly present on the *marae*. All the group, living and dead members alike, are brought together, making a long unbroken chain of kinsmen that stretches right back to Hawaiki and the Pō (Underworld).

The calls continue throughout the *pōwhiri* (action chant of welcome), and well into the *tangi* or wailing. In some tribes, particularly the Waikato, *karanga* are used as a general mark of appreciation throughout the *hui*. The old women *karanga* when gifts are laid down on the *marae*, when they enter the dining-hall and when they come out again. They *karanga* a concert party that stands to entertain them, and they *karanga* their friends as they start up the *kopikopi* (hula). One call I heard in this

107. Biggs ed. (1963), p. 16.

context went *"Korikori rā ngā putiputi o te taumata, korikori rā!"* (Shake, flowers of the summit, shake!") Visitors are *karanga'd* over to press noses, or to come for a meal, e.g. *"He karanga nā ngā ringa wera, karanga kai, karanga whakakī kōpū!"* ("A call from the cooks, come and eat, come and fill your bellies!")

The *karanga* is an ancient part of the ritual of encounter, and it was witnessed by a number of early travellers to New Zealand, for example Nicholas in 1817: "The moment we were perceived, one of their women made a signal to us by holding up a red mat and waving it in the air, while she repeatedly cried at the same time, 'Haromai, haromai, haromai . . .' During the whole ceremony of our introduction, the old woman never ceased waving her red mat and repeating a number of words, which, according to Duaterra, were prayers exclusively designed for the occasion, and suggested the first moment she beheld us."[108]

The *karanga* should always be performed in a proper ceremonial welcome, and if it is left out, the guests have reason to feel insulted. Eruera Stirling tells of one Waitangi Day many years ago, when two buses of Auckland people travelled to the *hui*, bringing a substantial donation with them. When they stepped on to the *marae*, they were given a perfunctory welcome, and no old woman stood to call them in. In the opening speech from the visiting side, the main Auckland speaker began by asking the cooking fires of the *marae* (symbolic of hospitality) to give them welcome, since the local people were so remiss: *"Karanga mai ki a mātou ngā kōhua, ngā tikera, ngā rākau, ngā mea katoa"* (Call to us, cooking fires, kettle, firewood, everything). He ended by threatening to leave the *marae*, taking the donation with him. At once the local people leapt up to make apologies, more intimidated by the threat of desertion than by the possible financial loss. Eventually the Auckland people were pacified but their sense of injury remained with them throughout the gathering, and they never did present their *koha*.

Poroporoaki (farewell)
At the same time as the old women are calling, an elder from the visiting party sometimes calls out a *poroporoaki* or farewell as he enters the *marae*. This is most usual at a *tangi*, where the elder is addressing the spirit of the person who has died, but it can be used on other occasions as well. The *poroporoaki* is poetic, chanted out loud as the elder advances, brandishing his walking stick, and its words are taken from the speeches of farewell that will later be addressed to the body:

Haere, e hoa, haere!   Haere ki ngā tipuna kua riro ki te pō.
Go friend, go!   Go to the ancestors who have gone to the night.

108. Nicholas (1817), pp. 127-8.

Ki te pō uriuri, te pō tangotango, te pō hekeheke.
The dark night, the dense night, the bottomless night.
Kua mau ki a koe te kākahu taratara,
You have donned the rough cloak of death,
Nō reira e koro, haere, haere, haere!
So old man, go, go, go!

The *poroporoaki* is particularly common in Northland. When a Northern group enters the meeting-house for a *tangi*, their chief elder begins to farewell the dead as he walks through the door, and continues as he stands by the corpse, weeping and speaking together. This version of *poroporoaki* is long and elaborate, almost like a speech. The Northern *poroporoaki* can lead orators of other tribes to feel that their privileges as *tāngata whenua* are being usurped. At one major funeral, the welcome to a Northern group was stopped short because the local elders felt that the Northerners were trying to open the speech-making.

Pōwhiri (action chant of welcome)
The *pōwhiri* (or *pōhiri*) is performed as the visitors move into the *marae*. The local people are lined up in front of their meeting-house, old women in front and younger women and men behind, with fronds of greenery in their hands. The leader *(kāea)* starts up the chant: *"Hei runga, hei raro, hei runga, hei raro"* ("raise, lower, raise, lower"), and the group begin to move their greenery in rhythmic actions, up and then down to hit the thighs in time with the chant. The *pōwhiri* follows a 3/4 rhythm, with the first beat stressed, and once the leader has everyone moving in unison, the chant begins:

Kūmea mai   [All]   *te waka!*[109]
Haul   the canoe!
Tōia mai!   [All]   *te waka!*
Drag   the canoe!
Ki te urunga!   *te waka!*
To the pillow   the canoe!
Ki te moenga!   *te waka!*
to the resting-place the canoe!
Ki te takotoranga i takoto ai, te waka e!
to the lying place to lie, the canoe!

On the *e!* the greenery is lifted and held, quivering. Often this chant is followed by another:

---

109. In all chant texts, those words underlined are recited in unison by the chorus. Words not underlined are performed solo by the leader.

Ka mate, ka mate!
It was death, it was death!
Ka ora, ka ora!
It is life, it is life!
Ka mate, ka mate!
It was death, it was death!
Ka ora ka ora!
It is life, it is life!
Tēnei te tangata pūhuruhuru
This is the hairy man
Nāna i tiki mai whakawhiti te rā!
Who has made the sun rise!
Hūpane, kaupane, hūpane, kaupane
Up this step, that step, this step, that step
Whiti te rā!
The sun rises!

Ka mate has a special story attached to it. When the Ngāti Toa fighting chief Te Rauparaha was trapped by his enemies at Taupo, a "hairy man" hid him and provided him with a ladder so he could climb from his refuge into the light of day. Te Rauparaha climbed up its crosspieces, the *"hūpane"* and *"kaupane"*, and escaped, and later composed this famous chant in celebration.[110]

Both these chants are also performed as war dances, but although the words are the same the performance is very different. War dances are performed by men, and the actions are aggressive and masculine. *Pōwhiri*, on the other hand, are performed mainly by women, with a gentle rhythmic waving of greenery, and the two types of dance cannot be confused. In the earlier times both chants were used as canoe-hauling songs *(ngeri)*.

The *pōwhiri* is only performed for important groups of visitors, and the greater their *mana* the more people join in, the louder they chant, and the more chants are given. The most common cycle are the two chants given above, and they may be repeated twice or even three times, to symbolise the effort of hauling this "canoe" with its precious freight on to the *marae*. There are other chants in currency, for example *Nō wai te motokā e topa mai ngā rori* (Whose is this motor car speeding towards me on the highway?), a topical chant which differs from the others in that it is sung rather than chanted; and *Haere mai e te Manuhiri tuārangi* (Welcome, visitor from afar), derived from an ancient *karanga:*

110. Ngata (1943), p. 7.

Haere mai, e te manuhiri tuārangi
Welcome, visitor from afar
Nā taku pōtiki koe i tiki atu i taha atu o te rangi
Brought here by my loved one from the horizon of the sky
I kukume mai! Haere mai! Haere mai!
Dragged here! Welcome! Welcome!
Haere mai! Haere mai!
Welcome! Welcome!

The other chant is part traditional, part topical. The first verse refers to the main visitor of the day arriving in his motorcar; the second recalls the ancient custom of slashing the body with flakes of obsidian to mourn those who have died:

Nō wai te motokā e topa mai ngā rori?
Whose is this car speeding towards me on the highway?
Aue, Nou nei Kāwana
It is yours Governor-General
Tika mai nei tāua, i nawa!
Coming straight towards me!
Aue hi! Aue hi! Aue hā!
Aue hi! Aue hi! Aue hā!

Hōmai he matā, kia haehae au
Give me a blade of obsidian, to slash myself
Aue! kia kotia i te kiri
To cut the skin
I awhi ai tāua, i nawa
You often embraced
Aue hi! Aue hi! Aue hā!
Aue hi! Aue hi! Aue hā!

There are only a limited number of *pōwhiri*, perhaps less than ten, in popular use.

A last type of *pōwhiri* is used when a body is brought on to the *marae*, but this type is rare and found mainly in the Taranaki and Ngāti Porou areas, e.g.:

Ripiripia, hae! hae!
Cut   slash slash!
Ripiripia, hae! hae!
Cut   slash slash!
E ā, turakina!
He is felled!

Paranikia te ūpoko
Head smashed
Te ngārara kai-tangata, hue!
By the man-eating insect! (death).

Greenery used in this *pōwhiri* is preferably *kawakawa*, the creeper which symbolises death; but on other occasions the silver-backed fern (*mamaku*) is used to symbolise peace and welcome. In practice people use anything that grows nearby—macrocarpa, palm fronds, even lily leaves at one *hui* I attended. The leaves are carefully collected after the *pōwhiri* is finished, and are not left lying around on the *marae*, because they have become *tapu* from being used in the ritual. The *pōwhiri* seems to have evolved as an amalgam of the war dance, which was performed as a "dance of welcome" on friendly visits, and the custom of women "waving garments and boughs of trees"[111] to welcome visiting parties. Downes in his article "Maori Etiquette"[112] claims that in the Whanganui area, garment waving was called *"tauwhiri"*, and the term *"pōwhiri"* was reserved for the waving of branches. Whatever its origins, the *pōwhiri* today is intended to impress rather than to intimidate, and the predominance of women in the performance shows that no hostility is intended.

Tangi (weeping)

Tangi or wailing expresses the desolation of losing those you love, and the dead are remembered at every Maori gathering. The old women dress in black, the colour of mourning, and as they advance into the *marae* they begin a high, uncanny wail, sometimes beating their breasts with a slow, hopeless motion, or waving a handkerchief as they cry. The dead have been summoned to the *marae* by the callers, and this cry recognises their presence. The *karanga* reminds people of those they have lost, and both local people and visitors join in the weeping. Particularly at a *tangi*, the wailing is loud and long, because death is so immediate. The visitors advance haltingly into the *marae*, heads bowed and tears falling. *Haere atu, ka tū ka tangi, haere atu, ka tū ka tangi* (Move, stand, and weep; move, stand, and weep). The *tangi* gives a moment of union to the ritual, because people not only remember their own dead, but also show respect and sympathy for the other group and its bereavements. At some distance from the meeting-house the visitors stop and stand, and wailing reaches a crescendo. If they stop a long way back, it is said that "they have not felt the warmth" of their welcome, and local elders call out *"Neke neke mai, neke neke mai"* ("Draw nearer"). Some of the women wail with a high, almost melodious

111. Polack (1938), p. 114.
112. Downes (1929), p. 151.

keening, which rises and fades in a dying fall; others use a low-pitched moaning sound, falling off into the "hum-wail". The wailing is stylised, and combines into a throbbing, harmonious chorus of grief. The *tangi* is evidently an ancient custom, witnessed by the earliest explorers, and it seems to have changed very little since then. John Logan Campbell described the *tangi* as follows:

"They stood for a minute or two in front of poor dead Ngatai, hanging down their heads, then the old women of the party broke into a well-sustained hum-m-. . . . After getting into the full swing of the hum-wail, the next stage was to end this with a short ejaculatory sentence in eulogy of the deceased, and when they had reached the grand full swing, the hum through the nose had disappeared, and the true wail-cry was given out loud and strong. When they had exhausted their sentences of eulogy, they then fell back upon a more self-scarifying way of proving their grief."[113]

Some of these eulogic sentences were as follows: "*He . . . taku makawe . . . hi*" ("Oh, the glory of my head"—literally, "hair"—alas), for a man; and for a woman, "*Haere e hine i te ara o ou tupuna, kia karanga nui mai, kei o kui . . . ha, kei o matua, hei karanga mai ki a koe*"[114] ("Go, girl, to the pathway of your ancestors, call loudly to your female and male ancestors, they summon you"). Some of the most elderly women still use sentences like this when they wail. Europeans are nearly always puzzled by this part of the ritual. It appears to express unbridled emotion, but people leave off crying quickly, and are soon enjoying themselves again, even at funerals. Part of the wailing is emotional, particularly at funerals, but on other occasions it is also a ritual performance showing respect for one's hosts and proper "Maori heart" rather than any personal grief. At modern gatherings handkerchiefs are usually in evidence, but in earlier times there was a saying, "*Nā te hupe me ngā roimata, ka ea ai te mate*" ("By tears and nose mucus, death is avenged") and noses were left to drip unchecked. Also in earlier days, women took obsidian flakes and slashed at their bodies until they bled, but today emotion is more restrained, and often a group show their respect simply by standing in silence with their heads bowed. Only women wail, although men weep silently and bow their heads. If a great friend has died, a man might show his grief by wailing out loud, but this is very rare. After wailing for a time, close female relatives of the local people or the dead man leave their group, and join the local women on the porch. At this point one sometimes hears the *tangi ātahu* or *tangi kōrero* (talking wail). Here a mourner tells a friend of her grief by breaking out into a spontaneous chant, talking through her tears. A wife might tell how much she loved her husband who has just died, and

113. Campbell (1881), pp. 172-3.
114. Taylor (1855), p. 222.

recall the wonderful times they had together, or a friend might tell of her sympathy and grief. These chants are an expression of true emotion, and follow no set form. Baucke in 1905 recorded a woman addressing the son of the woman who had died:

"Weep, orphan, weep, not that tears bring back our dead, but they bring the loved one nearer to our hearts ... Orphan, my orphan, the bitter south wind blows; who will shelter you now? Who will look for your homecoming? Who will ask when you are absent—where is he now? Who will think of your comfort? A wife, maybe—when the time comes. A sister, maybe—but not for long! Does she see us? .. More now a mother than ever, for now we can see it. Now she is gone, we see things more clearly. We have angered her often; grieved her, flouted her wisdom; slighted her wishes; thought ourselves clever when we deceived her! But she has recompensed all with the love of a mother. Think of it, orphan! The love of a mother!"[115]

When the wailing has continued for ten or fifteen minutes, a local elder calls out, *"Kua ea, kua tae mai koutou, kua ea"* ("It is requited, you have come, it is requited"), and on this signal the visitors move to the benches that have been set out for them on the border of *marae ātea*. At a Northland or Tainui *tangi*, all the visiting women go at this point to sit with the mourners, but in East Coast areas, only close female kin of the deceased go to the porch or the "house of death."

Whaikōrero (oratory)

The greater part of *te kawa o te marae* or *marae* etiquette centres upon the regulation of oratory—who may speak, in what order, and how they structure their remarks. In this section we will first consider how the orators are selected; then the ordering of speeches between host and visiting "sides" and within each "side"; and finally the structuring of speeches and how they are evaluated. The exchange of speeches during the welcome is often described as *mihimihi*, and the term *"mihi"* broadly applied to the greeting ritual originates here. The less formal, more discursive speeches later in the gathering can be referred to as *take*, and in these speeches the orator emerges even more clearly as an individual, with his own opinions, sense of humour and idiosyncracies.

Orators

The orator is an esteemed figure in the Maori world. A skilled orator is a master of genealogy, ancient chants, local history and proverbs. Not only is he erudite, but a consummate actor as well. His movements are dramatic and timed to give the best possible effect to the statements he is making.

115. Baucke (1905), p. 34.

The finest orators are well-known throughout the country, and when one of their number stands to speak on the *marae*, even the cooks leave what they are doing and come to listen. Oratory is the way for a man to win fame in Maori circles, and these men move about to a great many *hui* every year. On each *marae* their words are listened to with respect, and their performance watched with interest.

The pathway to these heights begins on the home *marae*. Men with *tāngata whenua* status in the district, either by long residence or by ownership of Maori land, who can also claim good descent, qualify as potential speakers. Men without these qualifications but with forceful personalities can also qualify, although their path is a little more difficult. As these men approach *kaumātua* status (from fifty on), they begin to groom themselves as speakers, attending many *hui*, learning chants and sometimes acting as back-up speakers for their group. If such a man shows confidence and ability on the *marae*, by the time he is fifty or so he will probably be acting as a regular speaker, both on the home *marae* and on visits to other districts. Each *marae* has its recognised complement of speakers, perhaps two or three elders and several back-up speakers; and at a very large *hui* speakers from other *marae* in the district are recruited to join the local "side". With the urban drift, some rural *marae* are left very short of speakers, and one or two remaining elders in the area may find themselves acting as regular speakers on perhaps four or five local *marae*.

A recognised local speaker learns the intricacies of local genealogy and history, and acquires an adequate arsenal of chants, but if he wants to become widely known as an orator, this is not enough. "You'll never be a man if you stay at home," one of my informants was advised when he was a young man, "you have to show your face around." Speakers who aspire to join this exclusive cadre of well-known orators attend every major *hui* they can, making dramatic speeches at moments of peak attention and fixing themselves on the memories of those who attend. In this way a man can become "known" to thousands of *hui*-goers, and over the years he builds up a reputation which assures him of a respectful hearing. To maintain this reputation he continually extends his mastery of genealogy and chants, and attends major *hui* at frequent intervals. One dramatic gesture on the *marae* and a man will be talked of for months later. At one recent *tangi* the body was laid out in a marquee so that the host of mourners could be accommodated. A well-known speaker who is also a minister stood up to criticise this arrangement, on the grounds that it was undignified for the corpse to be lying with his feet to the four winds. Before he launched into his impassioned denouncement, he tore off his clerical collar and hurled it to the *marae*, saying that on this occasion he preferred to speak as a man, not as a priest. The drama of the gesture was greatly appreciated, and is still talked of, almost two years later. Here the *marae* is very like the theatre. Certain actors become famous and widely acclaimed, and whenever they walk on to the stage, it is into an atmosphere of expectation.

Because the orator is so valued a role, there are many metaphorical names for him in Maori: *manu kōrero* (talking bird), *korimako* (bell bird), *pū kōrero* (talking flute), *waha kōrero* (talking mouth), and *māngai* (mouthpiece). The most common term, however, is simply *kai kōrero* or "speaker".

There are other restrictions about who may speak on the *marae*. In many areas sons are forbidden to speak while their fathers are alive, and younger brothers may not speak, while their elder brothers are alive. This principle is exemplified in the proverb *"He nui muringa hei kī mai i tōna angaanga"* ("No matter how important the younger may become, he must defer to his elder brother"), and it is particularly followed in the Te Arawa and Tūhoe areas. The *tuakana-teina* (elder brother-younger brother) distinction ramifies throughout genealogy, so that senior male descent lines are said to be *tuakana* to junior ones, and a man might use this distinction in an argument, telling his opponent to sit down "because you are *teina* to me". This can, however, be a double-edged weapon, and the man in his turn might be told to sit down because he, too, is *teina* to someone else present. When the senior male in the family is absent from the *hui*, or if he delegates his right to speak to a younger kinsman, the rule can be by-passed, but often men are in their sixties or more before they first speak on the *marae*, and others never speak at all. One Northland elder whose father died at ninety-five, was seventy-five when he gave his first speech, and this sort of case is not uncommon.

The other great question on the *marae* is whether or not a woman should stand to speak. In most tribes the answer is emphatically "No", and only the most foolhardy female would dispute it. In these areas it is said that *whaikōrero* is *tapu*, and not fitting for women. In East Coast tribes, however, including Te Whānau-a-Apanui, Ngāti-Porou and Ngāti Kahungunu, high born women have the right to speak on the *marae*, and it is also said that this is true in parts of Northland; although this seems to be open to some debate. Certainly in early accounts of *hui* in Northland, women were recorded as delivering orations on the *marae*.[116] The custom is said to date from the time of the Great Fleet, when the Mātātua canoe made its landfall at Whakatāne. The men went ashore to explore, leaving the chieftainess Muriwai in charge of the canoe (some say it was her niece Wairaka). A tidal rip caught the canoe, dislodged the anchor and the Mātātua began to float out to sea. Usually only men were permitted to paddle a canoe, but in this moment of danger Muriwai took up a paddle, calling out, *"Kia whakatāne au i ahau"* ("Let me make myself a man"), and managed to paddle the Mātātua back to safety. For

---

116. Nicholas (1817), Vol. II, p. 111; Polack (1838), p. 119.

this heroic act, it is said, Muriwai's female descendants have been permitted to speak on the *marae* ever since.

After its landfall in Whakatāne the Mātātua canoe was taken to Northland by Puhi-Moana-Ariki, the founder of the Ngā Puhi tribe, and this could explain why East Coast and Northland share the custom. However, the Tūhoe people, who also descend from the Mātātua canoe, do not allow women to speak on the *marae*.

Famous female speakers of.the East Coast include Hine Matioro of Ngāti Porou, Materoa Reedy of Ngāti Porou, Mihi Kotukutuku of Te Whānau-ā-Apanui, and Hine Katorangi of Ngāti Kahungunu. When Hine Katorangi's friend Te Aputa, chieftainess of Ngāti Raukawa, died many years ago in the Manawatu area, Hine Katorangi came to her *tangi* at Poutu *marae*. After local speakers had welcomed her party, Hine Katorangi stood to speak. The local elders led by the redoubtable Taite te Tomo, jumped up in a fury, telling her to sit down, that this was not their custom. Hine Katorangi turned on them with scorn, telling them she had no intention of addressing them, but she wanted to talk to her friend Te Aputa. She proceeded to farewell the dead woman, and the elders sat in silence, not daring to interrupt her again.[117]

The East Coast custom is occasionally used to infuriate guests, as visitors from other areas consider it an insult to be welcomed by a woman. Years ago Te Arawa and Ngāti Porou were competitors for a football cup. Ngāti Porou won it, but no sooner had they taken possession than Te Arawa challenged them again. and this time Te Arawa won. Ngāti Porou were annoyed by this, and when Te Arawa came to collect the trophy the local people sent up one female orator after another to welcome them. Arawa sat there fuming, but because they were visitors, there was nothing they could do about it.[118]

A final exploit of one of these intrepid women is the story of Mihi Kotukutuku, who lived at the turn of this century. The reader should first be reminded though, that if a speaker on the *marae* becomes impossibly offensive, the traditional way to silence him was for the old women to bend over and flip up their skirts at him *(whakapohane)*. This graphically expressed the opinion that the speaker was *noa*, like a woman, and should no longer speak on the *marae*.

Mihi Kotukutuku was attending a *tangi* in the Arawa country, where women are not allowed to speak on the *marae*. The hosts had opened the oratory, and now it was the guests' turn. The East Coast men were in a dilemma, because the old lady outranked them all and was properly their first speaker. After a pause, she stood, and launched into a chant. Seconds later the Arawa men led by Mita Taupopoki were on their feet yelling in

---

117. My thanks to Joan Metge for the details of this story.
118. My thanks to Tilly Reedy for this story.

outrage, cursing her and telling her to sit down. The old chieftainess serenely ignored them, and continued her speech to the end, then she looked over to the local elders and addressed them with all the pride of her descent. "You Arawa men! You tell me to sit down because I am a woman, yet none of you would be in this world if it wasn't for your mothers. *This* is where your learning and your grey hairs come from!" And turning her back on them, she bent over and flipped up her skirts in the supreme gesture of contempt. The Arawa men sat speechless, dumbfounded by the grandeur of the insult, and in that silence the old woman became a legendary figure. She left the *marae* unrebuked, and East Coast people have been telling the story ever since. The sequel to it came at Mihi Kotukutuku's own funeral, many years later. Three busloads of Te Arawa arrived outside the *marae*, and as they entered their chief elder Kepa Ehau began loudly to curse the old woman. "Mihi Kotukutuku! Good job you died! You were the first woman ever to trample the plumes of my ancestor, and now you will be the last! Good job you died!" At first Mihi's sons were astonished and furious, and wanted to throw Te Arawa off the *marae*, but then they remembered her famous exploit in their territory and realised that in a curious fashion Te Arawa were doing her honour. Only a most chiefly woman could be worth such abuse, and that they only dared deliver it once she was dead was a further tribute to her *mana*. As the saying goes, "A chief does not bother to quarrel with a commoner."[119]

This custom still persists in the East Coast, and high-born East Coast women occasionally assert their rights elsewhere. On one recent occasion when such a woman spoke on a Waikato *marae* one of the local elders switched off the amplifying system in disgust. An even more dramatic confrontation arose when a group of Ngāti Porou were attending an important Waikato funeral several years ago. During the visitors' speeches, a high-born young Ngāti Porou woman stood to address the gathering. Waikato elders jumped up angrily, telling her that in earlier years she would have been killed for such an outrage, and put into the *hāngi*. The Ngāti Porou men were also furious that such a young woman could shame them in front of their hosts, and were preparing to walk off the *marae* when one of their elders stood and began to speak. He gave the young woman's genealogy, tracing it through lines that were at every point senior to Waikato counterparts, and established her superiority over her detractors beyond any doubt. He closed by saying that if Waikato had in earlier times dared to offer such an insult to Ngāti Porou, they would have ended up in the earth oven. Waikato were silenced, but not the Ngāti Porou men, and their criticism of her conduct once the welcome was over was loud and abusive. However, these female orators are now few; the rural East Coast areas are becoming depopulated, and *hui* are far less

---

119. My thanks to Eruera and Amiria Stirling for this account.

frequent than in the past. When a woman speaks on the *marae* today she should ideally follow the male orators, and justify herself by referring to her illustrious predecessors.[120] In other areas women speak only in the meeting-house at night, and then only when they have something important to say.

Turns of talk

The first rule in the order of speaking is that one man speaks at a time. Once an orator stands on the *marae*, he should properly be immune to interruption. If someone is not qualified to speak and yet stands, he might be ordered to sit down *("E tau ki raro!")*, and if a speaker becomes impossibly offensive it has already been mentioned that the old women might bend over and flip up their skirts at him *(whakapohane)*. Long-winded speakers are not popular; after half an hour or so people start to get restless and call out, *"Kia poto te kakau o tō paipa"* ("Shorten the stem of your pipe"), and if the speaker doesn't take the hint one of the women of his group may stand and start up his *waiata*, effectively cutting him off. Drunks get similar treatment, but as long as a speaker does not seriously offend the decorum of the *marae* no-one is permitted to interrupt him. The greater the *mana* of the speaker, the more secure he is. Even if another group should arrive on the *marae*, the speakers have their say and the visitors have to wait.

Sometimes today when a *hui* is being run to a strict timetable (for example, if a distinguished visitor is expected shortly), a long-winded orator may be silenced by the younger men. This kind of interruption is not kindly received, and the elders resentfully mumur about *"ngā taita-mariki tukituki tahā"* (young men who like to break calabashes), or demand a public apology.

At King Koroki's funeral in 1966, when Te Arawa were being welcomed on to the *marae*, the Governor-General's aide-de-camp arrived, and Te Arawa were asked if they would mind cutting their speeches short. They took this as a grave insult. In retaliation their orators began delivering interminable speeches, using the longest chants and *waiata* they could think of, and they utterly refused, as was their right, to give up the *marae*. The Governor's aide had to wait, and the filibuster lasted for several hours. Round about mealtimes, the cooks may safely interrupt men of no particular importance, but if they should happen to cut short a well-known orator invective is liable to fly. Because of this rule of non-interruption, heckling is unheard of on the *marae*, and when some young Maori students tried it recently at the Waitangi Day celebrations, they were criticised for their want of manners.

120. For a more detailed account of female East Coast leaders, see Apirana Mahuika's excellent thesis on this topic.

Once in a while two men stand at once to speak. In this case, hosts should defer to visitors, and lesser men to those of greater *mana*. On one occasion, however, when the then Prime Minister, Mr Fraser, was being welcomed to Te Arawa, both men were hosts and of about equal *mana*. They glared at each other, but neither sat down: then they smiled, turned their backs on each other and proceeded to deliver simultaneous orations. This way neither man lost face, but theirs was a most uncommon solution.[121]

The order of speakers within a "side" is significant. In the East Coast area the most important elder speaks first, to trace genealogical links between the local people and the visitors. In many other areas, however, the position of honour is that of the last speaker, who puts down the gift and rounds off the discussion. His is the definitive speech, and it is a proud man who can say, "No-one can speak after me." It may well be that on the host side the most knowledgeable elder speaks first so that he can identify the visitors and cue the following local speakers; whereas on the visiting side the most important elder has the honour of handing over the gift. Whichever position he occupies, the main speaker is known as the *kākā kura* or red parrot, the bird that leads the flock, and he even more than the others speaks for his group. Sometimes the order of speakers is arranged in advance, outside the gateway of the *marae* or before the visitors arrive — at one *hui* I attended there were twelve speakers on the local bench who spoke in order from left to right. On other occasions the order is decided on the spot; the leading elder gives other speakers "the nod", or they confer in whispers for a minute or two before one of their number stands to speak. Sometimes the order is unpredictable, even to members of the group, and speakers simply stand when they feel like it.

Between sides, the order of speaking varies in different tribal areas. There are two main regional styles; *pāeke, pā harakeke*, or *taiawhiao*, where all the speakers of the local side are followed by all the visitors; and *utuutu, tū mai tū atu, tū atu tū mai, whakawhiti* or *tauhokohoko*, where local speakers and visitors alternate, local orators speaking first and last. To my present knowledge, the styles distribute as follows:

Pāeke (in blocs)		*Utuutu* (alternating)
Northland	Ngāti Porou	Te Arawa
Ngāti Whātua	Rongo-Whakaata	Tūwharetoa
Ngāti Awa	Te Aitanga-a-Māhaki	Ngai-te-Rangi
Tūhoe	Ngāti Kahungunu	Waikato tribes
Te Whakatōhea	Taranaki tribes &	Ngāti Raukawa
Te Whānau-ā-Apanui	Whanganui	Ngāti Toa

This regional variation is apparently long-established, and there is evidence for it in the writing of early observers. In 1814 Nicholas observed

121. My thanks to Jock McEwen for this story.

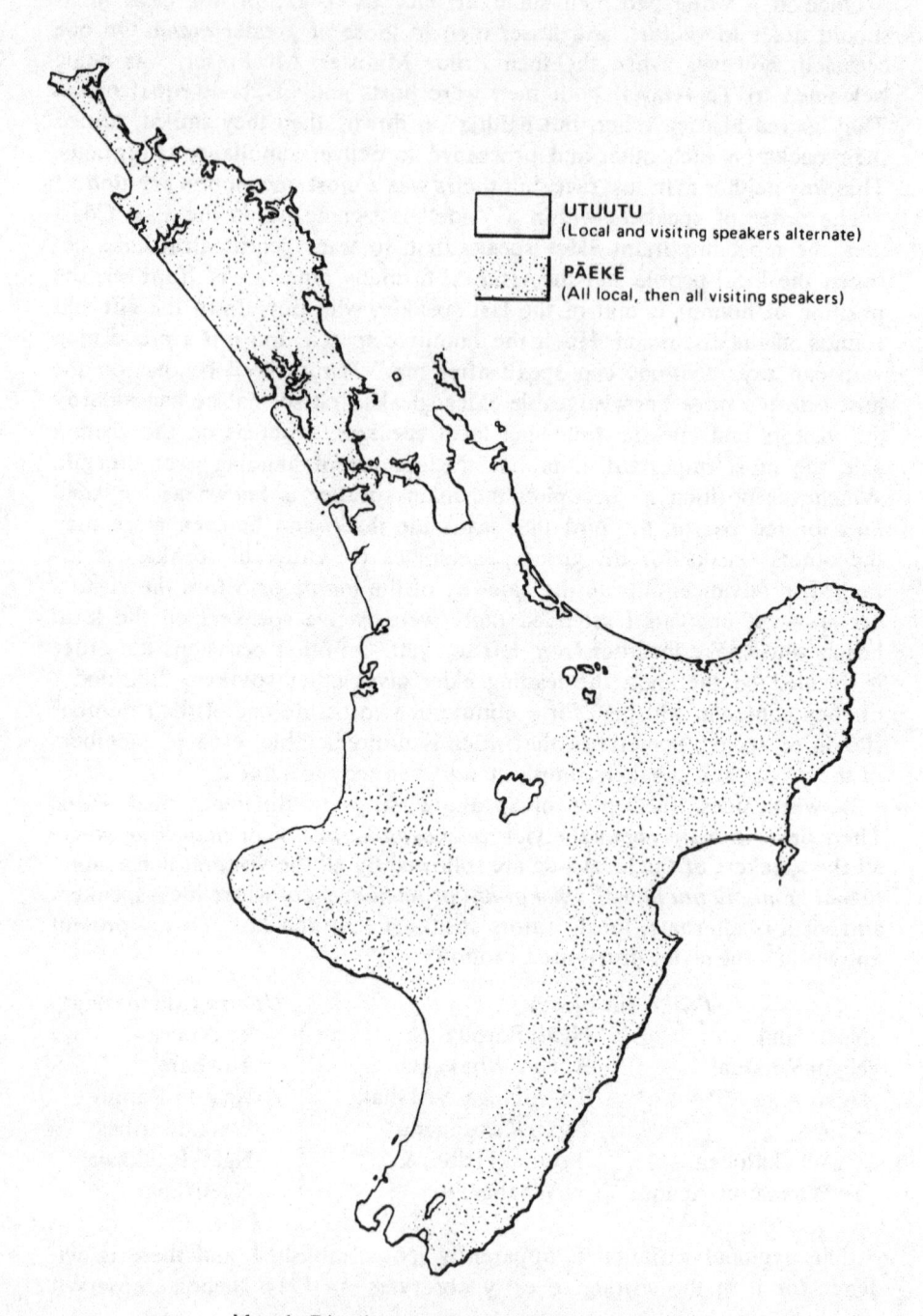

Map 6: Distribution of *Whaikōrero* Patterns

UTUUTU
(Local and visiting speakers alternate)

PĀEKE
(All local, then all visiting speakers)

the *pāeke* style at a *hui* in the Bay of Islands;[122] and in 1863 Maning described a similar etiquette for the Hokianga district, also in Northland: "His speech is ended and he 'falls in'. Some three or four others 'follow on the same side' . . . Then who, of all the world, starts forth from 'ours' but my diabolical old acquaintance the 'Relation Eater'."[123] On the other hand, E. J. Wakefield, visiting the Tūwharetoa people in about 1840, succintly described the *utuutu* etiquette: "An orator spoke from either party alternately."[124]

The *utuutu* etiquette seems to be broadly associated with tribes which stem from the Te Arawa and Tainui canoes of the Great Fleet. These canoes, according to legend, had close affiliations at the time of migration. The priest Ngātoro-i-rangi, who was supposed to travel on the Tainui canoe was lured on board Te Arawa instead by its captain Tama-te-kapua. To make matters worse, during the voyage he was cuckolded by the captain, and in his fury summoned up a storm which almost sank the canoe. When Te Arawa finally landed in New Zealand, they made landfall at Whangaparāoa shortly after the Tainui canoe. After that the two canoes went their separate ways. Te Arawa went to Maketu near Tauranga, now the district of the Ngai-te-Rangi people, and some of the crew travelled inland. The descendants of Tama-te-kapua settled around Rotorua and became the Arawa tribe, and the descendants of Ngātoro-i-Rangi settled around Taupo, and became the Tūwharetoa people.

The Tainui, on the other hand, sailed south from Whangaparāoa to the Tamaki Strait, just outside Auckland. The crew members went ashore to explore, and found that only a narrow isthmus separated them from another harbour, which they named the Manukau. They hauled the Tainui across the isthmus, and sailed down the West Coast to Kāwhia, where they finally settled. Their descendants spread out and became the Waikato people, occupying a large section of the North Island from south Auckland to Te Kuiti. Many generations later, when Te Rauparaha led a joint expedition of Ngāti Toa and Ngāti Raukawa warriors south in the 1820s, Tainui descendants were established in the southern part of the North Island as well.

The *pāeke* style seems to be associated with a different set of migrations, those of the Awa people. According to some legendary accounts,[125] Ngāti Awa were pre-Fleet occupants of Northland who migrated south to the Bay of Plenty and from there extended their influence right along the East Coast. Other accounts claim that the Ngāti Awa were brought to the Bay of Plenty by the Mātātua canoe, which later sailed to Northland. In

---

122. Nicholas (1817), Vol. II, p. 94.
123. Maning (1863), p. 47.
124. Wakefield (1845), Vol. I, p. 462.
125. For an account of the Ngati Awa history, see Smith (1896), pp. 38-47.

any case, there is a clear link between Northland and the Bay of Plenty and East Coast tribes, including Ngāti Awa, Tūhoe, Te Whakatōhea, Te Whānau-ā-Apanui, Ngāti Porou, Rongo-Whakaata, Te Aitanga-ā-Māhaki and Ngāti Kahungunu, all said to have been subject to the Awa influence. The Awa people later migrated to the Bay of Plenty to Taranaki, where they are known as Te Ati Awa, and from there to the district around Wellington. There are many conflicting stories about the directions of these migrations; for example the Taranaki people claim that the Awa people originated in Taranaki, and migrated from there to the North Cape, and later to the Bay of Plenty, but the general lines of migration are clear, and they do broadly link those areas which exhibit the *pāeke* style of oratory.

One unusual pattern occurs in Whanganui, where although the usual pattern is all host then all visiting speakers, at funerals the visitors in a party speak first. This is said to be because the dead person overshadows everyone else present, and visitors should farewell him without any preliminary greetings from their hosts. After the burial, however, things return to normal and the local people speak first. This custom finds some parallel in Northland, where the leading elder of visitors to a *tangi* farewells *(poroporoaki)* the dead upon entry. The *poroporoaki* is practised in other areas too, but in Northland it most nearly amounts to a speech. These practices often cause inter-regional difficulties. Visitors to a Whanganui *marae* may refuse to speak before they are welcomed, and if Whanganui orators attempt to address the dead in this fashion on an outside *marae*, they may be accused of following a "first come, first served" procedure. Northland speakers, too, may be met with disapproval for their prolonged *poroporoaki*.

Within these stylistic regions there may be local variations in etiquette due to peculiar historical circumstances, and on borders where the two styles meet there may be some overlap, with nearby communities practising different etiquettes according to their major affiliations, but generally speaking the styles distribute in solid geographical blocks (Map 6, p.154).

The most problematical area in this respect is Northland, where although the traditional and probably the dominant pattern is *pāeke*, a large amount of local variation seems to occur. Informants, even elders, from this area give quite diverse accounts of local oratory patterning, and a great many informants don't in fact seem to be certain about their local pattern. This contrasts strongly with all other areas, where decisive and consistent accounts of the oratory pattern are easily gained. It could be that in Northland there is a far greater tolerance for variation in oratory procedures, and that local pride is less strongly attached to this part of the ritual. On some Northern *marae*, for example, it is possible to honour a distinguished party of visitors by adopting their *kawa* (etiquette) for that occasion. At a recent *hui* in Waimā, the Waikato people brought the body of a Northland woman who had married into the Maori Queen's family back to her kinfolk for mourning. On this occasion the Waimā group adopted the Waikato alternating pattern, and held the speeches on the *marae* as a tribute to the *mana* of the Queen, but the body was placed inside the meeting-house in accord with local custom. Waikato people who did not wish to sleep with the dead were given the option of resting in a marquee outside.[126] Even this sort of concession to visiting custom, however, would be unthinkable in most areas.

There are two other factors which might explain the variability of Northland *marae* procedure. Firstly, it seems that in Northland, small-scale groups operating quite independently of each other were established long before European contact. Northland was one of the earliest areas of Maori settlement, and it provided an optimal environment for *kūmara* cultivation. Under these conditions one could expect a rapid rise in population, and certainly by the time of earliest European contact, there were a large number of groups of about sub-tribal size established in Northland, each occupying its own territory and communicating with other groups largely through warfare. In this situation one could expect marked local variations in *marae* ritual to have developed.

After contact, however, the established patterns were disrupted. With the arrival of the musket, a military leader like Hongi Hika could forge an unprecedented union of Northern groups, arm them, and lead them to military success. Northland also received the first and most devastating wave of European settlement. Most traders, whalers, missionaries and settlers came first to the Bay of Islands, and many of them went no further. There was no opportunity for gradual adjustment between *pākeha* and Maori, and so it was in this area that culture contact had its most massive impact. To the missionaries, for example, can be attributed the fact that in some Northern *marae* today, hymns are used instead of *waiata* (ancient songs) at the end of a speech, and Christian prayers replace *tauparapara* (chants) at the beginning. If one assumes an initial diversity of custom followed by a period of cultural attack, both local variation in procedure and some uncertainties about the "proper" pattern in Northland make a good deal of sense.

In all other areas, the rule which governs the choice of style is that visitors should follow the local pattern. Any attempts by a visiting group to impose their own rules of *marae* procedure on the host *marae* will be heartily resented. At one East Coast *tangi* a Te Arawa elder stood to criticize the local people for letting a younger brother speak in ceremonial welcome to their guests. He was quickly told to "put your *kawa* (etiquette) in your bag and take it home with you," and had to accept the rebuke. People prefer their own style of oratory, and criticise other patterns;

---

126. Pat Hohepa (personal communication).

for example those who follow the alternating etiquette say it is far better because it gives visitors an early opportunity to identify themselves and saves the local people from welcoming them in ignorance. Those who follow the *pāeke* pattern, on the other hand, say it is better because there is no need to match numbers, and no-one is missed out from the speech-making. Differences in etiquette can cause problems to visitors, and on occasion a party will blunder by following the wrong pattern. In this case the local people will correct them, often quite caustically, and the visitors lose face for their ignorance. Widely travelled elders with a knowledge of different local *kawa* are therefore a valuable asset to a visiting party.

The other major question to be decided in oratory is how many speakers should stand on each side. In the *pāeke* etiquette, where all the hosts speak in turn followed by the visitors, this is not really a problem. Each side sends up as many speakers as seems appropriate to the *mana* of the occasion and the number available on their "side", and there is no compulsion for the two sides to match numbers, although gross differences may signal differences in *mana*. Two or three speakers can give a respectable welcome; in Northland, perhaps only one local orator may stand. In the alternating *utuutu* etiquette, however, the sides must match, except that locals speak first and last. In this situation trials of strength readily develop, with one side trying to talk the other side into the ground. Visitors sometimes come with a high complement of orators, each speaker equipped with his own chants and *waiata*, and the local people have to try to round up a matching side. I have heard of cases where there were twelve, fifteen or even twenty speakers on a side, although a typical number would be three or four. In this case, when the losing side gives up, the winning side puts forward several more orators, breaking the alternating pattern and stressing their superiority. In these competitions the visitors have the whip-hand, because they can close off the proceedings by putting down their gifts. On the other hand if the locals cut out early the visitors may decide that they have been inadequately welcomed, and refuse to put down their gift at all.

Turns of talk are signalled in the alternating etiquette by the phrase "*Ka huri*" ("Over to you"), but in *pāeke* speakers of a side succeed each other without comment until their last speaker calls out, "*Kua pāhi tēnei taha*" (this side has passed), or "*Kua mutu mātou*" ("We have finished"). In both etiquettes, when all the speeches are completed a local speaker calls the visitors over to press noses and shake hands.

Structure of whaikōrero*

The structure of *whaikōrero* is properly a major topic in its own right, and a detailed study has in fact been completed by a native speaker, Robert

---

*Translations in this section were made in collaboration with Eruera Sterling.

Mahuta, at the University of Auckland. In this section, therefore, only the broad structure of *whaikōrero* will be examined, and illustrations will be confined to the better-known chants and sayings. Information for this section is taken from a sample of fifty speeches recorded in the field and transcribed by a native speaker, Mrs Rangi Motu; and from a wide range of interview material.

Typically, a speech begins with a warning shout *(whakaarara* or *whakatūpato)* which claims the *marae* for the speaker, and catches the attention of his audience. The most common shout is *"Tihei . . . mauri ora!"* or *"Tihere mauri ora!"* ("I sneeze—it is life!"). The orator shouts it from his bench then rises, ready to launch into chant. At a funeral he might call out *"Tihei . . . mauri mate!"* ("I sneeze, it is death"), as more appropriate to the occasion. There are a range of longer chants also known as *whakaarara*, once used by sentries patrolling the terraces of a fortified *pā* and of these the most common begins: *Kia hiwa rā! kia hiwa rā!"* ("be watchful, be wakeful!"):

Kia hiwa rā! kia hiwa rā!
Be watchful! Be wakeful!
Moe araara ki te matahi tuna
You have to stay awake to catch eels
Moe araara ki te matahi taua!
You have to stay awake to catch a war party!
Ka tiritiria, ka reareaia a tama tū ki tōna hiwa rā,
Scatter, rise up, stand in your places,
Kia hiwa rā! kia hiwa rā!
Be watchful! Be wakeful!
Kia hiwa rā tēnei tuku, kia hiwa rā tērā tuku
Be alert on this terrace. Be alert on that terrace
Kei whakapurua koe ki te toto,
Or someone will wound you and make you bleed.
Papaki tū ana te tai ki Te Reinga
The tide is beating to Te Reinga
Eke panuku! Eke Tangaroa!
Move on! Up Tangaroa!
Hui e! Taiki e!
Together! It is done!

The authority and drama of this initial call does much to capture the audience's interest, and a masterful speaker prolongs it while he takes off his coat and hat and prepares to take possession of the *marae*, as a useful piece of by-play.

Some speakers remain seated while they recite their chant or *tauparapara* as well, and this really arouses the audience's curiosity. A voice arises from the speaker's bench, but the orator is not immediately apparent. The *tauparapara* (also called *"tau"*; or *"pātere"* on the East Coast) is a class of chants used at the beginning of a speech to establish the orator's claim to esoteric knowledge. They are recited in a rapid rhythmic incantation, illustrated by gestures and brandishings of the orator's walking-stick. Usually he stands in one place for the *"tau"*, but some orators stride up and down the *marae* in time with the cadence of the chant. The chants are full of archaic words and obscure historical references, and they have a distinctive "spell" quality. The roll of the voice and the mystery of the words lend the *tauparapara* its dignity, and the recitation conveys *mana* and *tapu* rather than specific information. The text of the chant has to be followed exactly; an error or deviation brings bad luck, and in any case it will detract from the speaker's *mana*. These *tau* are not always used; on informal occasions they are not really appropriate, and some speakers do not know any. If a speaker wants to impress he may string two or even three *tau* together at the beginning of his speech, but this can be overdone. *Tau* may also be used in the body of the speech to illustrate a particular point the speaker is making. There are hundreds of these chants, and they are still being composed, although only by the most expert elders. Their origins are diverse, including chants originally used for tree-felling, carving, adzing, dragging canoes, paddling canoes and sentry watch, but today their function is generalised, and virtually any incantation can be given at the beginning of a speech.

There are a number of types of *tauparapara*, appropriate to different types of occasion. Some are used particularly at funerals, while others can be used on a wide range of occasions; some are used by locals, and others by visitors, and there are special chants to be used by visitors on their first visit to a *marae*. Most *tauparapara* are recited by the orator, but other chants, called *pōkeka, ngeri* or *manawa wera* are recited by all his group in unison, something in the manner of a war dance. These group chants are given at the end of a bracket of *tauparapara*, or they may be used right at the end of the speech, after the *waiata* (song). Each tribal and subtribal area has its own distinctive *tauparapara*, which should properly be used only by members of the group or by hosts welcoming them on to a *marae*.

One of the best-known all-purpose chants goes back through history to the homelands of Hawaiki and Rarotonga:

Tihei—mauri ora!
I sneeze, it is life!
Tihei uriuri, tihei nakonako
It is darkness, blackness
Ka tau, hā, whakatau ko te rangi i runga nei
Lay, ha, set in its place, the sky above

Ka tau, hā, whakatau ko te papa i raro nei
Lay, ha, set its place the earth below
Ka tau, hā, whakatau ko Te Matuku mai i Rarotonga
Trace back to Te Matuku from Rarotonga
Koia i rukuhia manawa pou roto
Who dived to the spirit within
Koia i rukuhia manawa pou waho
Who dived to the spirit without
Whakatina kia tina, Te More i Hawaiki
Fix firmly, Te More from Hawaiki
E pupū ana hoki e wawau ana hoki
Rising and falling
Tārewa tū ki te rangi
Rise and stand up to the sky
Aua kia eke, eke panuku, eke Tangaroa
Rise, rise together, up Tangaroa
Whano, whano, hara mai te toki
Go, go, bring me the adze
Haumi e, hui e . . . . taiki e!
Bind it, join it . . . . It is done!

At almost any *hui* this chant will be heard. Its words are ancient, and obscure.

Of the chants to be used at a funeral, a well-known example refers to the tide, flowing in to gather up the spirit of the man who has died:

Te tai rā, te tai rā
That tide, that tide
E pari ana te tai ki whea?
Where is it flowing?
E pari ana te tai ki te kauheke, kaumātua,
It flows to the elder, the old man,
He atua, he atua e!
He is a spirit! a spirit!

All the widely-known chants have a number of versions, different in small details of wording.

A *tauparapara* appropriate to local speakers welcomes the visitors, who are depicted as climbing up to the *marae*. This symbolism was no doubt apt in the days of terraced hilltop communities:

Piki mai rā, kake mai rā,
Climb towards me, climb on,

Hōmai te wai ora ki ahau
Give me the water of life
E tūtēhu ana te moe a te kuia nei
Troubled was the sleep of this old woman
I te pō, pō, ka awatea
Through the night, the night, until the day
Papaki tū ana te tai ki Te Reinga
The tides are beating to Te Reinga (where spirits jump off to the underworld)
Ka pō, ka ao, ka awatea.
It was night, then dawn, and now it is day.

A *tauparapara* for visitors to a *tangi* greets the local meeting-house:

A ... Porourangi, takoto ake
Ah, Porourangi, lying there
Ki waenga tō iwi
Amidst your people
Aue, aue, taukiri e!
Alas! alas! I mourn for you!

A string of *pōkeka*, usually recited at a *tangi*, refers to the dead in a series of poetic images:

Taka ka taka
It falls, it falls
Taka ka taka
It falls, it falls
Ka taka te motoi
The greenstone ear-pendant falls
E kapo ki te whetū
I snatch at the star
E kapo ki te marama
I snatch at the moon
E kapo ki te ata o taku raukura ka riro!
I snatch at the shadow of my lost feather plume!

Kimihia, rangahaua, kei whea rā koe e ngaro nei?
I search, I seek, where have you gone?
Tēna aua! Ka riro kei Paerau
Aua! You have been carried away to Paerau (a star)
Kei te huinga o te kahurangi ka oti atu koutou e tama e ...
To the assembly of those who will never return, my son.

A *ngeri*, used on the East Coast as a final *tau*, was once a canoe-hauling chant:

Uira te rā, wewero te rā
The sun sparkles, the sun glows
Ngā tāngata whakaririka
Everyone get ready
Mamau ki te taura e
Grasp the rope
Kia tū mātātohitia ake
Stand in line
Taku tū mātātoro e
I stand to give the order
O ihu, o waka, Turuki, turuki
The prow, the canoe, together, together
Paneke, paneke
Forward, forward
Turuki, turuki, paneke paneke
Together, together, forward, forward
Tēnei te tangata pūhuruhuru
This is the hairy man
Nāna i tiki mai whakawhiti te rā
Who has made the sun rise
Hūpane, kaupane, hūpane, kaupane
Up this step, that step, this step, that step
Whiti te rā!
The sun rises!

The famous chant *Ka mate!*, given on page 143, can also be used in this context.

An example of a local *tauparapara* might be the chant quoted at the beginning of this chapter, first recited by Apanui's parrot to warn him of danger. Rightly speaking, this chant should only be used by Apanui's lineal descendants, members of Te Whānau-ā-Apanui tribe.

There are a set of phrases which occur at the end of a great many *tauparapara*, used in most tribal areas. The first of these was originally used at the end of seafaring incantations, but has been generalised:

Eke panuku, eke Tangaroa!
Move up, up Tangaroa! (the sea god).
Hui e! Taiki e!
Together! It is done!

The other seems to have been a wood-working incantation:

Whano! whano! (*hara mai te toki*
                    (*hou*
                    (*tū*
Go!   Go!   (bring me the adze
                    (bind
                    (stand
Hui e! Taiki e!
It is joined! It is done!

An expert speaker has a wide repertoire of *tauparapara*, and on each occasion he will try to choose one which is most apt to the district, his role in the *hui* and the reason the *hui* was called. If a visitor recites a local *tau*, this is a great compliment to his hosts and a tribute to the range of his own knowledge. Most speakers use the same *tau* over and over again, and perhaps know only one or two. The most precious chants are those passed down through the family, to which the orator has an indisputable right; the more common chants lose a lot of their impact by constant repetition.

It has already been mentioned that *tauparapara* are not always used, and in this case there are certain standard phrases which can substitute. In the Tainui area, for example, a common opening is the phrase, "*Te mea tuatahi, kia wehi ki te Atua, kia whakahōnore tō tātou Kuini,*" ("The first thing is to fear God and honour our Queen"); and for visitors to any *marae*, a good opening counter is "*Te marae e takoto nei, te whare e tū nei, te wai e hora nei, ngā waka e tau nei, tēnā koutou, tēnā koutou, tēnā koutou*" ("The *marae* which lies here, the house which stands here, the river which spreads nearby, the canoes which have landed here, greetings, greetings, greetings"). These phrases, along with the texts of the chants, illustrate one of the main stylistic themes of Maori oratory—the repetition of symmetrical structures. These repetitions give balance and sonority to the speech, and they are one of the reasons why Maori oratory seems so effortless. If a speaker is at a loss for words, he can resort to one of the key expressions used in oratory, and repeat it with variations. This point will become clearer as we examine the body of the *whaikōrero*.

The central text of a *whaikōrero* is still highly stylised, but unlike the opening chants it is not completely predictable in wording. The orator cuts his cloth to fit the occasion, but weaves it out of a large set of phrases which are heard over and over again, in different arrangements. These phrases are poetic and mythological, providing a sort of verbal embroidery for the speech. Skilled orators use poetic sayings with an off-hand deftness, and it is these speakers who are most likely to abandon the well-worn repertoire for something more striking and original. They coin poetry of their own, or launch into vivid, witty prose, leaving aside the standard structures altogether. Most speakers follow through the ritual forms, repeating phrases of greeting and calling on the dead, but the best speakers end up discoursing on quite unexpected topics, moving their audience to laughter or tears at will. It is the hope of hearing one of these masters at work (along with other incentives), that brings people to one *hui* after another. People best appreciate a speech full of drama and fire—an impassioned denouncement, a series of sly digs or an inspired piece of clowning. For most of the time they are listening to one speaker after another through the ritual paces, and they do get bored. The speakers listen to each other in case there is something they can elaborate on later, but the rest of the audience chat, doze, smoke and otherwise divert themselves. The ritual has to be gone through if things are to be *"tika"* (correct), and people are philosophical about sitting through long hours of speech-making. For this reason, the occasional brilliant speech stands out all the more; the audience snap out of their passive monitoring of the ritual, and really begin to listen. When a succession of such speakers stands on the *marae*, each one picking up comments, embroidering on them, making jokes or giving vivid accounts of history, taking up errors and subjecting the perpetrator to good natured ridicule, the *marae* comes alive with attention. Just because these speakers work with the unexpected, there is really no way of describing the structure of their speeches. They make their impact by departing from the usual patterns, by innovating and inventing.

The usual patterns are, all the same, extremely important. They dominate the great majority of speeches and give *whaikōrero* its poetic, structured quality. The use of these phrases, plus a predictable broad sequence of topics, make a general study of *whaikōrero* possible.

One of the most interesting features of Maori oratory is its setting in a mythological landscape, one which would be quite unfamiliar to other New Zealanders. A totally different concept of the country and its history comes into play, and unless the listener roughly knows the landmarks of this landscape, he is liable to get lost. Places are called by their Maori names in direct preference to European equivalents (Tāmaki-makau-rau, not Auckland; Tūranga, not Gisborne), and places that are hardly noted on European maps become extremely important. Focal points of Maori settlement, such as Ruatāhuna, Ngāruawāhia, Ruatōria and so on, are insignificant communities in size and wealth, yet rich in history and *mana*, and they dominate the "Maori" map. Large cities on the other hand, are relatively unimportant, since they are European creations, and recent ones at that. Although increasing numbers of Maori people live in the main cities, they are still places without much *mana*. Their *marae* are new and the customs practised there are "half-*pai*". Regions in the landscape are referred to by their key mountains, rivers and ancestors. *"Ko Whanokao te maunga, ko Motu te awa, ko Apanui te tangata"* ("Whanokao is the mountain, Motu is the river, and Apanui is the man") means Whānau-ā-Apanui country; *"Ko Hikurangi te maunga, ko Waiapu te awa, ko Porourangi te tangata"* ("Hikurangi is the mountain, Waiapu is the river, and Porourangi is the man") is Ngāti Porou; and *"Ko Taupiri te maunga, ko Waikato te awa, ko Te Wherowhero te tangata"* ("Taupiri is the mountain, Waikato the river, Te Wherowhero is the man") refers to the territory of the Waikato tribes. Boundaries are mentioned that have nothing to do with current administration, for example, *Mai i Tikirau ki Ngā Kuri ā Whārei* (from Tikirau, a mountain at Cape Runaway, to Whārei's Dogs, a range of hills east of Tauranga), the boundaries of the *Mātātua* tribes. Even the orientation is different. "Up" is the southern part of the North Island, and "down" is the Far North. This relates to the legend that the North Island is in fact the petrified body of a great fish, caught by Māui with his grandmother's magical jawbone. The tail of the fish is in Northland and its head is near Wellington, with its eye at Lake Taupō. The North Island then becomes *Te Ika-roa-ā-Māui* (Māui's long fish), and the South Island is his petrified canoe. New Zealand as a whole is called *Aotearoa* (the land of the long white cloud), a name said to have been given to it by the early Polynesian navigators. The South Island is *Te Wai Pounamu* (the jade water), because it was the original source of greenstone, prized for weapons and ornaments. The Chatham Islands are called *Wharekauri* (House of Kauri); and Stewart Island is *Rakiura*.

In this mythological landscape, spirits at death journey north to Te Reinga at the tip of the North Island, there to leap over a cliff and join their myriads of ancestors in the Pō, a dark underworld: *"Te Pō nui, te Pō roa, te Pō kerekere, te Pō uriuri, te Pō tangotango"* (The Great night, long night, deep night, dense night, dark night"). If a man is a chief, his right eye becomes a star *("kua whetū-rangitia")*, joining constellations that were named by his ancestors. The earth itself is Papa the earth mother, swept by four winds from caves on the three major coasts of the island—Tai Rāwhiti (East Coast), Tai Hauauru (West Coast), Tai Tokerau (Northern Coasts) and from the South Island. When a man is buried, he returns to her womb. Somewhere to the north-east of Aotearoa over the Great Sea of Kiwa lies Hawaiki, the homeland, left by the ancestors in their canoes and still vividly remembered—Hawaiki nui, Hawaiki roa, Hawaiki tawhiti, Hawaiki pāmamao, Hawaiki i hono i wairua (Great Hawaiki, Long Hawaiki, Distant Hawaiki, Hawaiki Far away, Hawaiki the joining-place of Spirits).

This Maori landscape (Te Ao Maori) is peopled with ancient gods, spirits, and mountains with personalities. Its heroes are men like Tāwhiao, the second Maori King, Te Kooti the prophet, and Sir Apirana Ngata. Meeting-houses are talked to and the dead can still hear you. It is a world where events several centuries ago explain what a man says on the *marae* today. It is no longer a full-time world. A man who on one day of the

THE RITUALS OF ENCOUNTER

week is a freezing-worker, pragmatic as any of his mates and operating in the same social and economic world, on another day stands to speak on the *marae*, summoning up memories that they could not share, and set in his place by a net-work of tribal and genealogical ties. This separation of experience is sharper in the cities, hostile environments for a world tied closely to nature, and for some of the younger generations the Maori landscape is lost altogether. The point is clear—that people living side by side in a country may yet have a very different experience of it; and for the Maori people, their separate vision comes into clearest focus on the *marae*. Only in this context can *whaikōrero* be properly understood. If it seems mysterious and obscure, it is because it is set in another landscape, which only its native inhabitants can fully comprehend.

It is a true example of "in-group" language, clear only to initiates, and this at least in part is the reason it is so highly valued. Maori people have also learnt their way about the European cultural map, but on the *marae* this is left behind, and they return to a world different to that of their ancestors, but with common and ancient qualities.

The central text of a *whaikōrero* gains its structure from the prescribed sequences of topics, which vary according to the occasion and the role of the speaker, and are expressed in phrases taken from the mythological repertoire. At a *tangi*, for example, local speakers welcome visitors and identify them for the dead person, asking them to lay their own dead on the body of the man who has just died, to be wept over together. They outline his career, farewell him, and mention which groups have already arrived at the *marae*. Visiting speakers, on the other hand, farewell the dead directly, sending them on their way to the underworld (Pō) with grief and lamentation. Only at the very end of their speech do they greet the living—the mourners, the hosts, and the other tribes who have come to the *marae*. In all these speeches it is understood that the dead person is listening, appeased by the public display of grief, and dissuaded by it from returning to torment the living as a ghost. He is addressed as a great tree, felled by the adze of death; a talking-bird that has flown away; and the greater his *mana* the more elaborate is the poetry of his farewell. At this time too, old scandals and grievances are brought out into the open and forgiven, because the *marae* is a traditional place to heal quarrels.

The speech of farewell is called a *poroporoaki*, and it might run as follows:

Takoto e koro, takoto.
Lie there, old man, lie.
Takoto i te roro o tō tipuna whare,
Lie in the porch of your ancestral house.
takoto i runga i te papa i takatakahia ai e ō mātua, ō tipuna;
Lie on the ground trodden by your parents, your ancestors;

takoto i te tau marumaru o tō maunga, e koro, haere!
lie in the shadow of your mountain, old man, go!
Haere, kua ūhia koe ki ou taonga, ki ngā kākahu o tēnei hunga o te mate;
Go, you have been wrapped in the precious clothes of this thing, death;
kua takaia koe ki te kupu kōrero,
you have been clothed in the words of farewell; and
ki te puna roimata;
immersed in an endless spring of tears;
kua mihia ki runga ki a koe.
these greetings we have given you.
Nō reira, haere, haere, haere!
So leave us, go, go, farewell!
Haere te uri o ngā tipuna,
Go descendant of the ancestors,
haere te rata whaka-ruruhau,
go, the sheltering rata tree,
haere i runga i tō papa,
go upon your land,
haere i runga i tō moana,
go upon your waters,
ki ngā kupu kōrero e kōrerotia atu nei,
borne on the words we have spoken for you,
ki te Pō uriuri, ki te Pō kerekere, ki te Pō tangotango.
to the dark night, the deep night, the dense night.
Haere ki te pūtahitanga a Rēhua,
Go to Reehua constellation,
ki te huihuinga o te mano,
to the gathering of the thousands,
Noo reira, ahakoa te aroha, haere, haere, haere!"
Therefore despite love, go, go, leave!"

This *poroporoaki* has been impersonalised. Normally it would include the names of mountains, canoes and ancestors associated with the man who has died; his career would be remembered and shared experiences recalled, and his identity would be made very clear.

The *poroporoaki* is perhaps the most distinctive type of speech. Other speeches vary mainly according to whether the orator is local or visitor, and follow a typical pattern. Local speakers begin by issuing a general welcome to the visitors who have arrived on the *marae*. If they are clearly identified as members of a single tribe they will be welcomed by their tribal name or that of their ancestral canoe, and their appropriate local proverb may be quoted; e.g. *"Ko Tongariro te maunga, ko Taupo te moana, ko Te Heuheu te tangata"* ("Tongariro is the mountain, Taupo is the lake and Te Heuheu is the man"), for Tūwharetoa. In the more common situation of a mixed party, or one whose identity is not known to the local people, the speaker takes refuge in a series of greetings designed to cover everybody. e.g.:

Whakatau mai, whakatau mai, whakatau mai, whakatau mai.
Land here, land here, land here, land here.
Whakatau mai e ngā iwi, whakatau mai e ngā reo,
Come tribes,　　　　　　come the voices,
e ngā mana, e ngā waka o runga i te motu,
the great ones, the canoes of the island,
i raro i ngā hau e whā.
from beneath the four winds.
Haere mai ngā iwi o tēra tai, o tēnei tai,
Welcome the tribes of that coast, of this coast,
o te tuawhenua; haere mai ngā rangatira o te motu.
of the interior; welcome, chiefs of the island.

Now the speaker talks of the dead, those brought to the *marae* by the visitors, and those that belong to the local people:

Nō reira, ka hari te ngākau mō koutou ngā rangatira o te motu,
Now, my heart is glad for you the chiefs of the island,
kua tae mai ki konei, ki te mau mai i tō koutou aroha,
have come here,　　　bringing your love.
i tō koutou tangi ki ō tātou tini aituā,
and your tears to our myriad dead,
e hora nei rā i ngā marae maha o te motu.
scattered over the many *marae* of the island.
Nā koutou i tangi, nā koutou i mihi,
You have wept for them, greeted them,
nā koutou i tuku atu ki te kōpū o te whenua,
and let them into the belly of the land,
aa, nā tātou katoa.
and so then have we all.

Having evoked the dead, the speaker farewells them:

Nō reira, haere ngā mate, haere ngā mate,
Therefore, the dead, go, go,
haere ngā mate.
leave.
E koro mā, e kui mā, haere rā. Ngā tōtara nunui o ia wāhi,
Old men, old women, farewell. The great totara trees,

o ia wāhi i roto i te wao nui a Tāne,
from every part of Tāne's forest.
e hoki ki Hawaiki,
return to Hawaiki,
ki ngā takahinga o ngā tipuna kua ngaro.
in the footsteps of your ancestors.

From the dead he turns to the living, perhaps with the phrase *"kāpiti hono, tātai hono, rātou te hunga mate ki a rātou; kāpiti hono, tātai hono, tātou te hunga ora ki a tātou"* ("Join, join the descent lines, they the dead to the dead; join, join the descent lines, we the living to the living"). The orator might bridge the gap between the dead and the living, and between hosts and visitors, by reciting a genealogy that unites them all. Genealogy converts strangers into relatives, an invaluable alchemy in different *marae* situations. It demonstrates the orator's right to speak, and his expert mastery of past events. Only the most confident speaker will *"whakapapa"* on the *marae*, as his critics on the opposite bench are sure to pick up any errors. As one old man expressed his caution: "Don't wear your religion, your politics or your *whakapapa* on your sleeve."

Now that the visitors have been genealogically located, they are welcomed once again, and the speaker greets old friends by name:

Ngā mōrehu o aituā,
The survivors of those who have died,
tēnā koutou i runga i tō tātou moutere.
greetings to you on our island.
Ahakoa kei tērā paihau o te motu,
Although you dwell at that horizon of the island,
kei te rerenga o te rā, ahakoa kei te tōanga o te rā,
at the rising or the setting of the sun,
kotahi tonu tō tātou karangatanga, he iwi Maori.
our divisions are one, one Maori people.

Finally, the speaker discusses the reason why the *hui* has been called, and identifies parties of visitors who have already arrived at the *marae*. This order is not invariable, but it generally holds true. First, the guests are welcomed, and the dead are welcomed and farewelled; then the visitors are greeted in more specific terms, and the speaker outlines any *take* (specific topics) which relates to the occasion of his own preoccupations. Common topics are land, Maori language, the Treaty of Waitangi or the need to hold fast to Maori culture. Throughout the speech the orator uses appropriate proverbs to further illustrate his command of traditional wisdom.

THE RITUALS OF ENCOUNTER

Visitors begin their speeches differently from local orators, addressing themselves first to the *marae* and the meeting-house:

E tama rā, e Papa-tua-nuku, tēnā koe, tēnā koe,
Child,   Earth Mother,   I greet you, I greet you.
tēnā koe.   Tēnā koe e Papa-tua-nuku,
I greet you, I greet you Earth Mother,
hei tūnga mō ngā uri whakatipu.
as a standing-place for the rising generations.
E koro, te tipuna whare, e tū, e tū.
Old man, ancestral house, stand there, stand.

After the opening, however, the speeches follow similar lines, mentioning the dead, their hosts, and the main event of the *hui*. In all speeches, proverbs, historical and mythological allusions decorate the topical structure, and although the audience can broadly predict its content, still the artistry of its expression holds their interest. The topical structure of *whaikōrero* thus can be outlined as follows:

[Local: greet visitors]   +   Greet   +   Greet   +   *Take*
or   dead   living   (specific topic)
[Visitor: greet *marae*,
          meeting-house]

The *take* is optional, and many speeches follow through the ritual greetings without ever launching into general discussion. Orators do abandon this sequence in moments of particular inspiration, but usually they follow it closely, and address their inventiveness to its poetic embroidery instead. When in the course of his oration the speaker makes a good point, the other speakers raise a hand in acknowledgement, and call out *"Kōrero!"* ("Speak"); *"Tautoko!"* ("I support that!"), *"Kia ora"* ("Thank you"), or "Hear! hear!" If they disagree with what he is saying they sit in silence, eyes fixed on the ground. In general, orators watching another man speak sit impassively and withdrawn, being careful not to look too impressed. Only when he makes a joke or turns a particularly fine compliment do they smile and wave a hand.

Spatial Structures and Movement

Throughout the speeches local and visiting orators sit on opposite benches, facing each other across the *marae*. The local people sit on a group of benches to one side of the meeting-house, sometimes to the left and sometimes to the right. In the East Coast the local benches are often to the right of the house, (facing out), and in Tūhoe to the left, but this position may vary from one *marae* to another in the same district. The visitor's benches are placed opposite the local people, or facing towards the meeting-house.

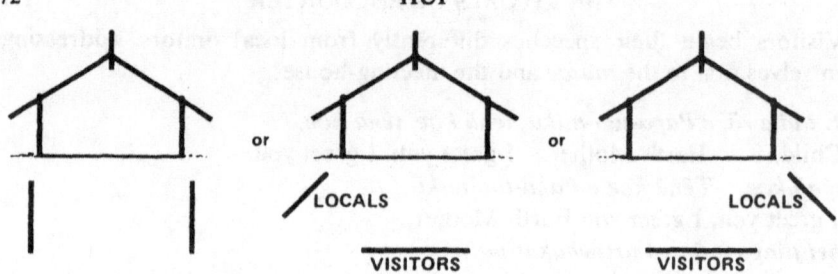

In all these arrangements, the orators sit on the front benches, with the old women behind them, and then the rest of their party. They are dressed in dark suits and tie, wearing a hat and overcoat as well in colder weather. It is not really proper for a man to speak in any other uniform. On occasions of particular pageantry, perhaps a welcome to Royalty, the main speakers wear feather cloaks over their suits, as a symbol of chiefly status. When an orator is ready to speak, he calls out his warning—"*Tihei . . . mauri ora!*" and stands, stripping off his overcoat and hat and picking up his walking-stick, then strides on to the *marae*. The carved walking-stick *(tokotoko)*, a whalebone *kotiate* or a *mere* (hand weapons) are indispensable props for a dramatic performance, and some people say they repel *mākutu* (black magic) as well. They give the orator authority, and lend emphasis to his gestures. Sometimes the speaker has no walking-stick, so he picks up an umbrella instead and uses that in his oration.

Speeches are illustrated with a wealth of gesture, tailored to the meaning of the words and graphically underlining them. A man who speaks with his hands in his pockets is scorned; people say that this is a sign he does not speak his mind. The best orators stand confidently on the *marae*, gesturing strongly and moving lightly. This type of stance is *tama tāne* or manly; the hesitant, apologetic stance is called *tama wahine*, a woman's way of standing.

Most orators today stand in one place, facing the benches opposite or the meeting-house. A few *marae* provide amplifying systems, which anchor the speaker to a microphone. The best speakers, however, move freely on the *marae*, striding backwards and forwards, leaping on their turns *(pekepeke)*, quickly stamping their feet and lunging into powerful gestures. They move like warriors, agile and strong. Local orators walk across the face of their meeting-house, weapons in the outside hand, taking care not to turn their backs on the ancestral building. Visiting orators follow two main styles. In most areas they move parallel to their hosts, but in a few tribes the visitors charge straight towards the meeting-house, then return walking backwards or turn round and walk back to their own group. In this style, the orator has been known to say one thing as he approaches his hosts, and the direct opposite in an aside to his own people on the return trip. When a speaker strides back and forwards on the *marae*, he delivers his speech in a sentence at each turn, or speaks as he moves in one direction, then turns and slowly walks back, head down, thinking of the next phrase to follow. As he gets more and more worked up, he almost runs while he is speaking, but turns and walks back as imperturbably as ever. There are now only a few speakers who use this dramatic style of delivery, but they are inheritors of a long tradition. Maning described an oration delivered on the occasion of his arrival in New Zealand in 1833, which in its style is almost indistinguishable from a fine *whaikōrero* of today. He was being carried from a row-boat to the shore on his first arrival in New Zealand, dressed in all his finery to honour the occasion, when his porter slipped, and Maning got a ducking. He stripped off his coat and shoes, and got into a wrestling match with the fellow, a man called "Melons". The chief arrived, and begins "to 'blow up' all and sundry, the tribe in general, and poor 'Melons' in particular. He is really vexed, and wishes to appear to me more vexed than he really is. He runs, gesticulating and flourishing his *mere*, about ten steps in one direction, in the course of which ten steps he delivers a sentence. He then turns and runs back the same distance, giving vent to his wrath in another sentence, and so back and forward . . . till he has exhausted the subject, and tired his legs. The Englishmen were beside me and gave a running translation of what he said: 'Pretty work this', he began, '*good* work; killing my *pakeha*—look at him! (Here a flourish in my direction with the *mere*). I won't stand this—not at all! not at all! not at all! (The last sentence took three jumps, a step, and a turn-a-round, to keep correct time.) Who killed the *pakeha*? It was Melons. You are a nice man, are you not? (This with a sneer). Killing my *pakeha!* (in a voice like thunder, and rushing savagely, *mere* in hand, at poor Melons, but turning exactly at the end of the ten steps and coming back again.) It will be heard of all over the country; we shall be called the '*pakeha* killers'. I shall be sick with shame. The *pakeha* will run away, and take all his *taonga* along with him. What if you had killed him dead, or broken his bones? His relations would be coming across the sea for *utu*. (Great sensation, and I try to look as though I would say 'of course they would!') What did I build this *pa* close to the sea for? Was it not to trade with the *pakehas*? And here you are killing the second that has come to stop with me. (Here poor Melons burst out crying like an infant.) Where is the hat?—where is the long coat?—where are the shoes?—The *pakeha* is robbed, he is murdered!' (Here a howl from Melons, and I go over and sit down by him, clap him on the bare back, and shake his hand.)"[127]

On more formal occasions the chiefs sat on the *marae* in a semi-circle, and the orator paraded in front of them. Logan Campbell in 1881

127. Maning (1863), pp. 34-35.

observed this oration at a *tangi*. "Suddenly he stops, faces about, and with slightly quickened step paces back towards the body lying in state, and delivers a sentence of his oration, arresting his further advance close to the chief. He now turns round again, and walks deliberately in silence back to the starting point, then advancing this time more quickly than the last, he delivers another short sentence—never more than eight or ten words. Gradually, as he warms to his theme, he makes his advance and delivers his sentence at an increased rapidity . . . Wonderfully strange is the effect that this at last produces when the speaker has worked himself to the highest stage of intense action, when he rushes forward, his mat flying wildly around him, brandishing with a peculiar quivering motion a *taiaha* rushing forward with high-toned voice and hastily-spoken words, ending his advance with a sudden jump in the air, and in a moment assuming the most statuesque repose, and in the most quiet dignified manner again pacing back . . . At last the hurricane has expended itself; all the warlike deeds and acts of prowess of the dead chief have been held up for emulation; and he ends with a dirge chanted in a low monotonous tone."[128]

This "dirge" is the final element in the *whaikōrero*, a *waiata* or traditional song, sung in unison by the speaker and his group. *Waiata* have been recorded since the earliest days of contact. Sir George Grey, an early Governor of New Zealand, published a collection of texts in 1854 (republished 1885, 1928, 1971), and Sir Apirana Ngata in 1928 published *Nga Moteatea* (republished 1959, 1972), a collection of almost 100 songs annotated in Maori, and translated into English by Dr Pei te Hurinui Jones. In more recent years Dr Mervyn McLean, an ethnomusicologist, has taped and transcribed a large number of *waiata*, now stored in the Archives of Maori and Pacific Music at the University of Auckland. *Waiata*, then, are a specialist topic, which is being thoroughly investigated by qualified scholars.

As with the *tauparapara*, there are many types of *waiata*, and orators try to choose one appropriate to the occasion. *Waiata tangi* (laments), *waiata aroha* (love songs), *oriori* (lullabies), *pao* (topical songs) and *pūtere* (songs composed by slandered women) can all be performed at the end of a speech. The orator calls for women of his group to support him; or he starts up his *wai* alone, and people move from their benches to stand beside him on the *marae*. If he can't think of a *waiata* or doesn't know one, one of the women might stand and start up a song for him, otherwise he has to sit down amidst cries of *"Tō wai! tō wai!"* ("Your song! your song!") Once in a while if the speaker is too garrulous, a woman stands beside him on the *marae*, announces *"Anei tō wai!"* ("Here is your song!") and cuts him off. Usually, though, the *waiata* is a chance for other people to show solidarity with the speaker, and even relatives from the

---

128. Campbell (1881), pp. 176-7.

other side of the *marae* stand to sing with him if he needs their support. Both men and women join in but the *waiata* is dominated by the womenfolk. They grumble if a man starts up the *wai*, because sometimes the note doesn't suit them and they end up squeaking in the upper registers, or growling in basso profundo. Favourite *waiata* are performed with enthusiasm, and once they get into the rhythm of the chant, the women begin to improvise actions, quivering their hands *(wiriwiri)* and giving *pūkana* (rolling the eyes down and making a comical face) to add to the flavour of the performance. The *waiata* is in fact called the *kīnaki* (relish) to the speech. On one memorable occasion I attended a female singer chanted with such enthusiasm that her false teeth flew out and landed on the *marae*. A prime rule in performing a *wai* is that its continuity must not be broken *(kaua te waiata e whati)*, and if there are only a few singers, the lead singer and supporters must be careful to breathe at different places, so that there is no break in the chant. Nor should a *waiata* be sung twice in the same ritual of encounter, although this sometimes happens. If a group knows only one or two *waiata*, it is better if these are rare ones, or they may be caught out. At one *hui* I attended the visitors knew only one *waiata*, the famous song "E Pā tō Hau". Just before their speaker stood, the preceding local speaker started up the chant. The visitors looked dismayed, and at the end of his speech their speaker had to confess that "You of the many chants have stolen our one!" This would not have happened to a group of well-versed elders, who usually share at least three or four *waiata*. The typical group has one or two main singers who know the chants by heart, and the others join in the parts they can remember. This is the way people gradually learn a *waiata*, by standing up to sing it again and again at many different *hui*. Today the *waiata* is sometimes replaced by an action song or a hymn in Maori, but these are not really regarded as adequate substitutes. A speaker who is acting the goat might even sing a Hit Parade favourite like "Please Release Me" or "Cheryl Moana Marie".

At a *tangi* people sing the favourite *waiata* of the person who has died, or action songs that he composed. On one occasion the singer completely forgot the words of the long and complex *waiata* he had started, but saved face by impudently suggesting that the dead man (a well-known expert), could finish it off, since he knew it by heart anyway. On a visit outside the home area, people may learn a *waiata* that properly belongs to their hosts, by way of compliment. *Waiata* are still being composed, particularly as laments for well-known leaders, but their music is gradually being modified in the direction of European melody. The words are poetic and mythological, summoning images from nature and the past. One *waiata*, lamenting the loneliness of an old woman, begins:

Engari te titi e tangi haere ana, e
Even the *titi* as it goes, crying

Whai tokorua rawa rāua
Travels in a pair
Tēnā ko au nei, e manu e
Oh bird! I am like
Kei te hua kiwi i mahue i te tāwai
the kiwi egg abandoned on the beech tree
Ka toro te rākau kai runga e
The roots grow over it
Ka hoki mai ki te pao
When the mother returns for the hatching
Ka whai uri ki ahau.
The offspring are trapped, like me.

The *waiata* can be rounded off by a chant or *pōkeka*, recited in the manner of a war dance.

Now the orator speaks a few last words, a reiterated welcome or simply *"Tēnā koutou, tēnā koutou, tēnā koutou katoa"* ("I greet you, I greet you all"), and moves back to his place. The *whaikōrero* is over. If the speech has been brief (say ten to fifteen minutes), dramatic and well-delivered, he has won more *mana* for his group. The last speaker for a visiting side puts down the *koha* (gift) at this point, signalling the end of their part of the oratory. In the Waikato area, this is answered with a *karanga* (call) of thanks from one of the local old ladies.

Whaikōrero are not limited to the rituals of encounter. Oratory is a main part of the *hui*, and people stand to speak after meals, in quiet moments, and in the meeting-house until the early hours of the morning. These later speeches, however, are less concerned with greetings, and more preoccupied with *take* (special topics). In some areas people make a deliberate policy of restricting the encounter speeches to ritual greetings, and keeping the *take* until later. In these later sessions of oratory the history, difficulties, and aspirations of the Maori people are discussed at length, in wide-ranging and unpredictable speeches. These speeches are political rather than ritual, and ritual restrictions on categories of speakers and proper topics are relaxed. In this context tribal policy takes shape as orators sway people in one direction and another, until gradually unanimity or at least a show of it is reached.

Hongi (pressing noses)
After the last visiting speaker has spoken, an elder stands from the local benches and calls the visitors over to press noses and shake hands: *"Haere mai koutou ki te rūrū."* The local people form a line across the front of the meeting-house, and the visitors begin to move along it, shaking hands with everyone in turn. In a few areas the local people come to the visitors instead,

a custom described by other tribes as *"Kua tae mai te wāpu ki te tima"* ("The wharf has come to the steamer"). The *hongi* line is friendly and relaxed; all *tapu* has been lifted. People greet each other according to age and sex. Most of the old people *hongi*, shaking hands and pressing noses two or three times, with everyone they meet. There are different types of *hongi*; in some places people press the sides of their noses together; in other areas people press foreheads together as well. The usual *hongi*, however, is pressing the bridge of the noses together, meanwhile shaking hands and giving a little sound of satisfaction, "mm, mm, aah". When old friends meet in the line they keep their noses together a long time, patting each other's backs and weeping in joy and sorrow. The *hongi* is said to have originated when Tāne created the first woman, breathing the spirit of life into her nostrils, but this explanation is not widely given. Mostly the *hongi* is regarded as comforting embrace, full of Maori *aroha* (love), and no one worries about its origins. Younger people meeting each other, shake hands and kiss cheeks, women to women and women to men, or simply shake hands saying *"Tēnā koe"* or *"Kia ora"* ("Hello"). As people move along the line, meeting and embracing, they chat, joke and call out "Never mind the kissing, move on to the *kai!"* The constraint of the ritual is over.

In Northland at a *tangi* the guests move straight in to *hongi* the dead, then move round the house to greet everyone present. If they are wearing greenery, they leave it at the foot of the coffin. This custom is not practised elsewhere, and other tribes find it strange, even frightening. If a Northern party follows this custom on a *marae* in another district the local people try to wave them back. Usually at a *tangi* only female relatives and close friends of the family come to *hongi* the mourners before the speeches are over.

On most occasions, then, the *hongi* signals the end of the welcome. The visitors have been greeted with due ceremony, and now they are called to share the hospitality of the local people in a meal.

The *mihi* (welcome) for each group is supposed to run right through without any interruptions, but sometimes when time is short another group enters and is welcomed at some point in the ritual. This might happen after the *tangi*, before the *whaikōrero* begins, and in this case the first group on the *marae* have priority in answering the local speeches. On other occasions the visitors may be called in during a pause between speeches, and the ceremony halts for a time while they enter, *karanga*, *tangi* and sit down. This interruption is less acceptable, and visiting speakers of the first party are entitled to get angry if they want to. If the group is not invited to enter, but barge in during someone else's welome, they will probably be sent out again; and the same thing happens if they enter while an orator has possession of the *marae*. Typically though, the ritual of encounter carries on from start to finish without any such complications. Its overall structure can be outlined (see next page).

178   HUI

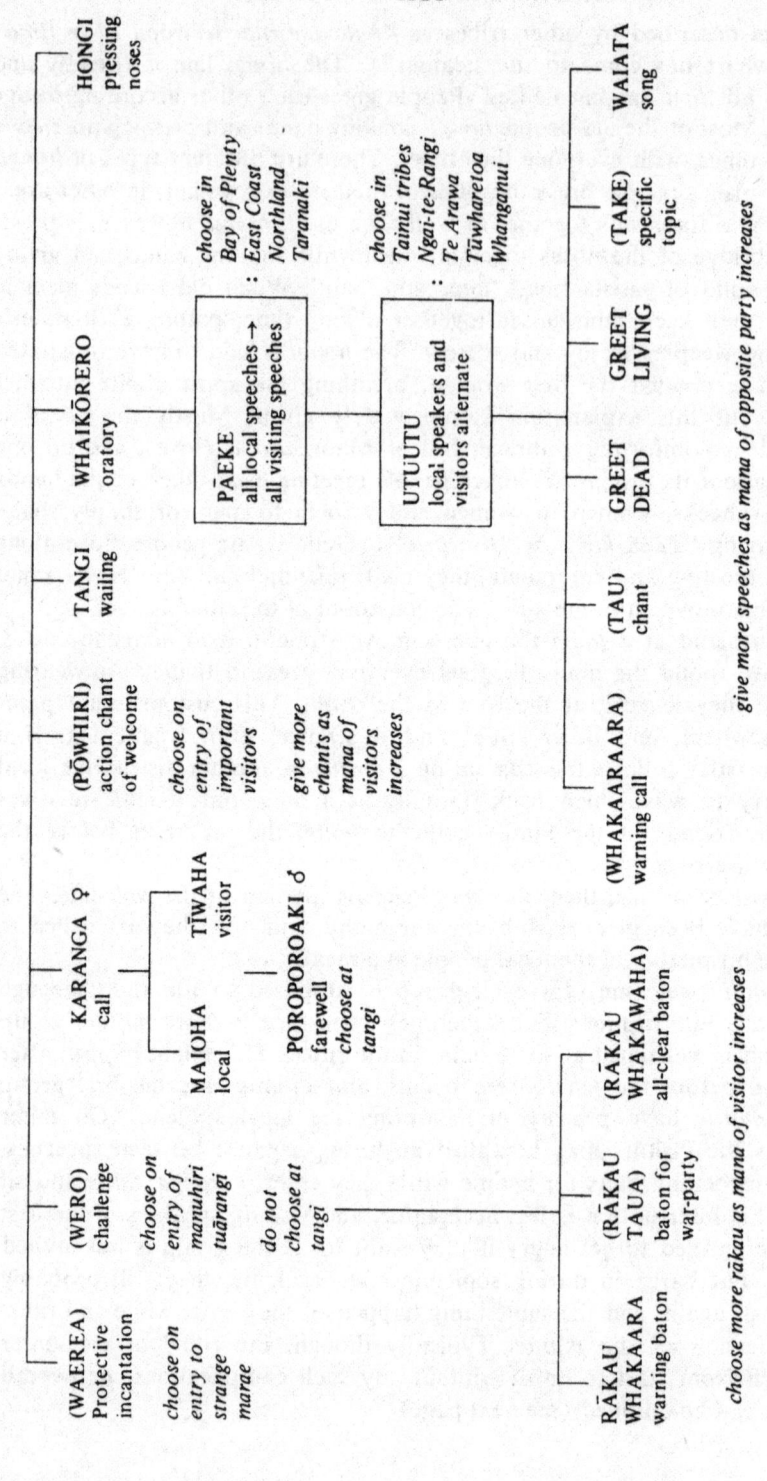

```
                                                              HONGI
                                                              pressing
                                                              noses

                                                                          choose in
                                                                          Bay of Plenty
                                                              PĀEKE      : East Coast
                                                              all local speeches →  Northland
                                                              all visiting speeches  Taranaki

                                              WHAIKŌRERO
                                              oratory                     choose in
                                                                          Tainui tribes
                                                              UTUUTU     : Ngai-te-Rangi
                                                              local speakers and  Te Arawa
                                                              visitors alternate  Tūwharetoa
                                                                          Whanganui

                                              TANGI
                                              wailing

                                                              choose on
                                                              entry of
                                              (PŌWHIRI)      important
                                              action chant   visitors
                                              of welcome
                                                              give more
                                                              chants as
                                                              mana of
                                                              visitors
                                                              increases

                              TĪWAHA
                              visitor
          KARANGA ♀
          call           MAIOHA
                              local

                              POROPOROAKI ♂
                              farewell
                              choose at
                              tangi

                              choose on
          (WERO)         entry of
          challenge      manuhiri
                              tuārangi

                              do not
                              choose at
                              tangi

(WAEREA)
Protective
incantation

choose on
entry to
strange
marae


RĀKAU        (RĀKAU        (RĀKAU
WHAKAARA     TAUA)         WHAKAWAHA)
warning baton baton for    all-clear baton
              war-party

choose more rākau as mana of visitor increases
```

```
(WHAKAARAARA)  (TAU)    GREET   GREET    (TAKE)      WAIATA
warning call   chant    DEAD    LIVING   specific    song
                                         topic

                        give more speeches as mana of opposite party increases
```

Figure 3: Structure of the Ritual of Encounter

CHAPTER SIX

CENTRAL ACTIVITIES AND *HUI* TYPES

Although the rituals of encounter are broadly similar for every type of *hui*, their central activities are markedly different. Each *hui* has its own *take* (cause for gathering), and these in turn dictate the activities of the main event. At a wedding, for example, the guests are welcomed on to the *marae* with *karanga* and oratory, but the main event is the marriage ceremony and the reception that follows. At the opening of a new *marae*, on the other hand, the welcomes follow a similar pattern, but the main event is the *whai-kawa* ceremony and the inspection of the new buildings. This distinction holds true for every type of *hui*, and in this chapter we shall discuss these central activities, and how they effect the broad staging of the *hui*.

Take fall into two main classes—those where the main event is a life crisis, centring on an individual; and those where the main event is centred on a group.

Life crises include funerals *(tangi)*, *kawe mate* (carry the death), the unveiling of memorial tombstones *(hurahanga kōhatu)*, twenty-first birthdays, weddings *(mārenatanga)* and anniversaries.

Group events include the opening of a new *marae*, the welcome given to distinguished visitors (Royalty, the Governor-General, the Minister of Maori and Island Affairs), and the gatherings of Maori organisations such as the King Movement, the Ringatū and Rātana churches, the Maori branches of the major denominations, the New Zealand Maori Council, the Maori Women's Welfare League and the 28th Maori Battalion.

These *take* can, on occasion, be combined. If an important dignitary comes to open a new *marae*, his welcome to the district may be joined to the opening of the new buildings. If some group is unable to attend a major funeral, or if a man is being buried away from his home *marae*, the death is "carried" *(kawe mate)* by the mourners to the next important *hui* in that district. Gravestones are often unveiled in groups, and double weddings or funerals are sometimes staged. In all these cases the central ceremonials are also combined.

An interesting feature of these ceremonials is that some are considered more "Maori", and their gatherings more truly *"hui"* than others. This distinction has a historical basis. *Hui* originally meant simply a "gathering or assembly", and all gatherings followed a similar etiquette. Since contact, however, the range of gatherings has changed, and new forms of etiquette have been introduced. Organisations such as the churches, the Maori Battalion, the New Zealand Maori Council and the Maori Women's Welfare League are introduced structures, and their gatherings follow committee procedures as well as traditional etiquette. Twenty-first birthdays, the marriage ceremony, and wedding anniversaries are all imported life crises, while the unveiling of gravestones is probably a replacement for the indigenous *"hāhunga"* or exhumation. Although the main events of these gatherings are not traditionally "Maori", they have acquired a Maori interpretation over the years of contact, and are preceded by some version of the rituals of encounter to mark the occasion as a *"hui"*. The *tangi* (funeral) and its affiliated *kawe mate* (carry the death), on the other hand, survive from the original life cycle, and require no extra interpretation to establish them as *hui*. The *tangi* in particular is revered as the most "Maori" gathering of all, and some informants in fact do not regard it as a type of *hui* at all but place it in a category of its own.

Tangihanga (*Tangi*)

The *tangi* takes precedence over all other *hui*, and indeed over all other activities. When a death occurs in the district, other gatherings are interrupted or cancelled so that the body may lie on the *marae*, and people leave what they are doing to visit the *tangi* or to help stage it.

When a man dies at home, the women raise the death-wail, and the news spreads from there around the community. People passing in the street call out *"E, kua mate a mea!"* ("So-and-so has died"), friends and relatives telephone each other, and the *marae* committee swings into action. In earlier days the kinfolk went outside and fired off muskets or lit a fire on the summit of a nearby hill to notify the district. If a man dies in hospital, the relatives have to wait until the body is released before they can take him home, and by then many of their friends and neighbours have already gathered in the house. The body is laid in the sitting-room or the main bedroom, dressed in his best clothes and surrounded by family portraits. Local people enter in groups with *karanga* and wailing; the men make speeches of farewell, and debate where the *tangi* is to be held. There may be considerable dissension over this point, especially if the dead person had close ties with several *marae*, and the argument may not be settled until the next morning. Once the decision is reached, however, the *marae* committee is notified and they begin to get everything ready. First, they prepare a place for the body to lie. In the Mātātua area, especially if the person was elderly or of high repute, a small shed is built to the left facing out from the meeting-house from timber and canvas or corrugated-iron, or a tent is raised. This is called the *whare mate* or *whare-ā-apakura* (house of death, house of lamentation), and it houses the mourners and the *tūpāpaku* (body) throughout the *tangi*, as well as keeping the *tapu* of death away from the meeting-house. Canvas is laid down on the grass inside the *whare mate*, with flax mats and then mattresses on top, covered by sheets. In Northland the body is placed at the back of the meeting-house with its feet facing the door, so that the spirit can readily find its way out on its journey to the underworld; and in most other areas the coffin is put on the meeting-house porch under the front window. Wherever the coffin is put, a place is prepared beside it for the mourners.

If a man dies away from home, perhaps in one of the cities, he is usually taken home for burial, even though it may be several hundred miles away. The coffin is placed in a hearse, a stationwagon, or on the back seat of the bus that the mourners have hired for the journey, and the party sets out. If he had been an important figure, the journey may be interrupted repeatedly by the requests of other tribes that he be allowed to lie on their *marae* for a short while. Once he reaches his own district, these requests become even more urgent, and people have been known to park a truck across the road or to form a human chain, so that the hearse cannot pass them by. On one occasion the hearse was stopped, but the undertaker refused to let the local people take the body on to their *marae*. The old women danced round the vehicle in a rage, wailing and howling and hitting it with sticks, until finally he relented.

As the hearse approaches the home *marae* the visiting party forms around it on foot, and the women begin to wail. A local woman calls out:

Hoki wairua mai e tama, hoki mai ki te wā kāinga,
Return in spirit, son, return to your birthplace.
Ki tō iwi, hoki wairua mai!
To your people, return to us in spirit!

A visiting caller replies:

Tēnei rā mātou e hari atu nei,
We are they who bring,
Tā tātou mate, kua wehea atu ki te pō!
Our dead, who have been taken to the night!

As the pallbearers carry the coffin into the *marae*, they may be greeted with a *pōwhiri* (action chant of welcome) for the dead:

He aha te tohu o te ringaringa?
What is the sign in our hands?
He kawakawa!
Kawakawa leaves (for mourning)

He aha te tohu o te ringaringa?
What is the sign in our hands?
He kawakawa!
Kawakawa leaves!
Aa, e tuku ki raro kia hope rā
Lower them to the waist
E horo kia hō, te whakatau a te mate!
Let them fall, death alights!

The coffin is set down in the *whare mate*, and the lid is removed to a crescendo of wailing from the women. The mourners drape feather cloaks across the body and pile flowers at his feet. Portraits of ancestors and deceased kinsmen are propped about the coffin, with a Union Jack draped across it from side to side if the man had been a soldier in either of the two World Wars. The widow is led to the left of the coffin, and her female kin and all the old women sit around her, dressed in black. As the wailing dies down the speeches begin, and local and visiting orators in their turn farewell the spirit of the dead man to the underworld. When the oratory is over, the people come to *hongi* with the mourners, carefully removing their shoes before they step on to the flax mats of the *whare mate*. They stand beside the coffin weeping, and in some areas (particularly Northland), they bend down and press noses with the *tūpāpaku* (body) as well. Each person in turn embraces the widow and all the female mourners, weeping with them and showing their sympathy as best they can. After the *hongi* the guests are called into the *whare kai* for a meal, but the mourners (*pani, kiri mate, pae mate*), stay beside the body and do not eat. They keep a vigil throughout the *tangi*, sleeping beside the body at night and sitting there during the day to keep the dead person company. The chief mourner (*tūpoupou*) in particular should never desert her post. Food is brought to them after sunset but because they are touched by the *tapu* of death, some women refuse to eat at all. In any case, they avoid the dining-hall and any place where food is being cooked (*noa*). The old people believe that if a widow should break her fast she will not be able to cry—"The tears won't come." One women told me that when she was young, she was the *tūpoupou* for an elder kinsman, and was told to fast. On the third day an old woman persuaded her to eat some jelly, but immediately afterwards she fainted, and then was very ill. She thought that if she had been older it would have killed her.

The first day of the *tangi* is set aside for local people to "pay their respects", and parties come and go all day. Men arrive in their gumboots and working clothes on their way home from work, because it is believed that one should never pass a *tangi* by without some token of sympathy, no matter how you are dressed. There is a saying *"Ki te kite koe i te ngārara e kurupae ana i te huarahi, kaua koe e whakawhiti—me peka"* (if you see a dragon lying on the road, don't go past it—turn aside), and people who pass a *tangi* by will be criticized as *whakahīhī* (stuck-up) and lacking in "Maori heart". Each party follows through the rituals of encounter in a sad and solemn atmosphere, though in between times people joke and chatter, and try to cheer up the widow with songs or memories of happy occasions. As each group enters the *marae* the men take off their hats and the women tie scarves and wreaths of greenery *(pare kawakawa)* about their heads, then they walk slowly on to the *marae* with an elder calling out a *poroporoaki* (farewell) and the callers exchanging *karanga:*

Local caller:
Haere mai rā e te iwi e
Welcome, people
Mauria mai te aroha ki tēnei a tātou
Bring your compassion to this one of us
Kua tīraha atu i te rā nei,
Who lies here today.
Haere mai, haere mai!
Welcome, welcome!

Visiting caller:
Haere atu rā e tama e
Farewell, son
Ki te paepae o Matariki
To the threshold of Matariki (Pleaides constellation)
O Rēhua
of Antares star
Haere atu rā!
Farewell!

The women carry wreaths and bouquets, or a photograph of the dead man, and lay these at his feet amid bitter weeping. The widow in particular must wail, and after three days of almost constant lamentation much of her initial emotion is purged. In Northern areas the body lies at the back wall of the meeting-house, and the greeting takes place inside. Visitors take off their shoes at the doorway, and enter to the sound of *karanga*, followed by wailing and an elder's *poroporoaki* (farewell) to the dead. As the *kaumātua* (elder) is speaking, the rest of the party stand weeping, then they move directly to the coffin, dropping their *kawakawa* leaves at its foot, and *hongi* with the dead man and the mourners. In other tribes only close kin approach the coffin, and the rest sit down while speechmaking begins. Speakers from the local party welcome the visitors, although close male kin of the deceased may not stand to greet their guests. The visitors reply.

addressing the dead man as though he could still hear them and farewelling his spirit to the underworld. When the last visiting speaker is about to end his speech he lays a *koha* (donation) on the *marae*, and on some occasions a cloak or an heirloom is presented as well to honour the dead man during his last days on earth. Now the visitors are called up to shake hands and press noses, and as they pass the coffin they lay their greenery at its foot, "leaving something of themselves behind". Before they go to the dining-hall they cleanse themselves (*whakanoa*) with water from a bottle left beside the meeting-house or a nearby tap, flicking water over face and hair to lift the last traces of *tapu*. Some people use dry bread instead, while others regard a shot of straight liquor as the most efficacious of all. The older people are particularly careful to take these precautions. "*Kia wehengia atu ngā kēhua*" ("To keep away the ghosts").

In the evening the coffin may be taken inside the meeting-house, especially if the weather is chilly, but in the more conservative areas they prefer not to have the coffin inside at all, and the mourners stay out in the *whare mate* or on the meeting-house porch. Food is brought to them on special plates, and they eat and then talk or weep quietly while inside the house, the elders talk on a wide range of topics, and argue where the body is to be buried and at what time. After the evening meal a church service is held inside the meeting-house, then the coffin is closed up for the night, unless a later group of visitors is expected. People wash and get into their pyjamas, then the oratory begins again, by no means restricted to the topic of the *tangi*. These speeches should continue until late at night, but at many *tangi* today the home people leave the *marae* in the evening and go home "to their feather mattresses and hot-water bottles", so that the mourners are left alone. This is regarded as a lamentable state of affairs, characteristic of the slipping-back of *Maoritanga* but people cheerfully acknowledge that they can't resist their comfort. At the same time they wistfully recall the days when the *marae* was "packed out" for every *tangi*.

On the morning of the second day visitors from other districts begin to arrive, and local people who come late on this day are tartly reproved: "Here these people have come all the way from Auckland, and yet they beat you no-good lot from just across the road!"

The day passes with the reception of visitors, and it is a sad time for the mourners if hardly anyone arrives. For an important man, busloads of people from all over the North Island and many private cars come to the *marae*, elaborate eulogies are delivered and wreaths are heaped up at the end of the coffin. Telegrams bearing messages of farewell and regret, often in the form of a *poroporoaki*, are read out to the gathering. The mourners are honoured by this attention, a final tribute to the *mana* of the dead man. That evening is his last night on earth, and it is the finest tribute of all if the speeches continue until dawn. The speakers recall his deeds, sing songs that he composed, and if the place of burial has not been settled they continue to argue until the first light of morning enters through the meeting-house windows. These arguments over the burial (discussed in an earlier chapter) are an honour to the man, though they may be very upsetting to the mourners if any serious split of opinion develops. Usually in the end, however, the wishes of the closest family or the dying wish of the dead man are followed, and the opposition shows itslf to have been more ceremonial than anything else.

On the morning of the third day the last visitors, including important dignitaries and local Europeans, are welcomed on to the *marae*. The funeral service is held at about 11 o'clock. The family kiss the dead person goodbye, and the coffin is closed for the last time, in a moment charged with emotion. The old women wail and spectators weep quietly. In earlier days on the East Coast, the younger women of the tribe were called forward at this time, and snippings of their long tresses *(uru māhora)* were taken and placed in the coffin as a last sign of love. Amiria Stirling told me "the girls in those days didn't just cut their hair like they do now. At the *tangi*, their *uru māhora* was cut, and that's all. I think its beautiful when I see it—there's one woman with the scissors, and she just takes what she wants, and cuts it—the tears of the *mokopuna* (grandchild.)" The bell is now rung to bring everyone to the meeting-house, and the funeral begins. There are often several ministers present, and they conduct the service in Maori, alternating prayers and Bible readings with well-loved hymns such as *"Tama Ngākau Mārie"* ("Son of the peaceful heart") and *"Mā te Mārie a te Atua"* ("With the peace of God"). After the sermon and the final prayers, there is an RSA service if the dead man had been a returned soldier, and the pallbearers, young male kin of the deceased, carry the coffin to the hearse, or to the graveyard if it is nearby. Women and children walk behind the coffin carrying bouquets and wreaths, followed by the mourners and the rest of the congregation in procession. As the hearse drives away to the cemetery, an old woman calls the saddest *karanga* of all:

Haere, e hoa, ki tō whaea, ki tō pāpā,
Go friend, to your mother and father,
Haere atu rā!
Farewell!

Close male kin of the deceased have already been down to the cemetery early that morning to dig the grave. In some areas they become very *tapu* by their activities, and have to cleanse themselves thoroughly in a nearby stream before they can return to the *marae*. When the cortege arrives at the cemetery, everything has been made ready, and the burial service begins. Local men lower the coffin on ropes into the grave, while the family cluster around weeping. Some visitors stay outside the graveyard fence, to avoid the strong *tapu* inside, while those who do enter turn out their pockets first. The person's clothes and most intimate possessions are put into the grave in suitcases and plastic bags—his pipe, his watch, his books, and anything else which is imbued with his personality. At one *tangi* I attended for a little boy, his tricycle was buried beside him. The service is recited in Maori and a last hymn is sung. Before the grave is filled an old woman *karangas:*

Haere ki te kōpū o te whenua!
Go to the belly of the land!

One or two elders give speeches of farewell, and women strew petals from the wreaths over the coffin. At an RSA funeral each returned soldier drops the red poppy from his lapel into the grave, and murmurs a few words of farewell. An old woman might sing a lament from the head of the grave, or in the Taranaki and Whanganui areas a *poi* chant is performed "to send him on his way". Members of the family throw handfuls of dirt over the coffin, and then the gravediggers begin to fill the grave. When they have finished the mourners lay wreaths on the mound, then walk slowly back to the *marae.* As they leave the cemetery they cleanse themselves with water from a bucket or a bottle that has been left outside the gate.

In some areas the *hākari* (feast) follows directly after the burial, though there is a trend to hold the *hākari* beforehand, so that guests can leave directly after the ceremony. In other places the bereaved family are taken back to the house by the elders, and the *takahi whare* (trample the house) ceremony is carried out. This ritual is designed to drive out any lingering traces of the dead man's spirit, and to purify the house for further occupation. In earlier times any building in which a death took place was burned. As the party approaches, an old woman calls out:

Haere mai rā e te iwi e
Welcome, tribe
Takahia mai rā ngā tapuae o tō koutou hoa
Trample in the footsteps of the friend
Ka ngaro i te rā nei, e, haere mai!
You have lost today, welcome!

The elders enter the house and walk around its rooms, reciting *karakia* (prayers) and sprinkling sacred water about from a leafy branch. The old women wail to drive away any ghosts *(kēhua),* and sometimes a church service is conducted as well. Speeches follow, welcoming the bereaved family back into their home, and assuring them that no harm will come to them now that the *tapu* has been raised. Food or liquor may be served to complete the deconsecration ritual. If there are no expert elders in the community the *tapu* may be lifted by a beer party in the house that evening, or several days later. The *takahi whare* is variously described in English as a "tramp-tramp", "de-lousing", or "driving out the devils".

When the mourners return to the *marae*, they are welcomed with weeping and calling:

Haere mai, te kāhui pani,
Welcome, the bereaved,
Hoki mai ki tō iwi,
Return to your people,
Haere mai, haere mai!
Welcome, welcome!

After the *hākari* most of the guests depart. The night after the burial is called the *pō whakamoemoe* (night causing sleep, or night causing marriage), and it was traditional for the guests to stay on the *marae* for merriment and matchmaking, to help cheer up the mourners. In some areas this custom is still followed, but in others, elements of the *pō whakamoemoe* are introduced into the night before the burial instead, while all the guests are still on the *marae*. People sing comic songs, perform war dances, tell jokes and persuade old women to do the *hula*. The entertainers are all the more uninhibited because some of them alternate their items with visits to the local pub or out to the cookshed, where a drinking party is often in progress. The elders may find this behaviour incongruous with the night before burial, and stand to deliver sharply critical speeches, but they are told that customs are changing, and that this is the way of *Te Ao Hou* (the New World). On most *marae*, however, the night before burial remains solemn, and merry-making is reserved for the next evening.

After the *pō whakamoemoe*, the *tangi* is over, and friends take the family back to their home and stay with them for a while to keep them company. The local people tidy up the *marae* and settle the accounts, and the community settles back into its usual routine. Some Maori funerals, especially in the cities, no longer follow the traditional pattern. The funeral is held in the chapel of the funeral parlour, and the undertaker manages the entire proceedings according to European etiquette. Some undertakers refuse to allow a "Maori wake" on their premises, and insist that they shall have complete control over the conduct of the funeral. Expense and the lack of appropriate facilities are also inhibiting factors. These funerals would not be labelled *"tangi"*, and are generally regarded as an inappropriate farewell for someone of Maori descent.

Kawe Mate ("carry the death")

The *kawe mate* follows the *tangi* by several weeks or even months, and it can be prompted by a number of circumstances. If a man has been buried away from home under protest from his kinfolk, the owners of the *marae* "carry the death" back to his original birthplace to settle any ill-feelings. If a great leader dies his death is "carried" to other *marae* with which he had close contacts, especially if they were unable to be represented at the *tangi*. The *kawe mate* may also be in the nature of a return visit to those groups who visited the *tangi* and important visitors must not be neglected. When Sir Apirana Ngata died a party of about 100 travelled many districts of the North Island after the *tangi*, staying one day in each place.[129] As they travelled up the East Coast on their way North, they decided to make their first stop at Te Kaha. This meant, however, that they would pass by the *marae* of Mihi Kotukutuku, the Whānau-ā-Apanui chieftainess. As soon as she realized this, she rang the Te Kaha people, summoned them to Raukokore and forbade them to prepare their *marae*. When the cars began to pass, she went to the gateway of her *marae* and began to call them in with a *pōwhiri*. Unable to ignore such an invitation, most of the group entered the *marae*, were greeted and stayed for a meal. When they made to leave they found that Mihi had taken the photograph of Apirana from the porch where they had left it, carried it inside the meeting-house, and was sitting beside it looking obdurate. "You can go if you want to" she said, "but Apirana is staying here with me." So they had to stay. Those of the group who had gone past Raukokore found Te Kaha *marae* deserted, and had to travel to Whakatane instead and stay the night in a pub.

There is no real central ceremony for a *kawe mate*. The rituals of encounter follow almost exactly the same form as when a coffin is first brought on to the *marae*, except that the group bring the spirit of the dead man instead; and it is the encounter itself that is all-important. Small children or female mourners dressed in black carry a photograph of the dead man at the head of the party, to symbolise his presence, and the group enter the *marae* amid a medley of calling and wailing. The following transcript is taken from an actual *kawe mate* entry:[130]

Local caller:
Haere mai, haere mai!
Welcome, welcome!
Hoki wairua mai rā e ngā tini aituā, e te iwi e,
Tribe, bring your many dead to us in spirit.
Haere mai, haere mai!
Welcome, welcome!

129. Phillipps (1954), p. 197.
130. Except that personal names have been replaced by anonymous terms.

CENTRAL ACTIVITIES AND *HUI* TYPES

Piupiutia mai rā tō koroua e te iwi e
Bring your old man, to us
Haere mai, haere mai!
Welcome, welcome!

Local *kaea* (leader for *pōwhiri*):
Kia rite!
Get ready!

Local caller:
Haere mai rā te mana ariki e,
Advance, prestige of chiefs.
Mauria mai o tātou tini aituā,
Bring our many dead,
Haere mai, haere mai!
Welcome, welcome!

Local *kaea:*
E, tēnā i whiua!
Begin actions!

Local party perform *Pōwhiri:* (Action chant of welcome).

Aue, hōmai he matā kia haehae au,
Give me an obsidian blade to cut myself,
Aue, kia kotia ai te kiri
To cut the skin
I awhi ai tāua i nawa,
You often embraced,
Aue hi, aue hi, aue hā! (2X)
Alas!

Visiting elder calls out *Waerea.*

Local party perform Action Song:
Kaea:
Kia rite!
Get ready!

Group:
Ngā whare pā, tēnā huakina
Open wide the meeting-houses
Te iwi tangihia
For those who mourn

Te mamae nei a te pōuri nui
The great pain we feel
Tēnei rā, tama mā,
Is for you, our sons,
Aue, hoki mai rā, hoki mai rā ki te kāinga,
Come back, return home,
E tatari atu nei ki a koutou
We have waited for you
Ngā tau roa
Through the long years
I ngaro atu ai, te aroha,
You were away, sorrow,
E ngau kino nei ahau, hi!
aches within me, Hi!

Local caller:
Hoki mai rā e koro ki te wā kāinga e,
Old man, return home,
Haria mai ngā aituā o tō tipuna e,
Bring the spirits of your ancestor,
Haere mai, haere mai whakaariki e,
Welcome, come and make us chiefs.
Haere mai, haere mai!
Welcome, welcome!

Visiting caller:
Haere mai rā e koro e
Come, old man
Whakataukia mai rā ō pōtiki pani
Bring your orphaned friends
I hurihia iho ai
Who have been turned out
E ngā tāngata ki te Ao tū ai e!
By men into the world to stand alone!

Visiting caller. *Tangi kōrero* (Talking wail).
Ei, whakataukia mai rā te rangi o te mamae e,
Bring the song of pain and lay it down,
Kia tūtaki mai ngā mate kua pā ki ahau!
So my dead may gather around me!

Visiting caller:
E koro whakatau mai rā i tō kāhui pani
Old man, alight on your grieving people

Hoki wairua mai rā e koro e,
Return in spirit, old man,
Karanga rā!
We call you!

Local caller:
Haere mai, haere mai!
Welcome! welcome!

Visiting caller: *Tangi kōrero* (Talking wail).
Hoki wairua mai rā e Pā e
Return in spirit, father
I runga i tō whānau e
Upon your family
I motuhia i roto i tēnei rā
Cut from you this day
Kei reira te hoa e
You are there, friend,
Kia tūtaki mai ngā mate kua pā mai
To meet the dead who have gathered
Ngā mate i te ao ki muri e
With the dead in the world beyond,
Ki te mamae e, ko ia ki te Matua!
The world of pain; he has gone to the Father!

Wailing follows, and then the speechmaking begins. Mutual compliments are exchanged, and the speakers farewell the dead man. If there had been any quarrel at the *tangi*, this is the time to settle it. At one *kawe mate* I attended the man had been buried in the town where his wife was living, so that she could regularly visit the grave. When the widow and her relatives "carried the death" back to his birthplace, the local people only half-jokingly suggested that she should marry one of their men, as a "fair swap" for the body of her husband.

If the visitors stay at the *marae* overnight the evening is spent in speechmaking and entertainment, and the group renew their bonds of kinship. The fate of the widow is discussed and debated between her kinfolk and her in-laws. In the morning the visitors may be taken to local graveyards, so that the spirit of the dead man can visit his friends and acquaintances. The significant thing about a *kawe mate* is that grievances are settled and signs of esteem and solidarity are exchanged between the groups.

Today it is common for an important death to be carried to a major *hui*, perhaps the Coronation or the *Hui Tōpu*, where it is certain that a large number of tribes will be assembled; and this saves the mourners from making many visits over an extended territory.

Hurahanga \
Whakaara } *Kōhatu* (unveiling)

The unveiling of a memorial gravestone takes place about a year after the *tangi*, as a final token of *aroha* (love) for the dead. Although in some areas this ceremony is dismissed as a European innovation, in most tribes it is regarded as a fitting end to a man's career on earth. The size and elaboration of the monument reflects the *mana* of the dead person, so that obelisks, carved angels or even statues of particularly venerated leaders may be raised. These larger memorials are sometimes placed on the *marae*. In most cases, however, the gravestone is a simple slab of polished granite, inscribed in Maori, with perhaps a small porcelain picture of the deceased, which is set over the place where the person was buried. The extended family pay for the memorial, and they often fashion its concrete setting themselves, painting it white and decorating it with polished stones. Every effort is made to show the dead person that they are still cared for and remembered.

When the gravestone is ready, invitations are sent out to representatives of groups who attended the *tangi*, and a date for the unveiling is set. Public holidays are favoured, especially long weekends like Easter, Queen's Birthday or Labour Weekend. Easter is a particularly popular time for unveilings in Northland, and many Northern communities hold mass unveilings (up to ten stones at once) at this time, followed by football and basketball competitions to attract the young people home from the cities.

People begin to arrive at the *marae* on the day before the ceremony, or early that morning. Photographs of the dead person and his ancestors are propped up in the porch of the meeting-house or against the back wall, and his female relatives cluster around, dressed in black. The setting is precisely as it was at the *tangi* a year before, except that the coffin is replaced by a photograph. Guests enter the *marae* ceremoniously, wailing and calling on the dead. The speeches recall the dead person and the events of his *tangi*, and the elders discuss who is to unveil the gravestone. Usually their choice settles on a favourite child, grandchild or niece of the deceased, although on some occasions representatives of each of the tribes to which he was affiliated may be jointly appointed to unveil the stone. At about 11 am on the day of the unveiling the elders call for everyone to move to the cemetery. They travel in cars, or on foot if the cemetery is nearby. The minister walks in front, followed by the immediate family and then the rest of the group. At the cemetery the stone has been covered with a black veil, and sometimes a Union Jack or a feather cloak as well. Flowers are laid at its base, and photographs of the dead person and his ancestors are displayed nearby. The minister stands beside the grave and conducts a dedication service in Maori, alternating prayers and hymns with readings from the Bible. At the appropriate point in the service he calls forward those people who have been appointed to unveil the stone, and they each take hold of one of the ribbons attached to the veil, slowly drawing it aside, while an old woman *karanga*s the memorial. An elder reads out the inscription, then the minister closes the ceremony with a benediction, sprinkling holy water over the stone. Before the people leave the cemetery one or two elders give speeches, commenting on the gravestone and its inscription, and complimenting the family on the fine job they have done. Now the dead will lie in peace, satisfied with the memorial they have been given. After the speeches everybody files past the stone, running a hand over it or bending over to kiss the porcelain picture, then they crowd round, reading the inscription and commenting on the way it has been designed.

When the visitors leave the graveyard they wash their hands to lift any *tapu*, then return to the *marae* for the feast. While they are waiting for cooks to serve the meal, the elders spend the time in further speech-making, commenting on the day's events. Now that the last obligations to the dead have been discharged, the widow or widower is declared free to remarry at will. When the call comes from the dining-hall, people line up outside the doorway for the *hākari* (feast). This signals the real end of the *hui*, though some of the visitors may stay at the *marae* overnight. In Northland sporting competitions follow, and the gathering extends over the full period of the Easter break.

The unveiling is an interesting ceremony, because although it takes the form of a church service and a European gravestone is used, it apparently replaces the pre-contact *hāhunga* or exhumation rituals. In pre-contact times the body was buried for a period, then exhumed, and the bones were scraped and coated with red ochre. A second mourning ceremony was held before the bones were finally hidden away in a secret place where malicious enemies could not desecrate them. With contact, this custom was discarded, and Maori people began to erect gravestones over their dead instead. The unveiling ceremony is not as a rule used by Europeans in New Zealand, except for public monuments, bridges or foundation stones, and it seems that in this case, elements of European ceremonial have been transformed during the period of contact into a peculiarly Maori event.

Mārenatanga (wedding)

Tomo (formal request).
Northland weddings are often preceded by a *tomo* or *tono* ceremony, when the boy and his family formally ask for the girl's hand in marriage. If a couple want to get married, the boy talks to his father, and if his family approves of the match they make up a party to visit the girl's home. The *tomo* may be forced upon the couple if it is suspected that they are sleeping together, and in this case it will probably take place at the *marae*,

during a *hui* or one of the regular Sunday gatherings after church. One such *tomo* has already been described on page 110.

In the more usual case of a formal visit to the girl's home, the boy's family headed by his senior male kinsmen arrive at the arranged time, and are formally welcomed inside with *karanga* and *tangi*. The men exchange speeches or greeting, during which they refer to the *tomo* only obliquely, and then the *tomo* proceedings begin. The girl and then the boy are asked, "*E tama, e whakaae ana koe ko — te tāne (wahine) māu?*" ("Child, do you agree to take — as your husband (wife)?") If they both assent, the relatives then discuss the match and its desirability. They comment on genealogy as well as character and family background, and try to establish some genealogical links between the couple, although these should not be too close, and the marriage of first or even second cousins would probably be opposed. Strong opposition to the marriage at this stage is unlikely, however, since the relatives have to give their tacit consent for the *tomo* to be staged in the first place, but a show of dissent might be made to stress the value of the boy or girl to their kinfolk. Once consensus has been reached, glasses of beer are passed round, and arrangements for the wedding are made in a convivial atmosphere. The wedding is traditionally held at the boy's family *marae*, but this is by no means inevitable today, and the venue may lead to disagreement or ill-feeling between the families. Various aunts and uncles offer livestock and food for the wedding, and someone may volunteer to sew the dresses for the bride and bridesmaids. The evening soon turns into a party, and the relatives get to know each other better. From the *tomo* to the wedding the couple are allowed to sleep together without criticism from their families.

The wedding is held perhaps several months later. Invitations are sent out giving the time and place, but these are not intended to be exclusive, and all friends and relatives are welcome to attend.

Mārenatanga (wedding ceremony)
By no means all weddings are held on the *marae*, and there is an increasing trend for the reception to be staged in halls, reception rooms, or at the family home. In the cities, caterers are frequently hired to provide the *hākari* (feast), and a careful guest list is drawn up. Although these practices are criticised as "*Pākeha*-fied", they are followed because of their convenience.

At a *marae* wedding the guests arrive the night before or early that morning, and are ceremonially welcomed on to the *marae*, although the degree of formality varies greatly. The wedding is usually held at about 11 am in a nearby church or on the *marae* itself. The bridesmaids and groomsmen have been carefully selected to represent both families, and there may be six or eight attendants not including flower girls and page boys.

When they are dressed and ready, the bridal party proceed to church, the young men in evening suit and black tie, and the girls in identical formal dresses. At some weddings, the couple wear *kākahu* (cloaks) as well. The groomsmen disappear inside the church, and the bride stands with her father in the foyer. At a signal from the minister, the congregation rise to sing a hymn in Maori, and the bride advances down the aisle on her father's arm, followed by her bridesmaids. If the wedding is staged on the *marae* the bridal party enter all together, and the best man leads in the bride. Now the service proceeds according to the practice of the church; hymns are sung, vows are exchanged, and the couple sign the register. After the wedding the bridal party go to have their photographs taken, and the guests return to the *marae* for the *hākari* (feast).

Hākari (feast, wedding breakfast)
When the couple return to the *marae* with their attendants, the pastor leads them in and the old people may accord them a full ceremonial welcome, sometimes even including a challenge. The old ladies *karanga:*

Haere mai e tama, mauria mai tō rangatira
Welcome child, bring your wife (husband)
Ki runga i tō marae, ki roto i tō iwi
To your *marae*, among your people,
Tēnei e karanga atu nei i a kōrua,
To those who call you both,
Haere mai!
Welcome!

The formality of this welcome again varies greatly. The bridal party move to the porch of the meeting-house, and sit there listening to the speeches of congratulation The orators recite genealogies that link the two families, and give the couple sly instructions about carrying on their descent-lines. After the *whaikōrero*, the couple shake hands and *hongi* with all their guests, then move into the *whare kai* for the wedding breakfast.

Inside the dining-hall the gifts have been set out in a lavish display, and the tables are laden with food. A special table for the bridal party is placed at the end of the hall, with the wedding-cake upon it. The bride and the groom sit behind the cake flanked on either side by attendants, parents and important elders. The minister stands to say grace, then the feast begins. After perhaps ten minutes or so the Master of Ceremonies rises and proposes the toast to the Queen, inviting all to charge their glasses. Subsequent toasts are proposed to the bride, the groom, their parents and to absent friends, in the form of good-humoured *whaikōrero* by local elders or members of the family. After each toast, people stand up to sing appropriate songs, and the atmosphere becomes increasingly jovial. The cooks sally forth from the kitchen to swap comic challenges in song with their guests, old women perform impromptu *hula* and the couple are roundly teased. When it is time for the cake to be cut, everyone is primed for enjoyment.

In Northland the cutting of the cake is accompanied by a special ceremony known as *karangaranga putiputi* (calling the flowers). The top tier is set aside for the christening of the couple's first child, and the flower-studded second or third tier is cut according to this ceremonial. A local elder or the MC calls out in turn the name of each sub-tribe represented at the wedding:

E karanga ana ki a Ngāti —, kia haere mai,
I call on Ngāti—to come and collect,
Ki tā koutou putiputi.
your flower.

Someone from that group, often a small child, is pushed forward to collect their piece of cake, and in return they have to perform an item. They sing a song, start up a *haka*, or sometimes just dissolve into tears, overcome by their sudden exposure to public attention. The cake is taken to an elder of the group, who cuts it up and distributes it.

The wedding breakfast continues until late that afternoon, when people begin to drift outside for a visit to the pub, or sit in the evening sun on the *marae*, chatting companionably. In the evening a dance is held as a finale to the celebrations. Everybody returns to the hall, which has now been cleared, and dance away the night to the music of a local band. The "Valeta", the "Gay Gordons" and waltzes follow one after another, and the bride and groom dance and chatter with their guests. At the end of the evening, after the last waltz, they return home or spend the night with their elders in the meeting-house. There is no need for a honeymoon, especially if they had a *tomo*, and after the wedding they settle directly into married life.

Birthdays and Wedding Anniversaries
Birthdays *(huritau)* and wedding anniversaries are very like weddings, except that there is no church ceremony and the proceedings are even more informal. Relatively few of these occasions are now held on the *marae*, since a public hall or the family home may be regarded as a more appropriate setting for this rather "European" sort of gathering, and no liquor licence has to be obtained. However, as long as some elements of the rituals of encounter are included in the celebrations, the occasion still qualifies as a *hui*. Birthdays are celebrated either for a twenty-first birthday ("coming of age"), or for the seventieth or eightieth or even ninetieth

birthday of an important elder. Wedding anniversaries are usually celebrated on the fiftieth or "golden" anniversary.

If the occasion is held on a *marae* the guests are welcomed on their first arrival. The main event is the *hākari* in the dining-hall, and this in its procedure is similar to a wedding breakfast. The guests enter, grace is said and the feast begins. After a short time the Master of Ceremonies (usually a kinsman) stands to propose a toast, impromptu items are performed and speeches are made in honour of the occasion. These speeches are informal and humorous, inevitably followed by calls of *"He wai, he wai!"* ("Song, song!"). The speaker starts up an action song (*"He putiputi koe"*, "You are a flower"; *"He aha kē taku uma pākikini nei"*, "What is this aching in my breast"; or *"E te hokowhitu atu kia kaha rā"*, "Soldiers, be strong". are among the favourites), a comic love song or one of the favourite "pop" tunes, and everyone joins in with gusto. After the speeches the cake is cut and distributed. That evening a dance is held to complete the festivities. and people sleep overnight in the meeting-house.

Birthdays and wedding anniversaries differ from weddings in that they are not invariably celebrated. If the family cannot afford a large gathering, or if they place little importance on these events, a twenty-first birthday or wedding anniversary may not be celebrated at all, or just with an informal family party at home.

Church Gatherings

Gatherings of Ringatū, Rātana and Te Whiti followers, and those of the Maori branches of major denominations (Church of England, Roman Catholic, Presbyterian, Methodist and Mormon churches), very often take the form of a *hui*. The Rātana church, for example, holds major gatherings on 25 January (the date of Rātana's birthday), at Easter and on 8 November, the anniversary of Rātana's revelation, every year. In these gatherings church members are formally welcomed on to the *marae* with *karanga* and the music of the Rātana brass band, and after *whaikōrero* (speeches), competitions in sports, brass band music, action songs and *haka* are held, as well as regular church services, and there are talent quests and dances in the evenings. These meetings are attended by several thousand visitors, many of them young people, and the church manages to attract such large numbers by adding non-religious activities to its programme.

The Roman Catholic church, to give another example, stages the Hui Aranga[131] every Easter for members of Catholic Maori clubs. The gathering begins on Holy Thursday with an evening mass, and early the next morning after breakfast a formal welcome is given to church dignitaries and club members, in which *whaikōrero* are exchanged. After the welcome

---

131. Bennet (1971).

clubs compete in oratory, sacred music, action songs and *haka*, religious quizzes, and sports including football, netball, tennis and table tennis. In between these activities there are regular masses and meetings to discuss church business, including the venue of the next Hui Aranga. On Easter Sunday there is a religious procession and an open-air mass, followed by the presentation of prizes that evening and a dance, and early on Holy Monday visitors are farewelled. This *hui* is also regularly attended by about 2,000 guests, most of them young.

In the Presbyterian Maori church, founded in the Tūhoe area by the Rev. J. Laughton, regular synods are held in May and August of every year at Te Maunga-ā-Rongo *marae* in Ohope.[132] The May synod is a larger, social affair, while the August synod is mostly restricted to the discussion of church business. On arrival at the *marae* visitors follow through the rituals of encounter, and speeches are exchanged. It is generally true that in church *hui*, church dignitaries rather than elders are the main speakers, although elders may also speak. After the welcome, church business is discussed in meetings conducted broadly according to committee procedure, and services are held at regular intervals.

The Methodist Maori mission also stages its own gatherings, including a regular Maori-language school for its staff, and an annual Hui-ā-Tau (Gathering of the Year).

In this section, however, I propose to discuss in some detail the gatherings of two "Maori" churches (the Ringatū church and the Te Whiti cult) and of one "European" denomination (the Church of England), to illustrate in greater depth the form that religious gatherings may take.

Hui Tōpu (Church of England)[133]

The Waiapu diocese of the Church of England conducts a conference called the Hui Tōpu in May of every year. The first Hui Tōpu was held in 1954, and since then it has become an institution, patronised especially by the tribes of the East Coast. Each pastorate in the diocese takes turns at sponsoring the Hui Tōpu, and this privilege is keenly sought. The successful candidates organise a Hui Tōpu committee with sub-committees for catering, accommodation, competitions and so on. They arrange a venue for the *hui*, sometimes a *marae* or group of *marae*, a school or a large hall. At the 1971 Hui Tōpu in Rotorua, for example, the Rotorua Racing Club was used for meals and meetings; the Rotorua Sound Shell for culture competitions, and about eight surrounding *marae* for accommodation, each Pastorate being allocated their own *marae*. Acting wardens are appointed as information officers and to help keep order throughout the *hui*, and the local vicar is in charge of overall arrangements.

132. Jackson (1970).
133. See also Paenga (1971); Wawatai (1970).

CENTRAL ACTIVITIES AND *HUI* TYPES

In the meantime the other pastorates of the Waiapu diocese (an area extending from Tauranga, round the East Cape, to Woodville in the South) begin to organise themselves for their part in the *hui*. A target of about $200 is set for the contribution of each pastorate to *"Te Perēti"* (the "plate"), and this is raised through sports days, card evenings, bring and buys, and by regular family contributions. Extra money may be set aside for the hire of the bus or buses that take the group to the *hui*. Choir rehearsals begin, and each pastorate forms a *haka* team for the culture competitions. Action songs are especially composed for the *hui*, costumes are prepared, and the rehearsals culminate with a public performance for the people of the district, who give their blessing to the party. Just before the group set out on their journey to the *hui*, a service is held by the local pastor to bring them safely home.

On the appointed day busloads of visitors begin to converge on the *marae* where the formal opening is to be held. Wardens handle parking and direct the traffic. The local people are already on the *marae*, with the local vicar in charge. At a signal from the vicar the local *kuia* (old women) begin to call, and the visitors advance slowly on to the *marae*. A party lined up on the *marae* starts up the *pōwhiri* (action chant of welcome), and when this is finished, both locals and visitors join in the *tangi*, remembering their dead. Now the guests move to their seats, with each pastorate sitting more or less together, and the speechmaking begins according to the etiquette of that *marae*. Speakers are both elders and ministers, because elders attend the Hui Tōpu in force as an enjoyable annual holiday. Greetings are exchanged, and visiting orators may make a bid for the next year's Hui Tōpu, seeking to clinch their claim by gaining the approval of the local elders. At the end of the speechmaking the local pastor announces where each group is to sleep, and gives the programme for the rest of the day. The visitors make their way to their quarters, unpack and wash up after their journey. Meal tickets are issued to representatives of each group, and members of the party present these at the door before every meal. Because there are well over 1,000 people to be fed, gatecrashers have to be avoided, although this is not really a problem if the *hui* is held in a rural area. After dinner Evensong is held in a nearby church, then the clergy and the youth-leaders hold their meetings and receive programmes and instructions for the rest of the *hui*. A dance follows for the young people, but they are usually off to bed early that evening, so that they will be fresh for the competitions the following day.

At eight the next morning communion is held, and it is expected that each pastorate should be fully represented, though this is not always the case. Breakfast follows, and then the formal conference begins, with the election of officers for the following year, the presentation of parish reports on particular topics (the Prayer Book Commission, Church Union, the church Maori boarding schools, etc.). The Bishop of Aotearoa delivers an address to the conference delegates, and then topics such as church finance, the urban church, and the venue for the next Hui Tōpu are discussed. Most of the discussion is conducted in English according to committee procedures, with the Bishop in the chair, but comments or short speeches in Maori are sometimes introduced, and many speakers preface their remarks with a brief series of greetings in Maori. The conference adjourns for lunch after a short service, then resumes its discussions in the afternoon. In the evening the competitions begin. Groups compete in two main categories of performance—choral music, including Maori hymns; and cultural items, which include action songs, *haka* and *poi* dances. Points are allocated for costume, staging, sound quality, and for the virtuosity of the actions in the cultural items. Members of the public can attend the competitions, which are conducted in relaxed style by a Master of Ceremonies, and pastorate supporters enthusiastically barrack for their own groups. In the intervals, entertainment is provided by local talent.

The next day follows much the same programme, with discussions during the day and competitions in the evening. On occasion, a high dignitary from the Anglican or some other church is welcomed to the *hui* and the proceedings are temporarily adjourned to the *marae* for the rituals of encounter. When the competition results are announced there is jubilation in some camps and despair in others, and the judges are praised or criticised accordingly. On the last day of the *hui* a final service is held, and donations are ceremoniously collected from each pastorate in "Te Perēti". This is staged on the *marae*, with a jovial MC calling forward each pastorate in turn to submit their donations to the "plate". A local elder or the Vicar stands, gives a speech, hands over the gift, and then calls up his party to entertain the gathering with an action song or a comic skit. Several thousand dollars go into the "plate", and the expenses of the *hui* are usually met during this lighthearted ceremonial. After "Te Perēti", the closing feast is held, and the Hui Tōpu is officially over.

Ringatū Gatherings[134]
The Ringatū church, founded by Te Kooti, is often typified as the "most Maori church of all", and even non-believers regard it with a certain awe and respect. Its gatherings are surrounded by *tapu*, and its rituals display many traditional features, although they are closely united with practices based on the Bible. Ringatū gatherings are held on the twelfth day of every month, with special celebrations on 1 January, 1 June, 1 July, and 1 December of every year. Twelve is thought to be a sacred number, because Christ had twelve apostles, there were twelve tribes of Israel, and

---

134. See also Puna (1971); Misur (1971).

CENTRAL ACTIVITIES AND *HUI* TYPES

because there are twelve months in every year. These monthly services are held on established circuits of *marae*, with each faction of the church having its own overlapping circuit. The special celebrations are supposed to be a mass gathering of the Ringatū faithful on a single *marae*, but in practice each faction assembles separately.

Visitors to a Ringatū gathering are enjoined by a *tapu* law to arrive before sunset on the day before, and they may not leave until after sunset the next day, so that while the gathering is in progress the *marae* is cut off from the outside world. As each group arrives on the *marae* an old woman *karanga*s, and a local *tohunga* (priest) rings a bell on the porch of the meeting-house and leads them in prayers. After the short service the women weep if there has been a recent death, and the men exchange *whaikōrero* (speeches). The rituals of welcome are, however, abbreviated, and include Ringatū prayers. At the conclusion of the ritual, the visitors *hongi* (press noses) with their hosts, and enter the meeting-house.

Inside the meeting-house members of the congregation are seated around the walls on mattresses and mats, *marae*-style, and they sleep here overnight as well. The gathering begins with a service in Maori, led by the chief *tohunga* (priest). The *marae* "policeman" rings the bell outside, and everyone assembles in the meeting-house. No-one may leave or enter the house once the service has begun. Ringatū services follow a cycle of texts called *hīmene* (hymn), *pānui* (reading) and *waiata* (psalms), which are memorised by the priests and members of the congregation. The *tohunga* may dictate that the cycle shall be completed two or three times, by six or nine priests, or that all the congregation shall participate. In this case, the service begins with the chief *tohunga* (*"pou"*) standing to recite prayers (*inoi*) and a "*hīmene*" from his place by the door. He leans his hand against the wall and chants the text in a rapid incantation, with the congregation joining him rather in the manner of an ancient *waiata* (song). The person sitting next to him stands to recite a "*pānui*," the third person gives a "*waiata*", and so on right around the house. This recitation of Biblical passages from memory is one of the most impressive features of Ringatū practice, and it reflects an older oral tradition, in which memorisation was the key to knowledge. Great emphasis is placed upon being able to go right through the text without pause or error, and some of the more expert *tohunga* can recite a wide range of long passages faultlessly. If the service is restricted to *tohunga*, equal numbers of visiting and local priests may be appointed to carry out the order of service. Once the correct number of cycles has been completed, a priest gives a short address which closes the religious proceedings, and the men stand to exchange *whaikōrero* (speeches).

Services continue throughout the gathering at regular intervals, during the night as well. The second service is held late on the first night, and early the next morning there is a service at about 6 am. Breakfast that morning is a *hākari* (feast), and a table is set outside on the *marae* for the deity, with a box in front of it to receive offerings from the congregation. The feast used to be held outside on the *marae*, but today the dining-hall is used instead. After the *hākari* the people return to the meeting-house to discuss church business and to settle upon the venue for the next twelfth. A second service follows, then lunch, and a third service afterwards. There is a fourth service before dinner, and the fifth service, after dinner, is conducted by the *tohunga* when they return from the "sacred fire". They have taken sacrificial offerings in the form of money and written confessions to a place away from the *marae*, and burnt them in the fire. This ritual cleanses believers of their sins, and saves them from supernatural retribution. The sixth service held late that night is a farewell meeting, in which local people and visitors exchange prayers for each other's safety and well being. In the speeches that follow the visitors speak first, and only when they have finished do their hosts reply. The congregation stay overnight in the meeting-house, holding a seventh service at about 3 am, and early the next morning at a dawn service, the sick and ailing can be given healing by the priests, who sprinkle them with sacred water. After this ceremony speeches are exchanged, and breakfast is served in the *whare kai* before the congregation return to their homes.

Ringatū gatherings have many elements of *marae* procedure. The rituals of welcome, though they are abbreviated and include Ringatū prayers, follow broadly the typical pattern of the area. Throughout the meeting the congregation sleep in the meeting-house and eat in the *whare kai*. The services themselves show many elements that derive from *marae* procedure, for example the reciprocity between locals and visitors, the delivery of the chanted texts, and the *hākari* (feast) held on the main day. Some *marae* are known as "Ringatū" *marae*, and in fact have been built by the faithful to accommodate their gatherings, although other *hui* may be held there as well. These *marae* retain an aura of special *tapu*, and in some cases their *tapu* may intensify so greatly over time that they are no longer used even for church gatherings and no-one goes there at all.

Te Whiti Gatherings

Te Whiti's *marae* at Parihaka in Taranaki still stands, almost 100 years after it was besieged in 1881 by Government troops. The buildings are falling down and some have long since been demolished, but a small group of followers continue to gather at the *marae* on the eighteenth day of every month, and on 6 November, the date of the Parihaka siege. The regular meetings are small, attended by elderly people whose parents lived at Parihaka, but on 18-19 June, the main gathering every year, about 100 people assemble, first at the upper *marae*, in memory of Te Whiti, and then on the lower *marae*, in memory of his lieutenant (and later his rival), Tohu.

These gatherings are not so much religious meetings as days of remembrance, and the people come together to talk about Te Whiti, to sing his *poi* chants and quote his sayings. They assemble in the living-room of a house that still stands on the *marae*, and seat themselves about the walls on mattresses and mats. In cold weather a fire burns at one end of the room. As each group of visitors arrive, an old woman *karangas* from outside, and then the door opens and they enter, wiping their feet and taking off their shoes before they step on to the mats inside. The women call and answer, and then they *tangi* with their heads bowed, white feather in their hair recalling Te Whiti's symbol of "peace on earth, goodwill towards men". When the weeping is over the visitors move round the room, shaking hands and pressing noses with everyone in turn, and speeches are exchanged according to Taranaki etiquette.

At about midday a *hākari* (feast) is held in an adjoining room, where the walls are covered with pictures of Parihaka in earlier days. An elder says grace, and the people seat themselves round a long table for the plentiful meal. The rest of the day is spent with reminiscences and discussions of the past. In recent years some of the young people in the district have planned to rebuild Parihaka as a cultural centre, and their plans may be debated. In the evening, the people drift off to sleep while the elders continue to talk, or stand to sing Te Whiti's rhythmic chants.

King Movement Gatherings

The Maori King Movement stages a great many *hui* every year, most of them in the Waikato area, but increasingly outside it, as other tribes acknowledge the *mana* of the Maori Queen. The Queen is also represented at almost every major gathering in the country, and her party of elders and old women, with its core *te Kāhui Ariki* (the paramount family) are probably the most active *hui*-goers in New Zealand. They might attend eighty or more *hui* a year, as opposed to an average twenty to twenty-five a year for active elders in other areas. The two main categories of gatherings sponsored by the King Movement are the *poukai*, an annual cycle of visits by the Queen to loyal *marae;* and the annual Coronation, probably the largest *hui* regularly staged in New Zealand.

Poukai

The *poukai* gatherings were instituted by the second Maori King, Tāwhiao, shortly after he returned from a trip to England in 1884 to ask the British Government for the return of unfairly confiscated Maori lands. The first *poukai* was held at Whatiwhatihoe *marae* in Pirongia, as a harvest festival, and the gathering was later transferred to Parāwera *marae* near Te Awamutu.[135] The *poukai* served as a regular gathering for the King's followers in March of every year, to celebrate harvest-time according to

---

135. Te Awamutu *Courier*, 10.3.71.

Biblical precedents, and also according to some sources, to allow Tāwhiao to heal the ailing and infirm among his tribesmen. The meaning of the term *"poukai"* is obscure, although according to one source it was a metaphor originally used in oratory to denote the *mana* of a supreme chief.[136]

The modern *poukai* takes the form of a circuit of almost thirty *marae*, most of them in the Waikato area. In recent years, however, the *poukai* has been taken to Judea Pā in Tauranga by Dr Maharaia Winiata, and to the Tūhoe townships of Te Teko, Murupara and Te Whāiti by local elders. Each *poukai* is held on a set date at a given *marae*, and a list of the annual circuit is circulated among King Movement followers. The *poukai* binds the different *marae* loyal to the Queen into a single unit, and also gives an opportunity for deaths to be "carried" *(kawe mate)* from one *marae* to another within the King Movement's sphere of influence.

Each *poukai* is staged by the local *kōmiti poukai (poukai* committee) on the appointed day. Food is ordered and prepared, the *marae* is made ready, and the local people await the arrival of the *kāhui ariki* from Ngāruawāhia. The Queen usually attends the *poukai*, but sometimes she may be called to some other *hui* and her elders *(māngai*, "mouthpieces") speak on her behalf. The Queen's supporters travel to the *marae* in a hired bus, and the Queen and her husband travel separately in their official car, a large black Pontiac. If the King Movement band is present, they come in one or several mini-buses.

At about 11 am the visitors arrive outside the *marae* and assemble in a group at its gate. The Queen, her husband and her chief elders are at the head of the group, with the old women, then the band, followed by the rest of the party. The band strikes up a quickstep, and the group enters the *marae*, with the old women calling back and forth:

Local caller:
Haere mai ngā mate i Waikato
Welcome, Waikato dead
Ki te rā o tā tātou Kuini
To the day of our Queen
Haere mai rā!
Welcome!

Visiting caller:
Karanga mai te reo aroha
Call us, voice of love
Ki te Kāhui Ariki, ngā iwi, ngā hau e whā,
Call the Queen's party, the tribes, the four winds.

136. Hammond (1924), p. 195.

Karanga mai!
Call!
Tēnei ngā mate ka tūtaki ki ngā mate i a koe
These are the dead coming to meet your dead
I te papa, karanga tāua!"
Upon this ground, let us call together!

The local people perform the *pōwhiri* (action chant of welcome) for their Queen, and a visiting elder calls out:

Karanga te pō, karanga te pō,
Call, night; call, night,
Karanga te ao, karanga te ao,
call, dawn; call, dawn,
Karanga te rā, karanga te rā,
call, day; call, day,
Ko tō tātou Ariki tēnei kua tae mai!"
This is our Queen who has come!

Now both groups stand with their heads bowed in respect for the dead, the women wail *(tangi)*, and the band moves to the local flagpole to play the hymn "*Tama Ngākau Marie*" ("Child of the Peaceful Heart"). A minister recites prayers to bless the gathering, then everyone takes their seats and *whaikōrero* (speechmaking) begins. The Queen is seated in a special armchair, with her husband, her chief elders and a lady-in-waiting beside her. *Whaikōrero* (oratory) follows the alternating Tainui pattern, except when the *poukai* is taken to Tūhoe, where the local *pāeke* pattern prevails. Each speaker exchanges greetings with his counterparts, and expresses his respect for the Queen. Matters touching on the King Movement may also be discussed, particularly in the later speeches. *Waiata* are sung after each speech, and although the contents of most speeches are fairly routine, since the Ngāruwāhia speakers in particular go through the *poukai* rituals many times each year, the *waiata* are performed with enjoyment and watched with interest. The importance of this part of the ceremonial can be judged from the fact that the elders have set up a weekly *waiata* class at Tūrangawaewae *marae*, to extend their mastery of these chants.

After the speeches the visitors are called over to *hongi* (press noses) with their hosts, and the Queen with her chief elders leads the way into the dining-hall. Two old women sit at the doorway of the dining-hall with flax kits or bowls in their laps, and visitors drop in a donation as they enter for the feast. A child might give 10 cents or 20 cents, and an adult $1, $2, or $5, depending on the fervour of their loyalty to the Queen and the state of their finances. Some of this money helps pay for the *poukai*, and some is returned to Ngāruawāhia. A *poukai* (feast) is always lavish, and as well as the standard menu of pork, chicken, beef, vegetables, trifle and jelly, there are special delicacies such as dried shark, *karaka* berries, *kānga kopiro* (fermented corn), dried mussels, or grapes and watermelon in season. The Queen sits at a special table at the head of the hall, surrounded by the chief members of her retinue, and is served by a special waitress. The old women are always in high good humour at this point in the gathering, and as they enter they jig to the time of a comical song, and *karanga* to the cooks.

In the afternoon people sit around and chat or play cards, and King Movement business may be discussed in a special meeting with the Queen and her elders. At about 5 pm the band stands around the flagpole playing the hymn *"Mā te Marie a te Atua"* ("With the Peace of God") while a local warden lowers the *poukai* flag. This is later taken to the next *marae* on the *poukai* circuit. If the party stay at the *marae* overnight, an evening service is held at about 7 pm, then there is a dance after dinner in the *whare kai*, attended by both the elders and the local young people. Early the next morning another service is given, then everybody rises, washes and packs their bags. After breakfast they assemble on the *marae*, and while the band plays catchy tunes around the flagpole the local people *kopikopi* (hula) out from the dining-hall, waving dollar notes which they present to the band. The visitors join in, and while the elders *kopikopi* the rest of the party watch their antics with great amusement. After a final service conducted by the minister, farewell speeches are exchanged and the guests depart. The *poukai* are highly valued as a binding link between King Movement *marae*, and a forum where the business of the Movement can be discussed and debated. The Waikato old people, many of them widows and widowers, also value the *poukai* as an enjoyable outing in Maori surroundings.

Koroneihana (Coronation)
The Coronation is held at Tūrangawaewae *marae* in Ngāruawāhia on 23 May of every year, to commemorate the crowning of Queen Te Ata-i-Rangi-Kāhu in 1966. This gathering is regularly attended by 5–6,000 visitors, who come particularly to see the competitions in sports and cultural items, (held on the nearest weekend), and to renew their contacts with *Maoritanga*. Because of the scale of the gathering, its organisation is complex, delegated to a range of committees, and a very large number of workers are involved in its staging.

The Coronation typically begins on a Friday, when parties of visitors from other tribes are formally welcomed to the *marae*. These welcomes occupy the entire day, and in the evening a dance is held for the young people. Early on Saturday morning the Coronation flag is raised on the *marae* flagpole with a special service, and after breakfast the formal rituals of welcome with visiting groups continue. These are interrupted at 10 am, when the Queen is heralded on to the *marae*, and other prominent visitors are accorded a special ceremony of greeting. After a mass service further speeches of welcome by local elders are addressed to the Queen and those tribes that are assembled on the *marae*. Once these formal greetings are completed, any elder may stand to speak his mind on current issues, and the Coronation provides a significant inter-tribal forum where Maori opinion on issues such as the teaching of Maori language in schools, the Treaty of Waitangi or South African rugby tours of New Zealand can be formulated in traditional fashion. After lunch the main sporting activities begin, including basketball and football competitions, while the elders continue their discussions on the *marae*. That evening after dinner a service is conducted on the *marae*, and a dance for the young people is held in one of the dining-halls. Sunday is usually the most popular day of the gathering. It begins in the same manner as the day before, with a flag-raising ceremony early in the morning, and later the ceremonial seating of the Queen on the *marae*. After the speeches of greeting to the Queen, however, the cultural competitions begin, and groups from all over the North Island display their skills in action songs, *haka* and *poi* dances to a large and appreciative audience. After lunch the main football matches are held on the sports grounds across the road from the *marae* in great numbers, and the wardens have a difficult job directing parking and traffic. In the evening many of the guests begin to leave, but not before the trophies have been presented. For those who stay on, an evening service is followed by a dance and talent quest to round off the weekend's activities. The Coronation is a gathering with wide appeal. The young people attend it for the fun of the dances, talent quests, sporting and cultural competitions. The elders enjoy the assembly of their peers and the exchange of speeches on the *marae*, and visitors find the Coronation a refreshing exercise in *Maoritanga* as well as a tribute to the *mana* of the Maori Queen.

Ceremonial Welcome
The ceremonial welcome of an important visitor (Royalty, the Governor-General, the Prime Minister, the Minister of Maori and Island Affairs, the Bishop of a major denomination, or a visiting rugby side) on their first visit to a district may be the sole pretext for a *hui*, or it may be combined with some other *take*, such as the opening of a new meeting-house. The main elements of these occasions are the rituals of encounter, and these are performed with full pomp and pageantry. The *wero* (challenge) is delivered as the official party approach the gateway of the *marae*, and the *pōwhiri* (action chant of welcome) is chanted as they walk to the dais, set up facing the meeting-house. On very important occasions such as the Royal welcome to Gisborne in 1970, the ceremonial may be staged in

a major public facility (in this case, Rugby Park) to accommodate the thousands of visitors who attend. Speakers are carefully selected from the most prominent elders of each group and they pay tribute to the occasion by wearing Maori cloaks over their suits. Speakers from the official party also follow a pre-determined programme, with the guest of honour delivering the final address. After the speechmaking the visitors are entertained with a display of action-songs, *haka*, poi-chants and stick games from the finest concert parties available. These welcomes combine *marae* procedures with aspects of European pageantry (e.g. the detailed programme of speakers, careful reporting by newspapers and television, and dais for the official party), and they represent a self conscious display of Maori "culture" to an honoured European guest.

Meetings and Conferences
When groups such as the Maori Women's Welfare League, the New Zealand Maori Council, the Maori Graduates' Association and the Maori University Students' Association hold their meetings and conferences, the greater part of their activities are conducted in English according to committee procedures, and the gatherings only marginally qualify as *hui*. More often than not they are staged in public halls, schools, universities or some other public facility, rather than on a *marae*, although in the last year or so, *marae* have become an increasingly popular venue. The feature that marks them as *hui*, however, are the rituals of welcome or at least some version of them, that formally open the proceedings.

These rituals are usually abbreviated and modified along European lines, particularly when the gathering is not staged on a *marae*. At the opening of a conference, for example, a concert party lines up at the front of the hall, and as the official party enter they are greeted with a short *karanga* and a *pōwhiri* (action chant of welcome). When the visitors are seated on the stage they are entertained with action songs and *haka*, a minister recites prayers of invocation, and the speeches begin according to a programme announced by the Master of Ceremonies earlier in the evening. Local speakers may precede speakers from the official party, but often no local-visitor dichotomy is clear, and elders alternate with the local mayor, councillors or Members of Parliament who accompanied the official party, in welcoming the guest of honour. Maori speakers use both Maori and English, although some speakers prefer to deliver a *whaikōrero* (speech) in Maori strictly according to traditional patterns. Interpreters are in any case provided for the offical party. The last speech is delivered by the guest of honour, who formally declares the conference open at the conclusion of his remarks. After the speechmaking, items are performed by the concert party, and supper is served to conclude the evening. The rituals of encounter for these occasions have much in common with the ceremonial welcomes described in the previous section, except that they formally mark the opening of the occasion as well as the welcoming of the guest of honour.

At a conference the deliberations that follow are usually controlled committee-style by a chairman. Motions are put and passed or defeated, points of order are raised and remits are voted upon. There are some aspects of the procedure, however, that derive from more traditional methods of debate. The chairman typically waits until some kind of consensus is apparent before he puts a motion to the vote, and unanimity is highly valued, although it may be elusive on controversial issues. Some speeches are delivered in Maori or prefaced with Maori greetings, and ended with a *"wai"* (song). Elders are accorded high respect, and their opinions on some issues may be taken as definitive. Anyone who wants to speak their mind can do so, and committee procedures are often bent or even discarded to make this possible. The chairman acts as an arbitrator rather than an impartial enforcer of rules, and offers compromise solutions when the discussion has reached an impasse. Many of these gatherings are staged if not on a *marae*, at least in some facility where the people can sleep and eat communally, *marae*-style. One notable exception is the annual Maori Women's Welfare League conference, where the delegates stay in hotels. They are mostly middle-aged women, the cooks at any traditional *hui*, and for their own conference they prefer to escape from this role.

Despite such similarities to *marae* procedure, these gatherings in their organisation and conduct have more of the quality of a European conference than of a traditional *hui*, and they only marginally enter into this category.

This chapter is not a complete survey of Maori gatherings, but rather a description of the main types of *hui*. I have attempted to concentrate on those types of *hui* that were studied in the field, and to abstract a portrait of each type from specific cases. Case studies are not included in the account because they would be clearly recognisable and might constitute a violation of privacy. Instead, the account of each type is made as detailed as possible, and illustrative material from field notes is given wherever possible.

CHAPTER SEVEN

EPILOGUE

The *hui* has a life and validity of its own that is quite independent of anthropology. The actors move about on the *marae* with certainty, their activities follow in due order, and the total event is regulated by a series of clearly understood rules. The task of the anthropologist is to describe this reality as nearly as possible in its own terms, reflecting its structure in the structure of the description, and remaining faithful to its boundaries and definitions. For the *hui*, this meant discriminating "staging" activities from ceremonies on the *marae*, sorting out actors according to the roles they are given, and describing the ritual activities in the order they follow in actual performances. As far as possible theory has been kept in the background, and its categories (e.g. "Political Aspects of the *Hui*", "Religious Aspects", "Economic Aspects", etc.) have not been allowed to dominate the description. Now that the description is over, however, we can try to discover what theoretical insights proceed from the study of the *hui*.

In the first place, the *hui* and formal Maori culture in New Zealand today largely coincide, and it has been pointed out that an "occasional" strategy is perhaps best suited of all for the study of modern *Maoritanga*. In the *hui*, *Maoritanga* comes into its sharpest definition, whereas in other situations, especially in the cities, it plays at best a background role. This kind of cultural adaptation is by no means unique to New Zealand. In contact situations everywhere, minority groups maintain their distinct identities in episodic sub-cultures, which carry over from one special occasion to the next. In everyday life, in schools, offices, and even to a large extent in the family, the sub-culture is no longer adaptive, but it continues to flourish in gatherings where members celebrate its significance in their lives. This "occasional" quality of such sub-cultures is also their best protection. Since they are only reaffirmed among members, the majority group remains largely unaware of their survival, and missionary attempts at assimilation are by-passed. It is suggested here that the "anthropology of occasions" is likely to prove the most appropriate strategy for studying sub-cultures of this type.

Nor is the value of the approach limited to culture contact situations. The life of many institutions, perhaps of all institutions, is essentially